[ KITCHENS ]

BETA-PLUS

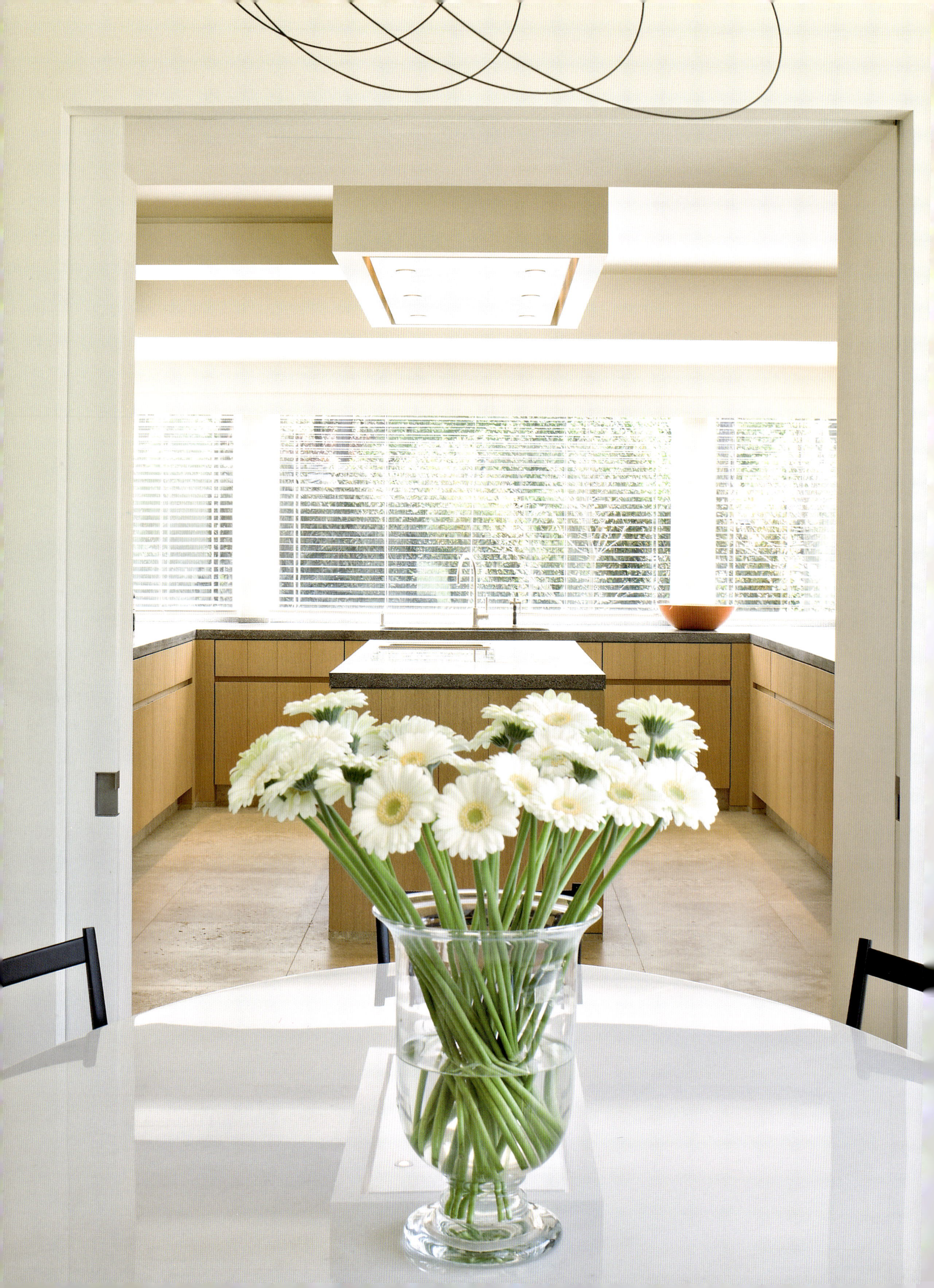

# [ KITCHENS ]

This kitchen was designed by Pierre Daems, interior architect with Obumex.

**4-5**
The natural stone company Louis Culot, which specialises in exclusive tailor-made kitchen worktops, crafted this worktop in flamed Grigio Quartzite.

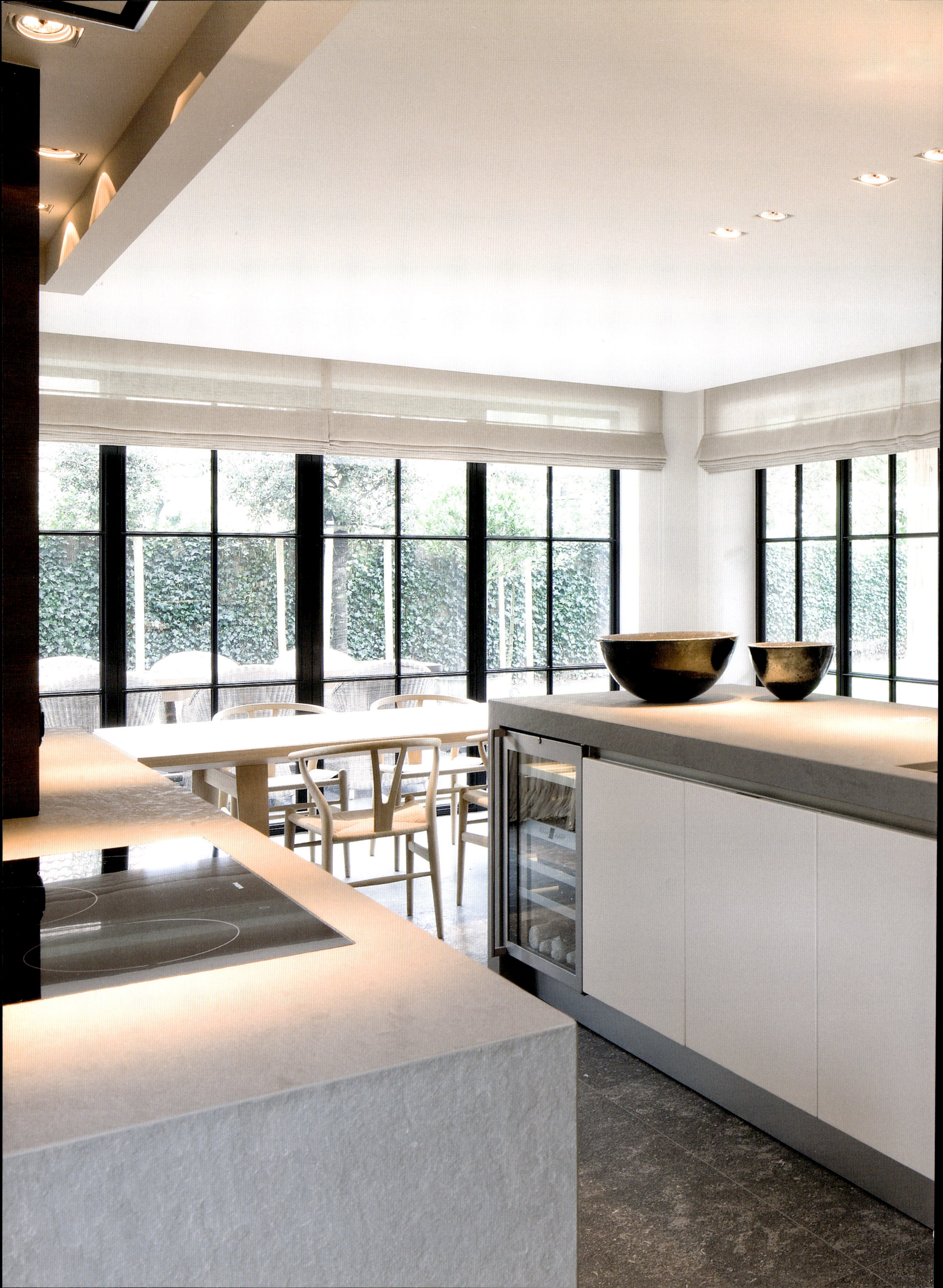

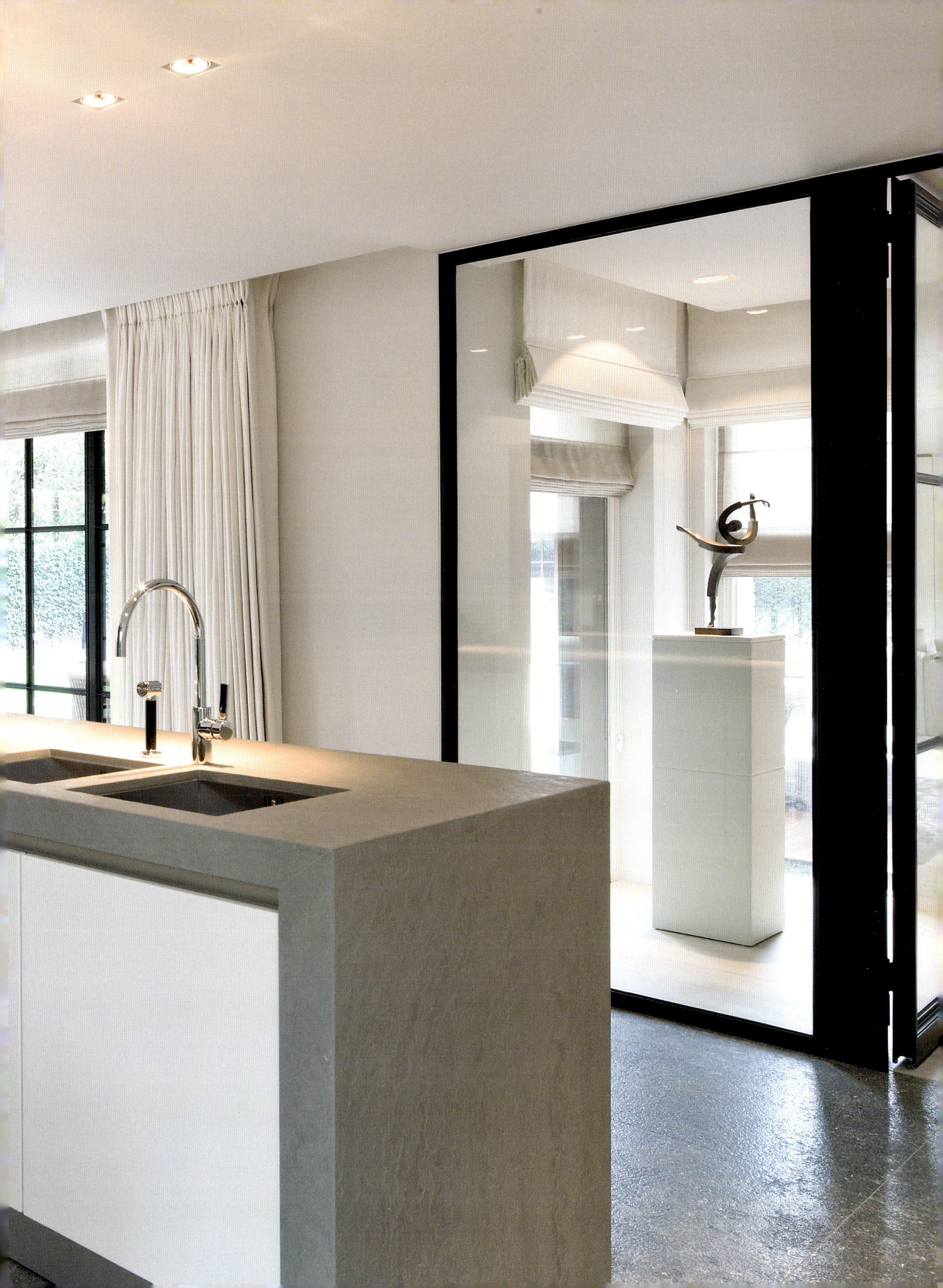

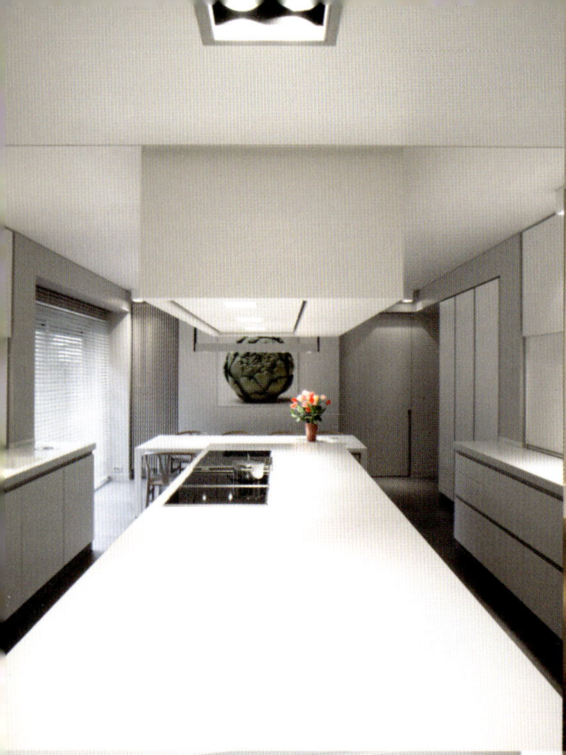
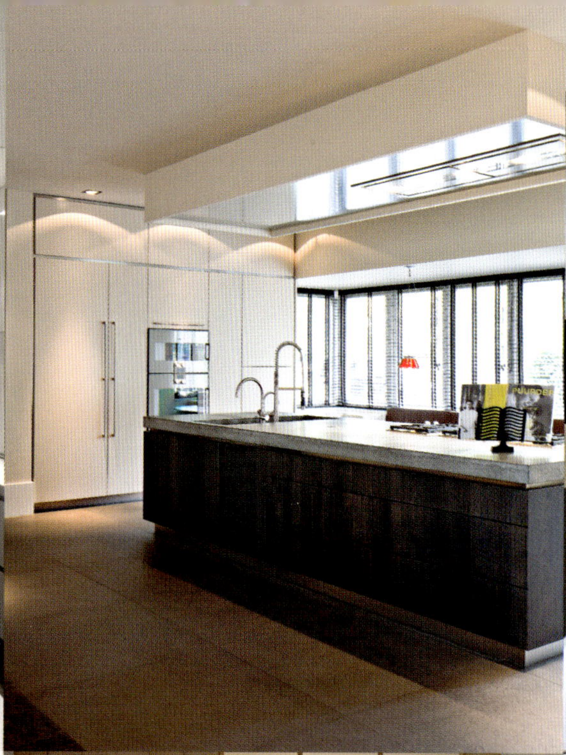
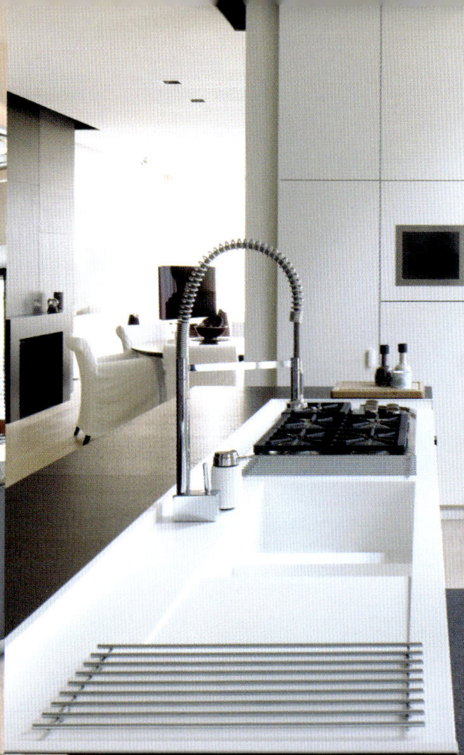
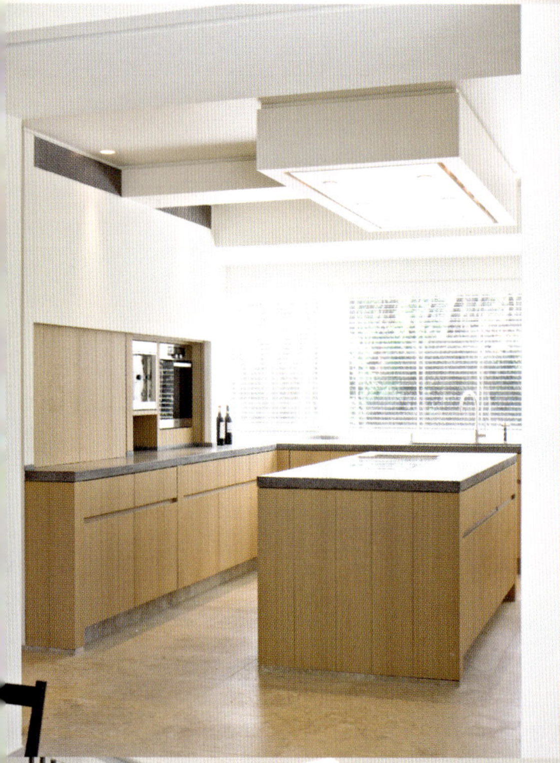
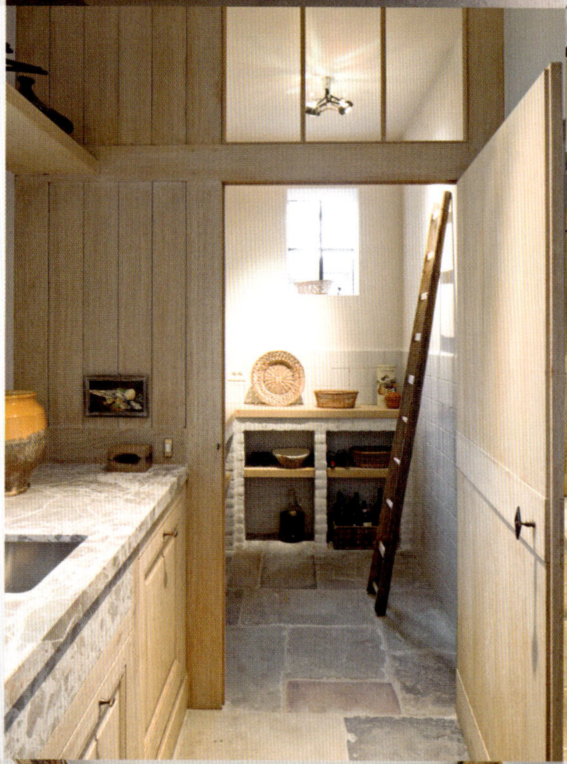
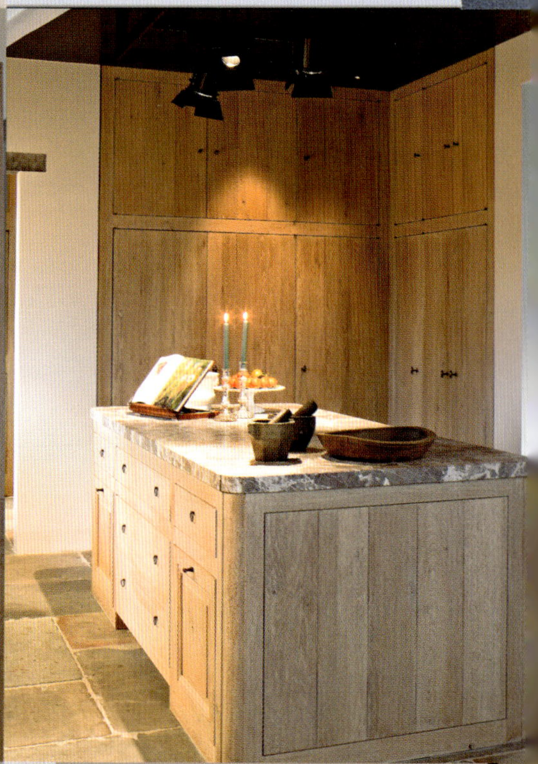
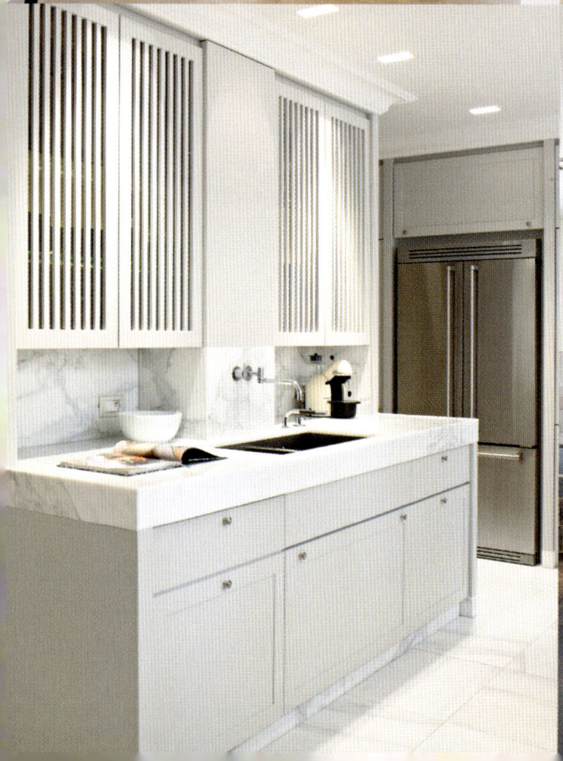
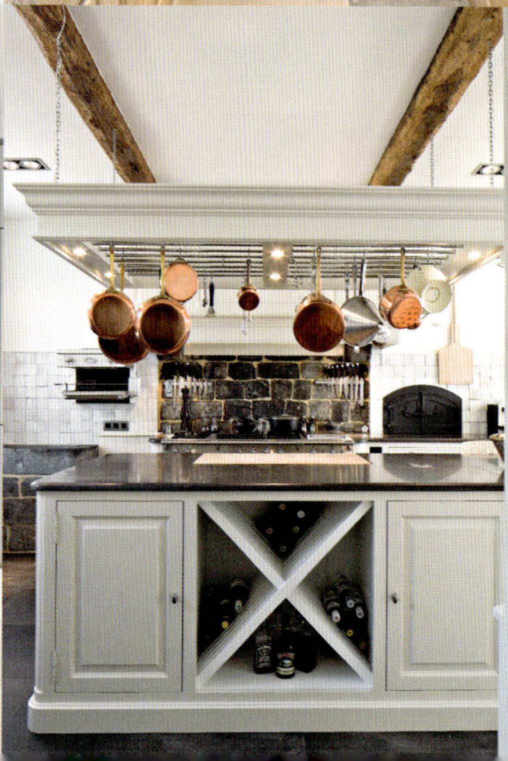
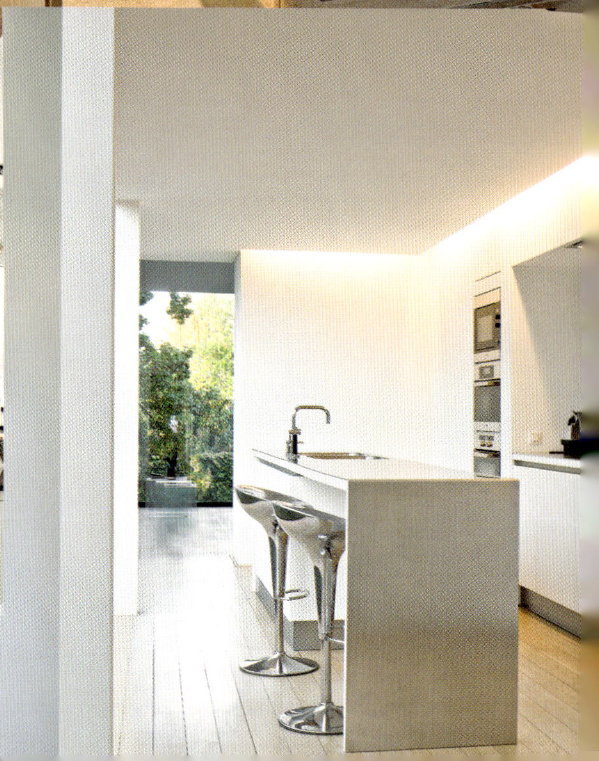

# [ CONTENTS ]

| | | |
|---|---|---|
| 11 | \| | Foreword |
| 12 | \| | A kitchen fit for a king - or a queen |
| 18 | \| | Contemporary classic in the heart of Bruges |
| 22 | \| | Constantly striving for perfection |
| 28 | \| | Kitchen with superb garden view |
| 36 | \| | A kitchen and dining room combined |
| 40 | \| | A feeling of warmth |
| 48 | \| | Kitchens with ambiance |
| 54 | \| | A blend of Provence and Old England |
| 58 | \| | A unique specialisation: kitchen worktops |
| 64 | \| | A passion for perfection |
| 70 | \| | Passionate and poetic, yet extremely professional |
| 74 | \| | Traditional craftsmanship coupled with practical contemporary design |
| 82 | \| | Country inspiration |
| 86 | \| | A novel cooking experience for inside and outside |
| 94 | \| | Exclusive kitchens for connoisseurs |
| 99 | \| | Country style but modern |
| 102 | \| | A blend of walnut and Marron Emperador |
| 106 | \| | Monochrome white and stainless steel |
| 110 | \| | An infinite source of inspiration |
| 122 | \| | Exclusive furniture fittings: the finishing touches that make a high-quality kitchen complete |
| 128 | \| | Functional and timeless living kitchens with character |
| 140 | \| | A commitment to openness and spaciousness |
| 144 | \| | Unrivalled culinary ergonomics |
| 150 | \| | Classical style at its best |
| 154 | \| | A personalised approach to each project |
| 164 | \| | Client-oriented and innovative |
| 178 | \| | A blend of cosiness and *joie de vivre* |
| 194 | \| | Addresses |

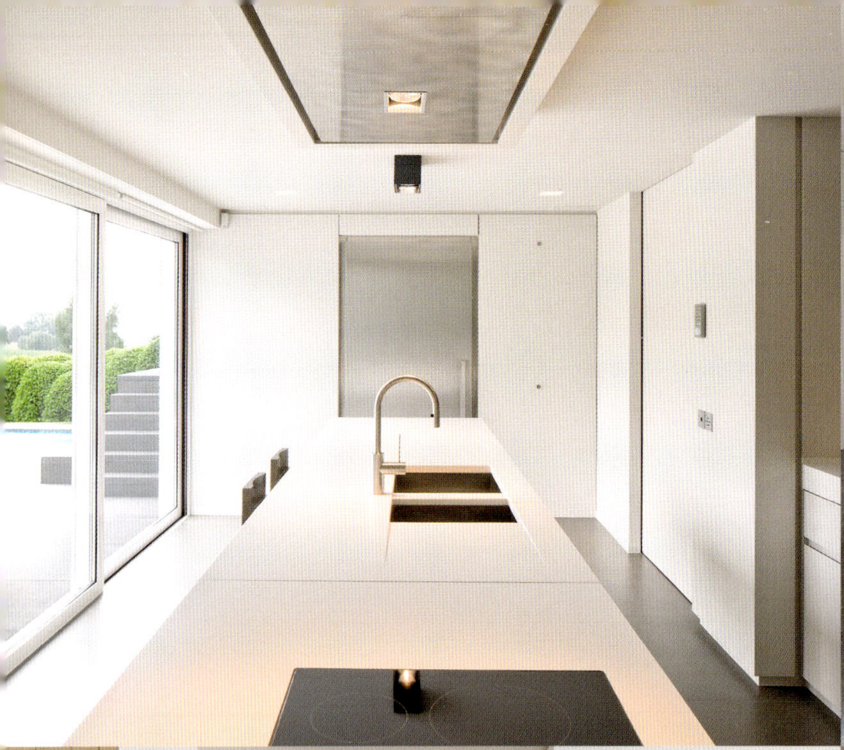
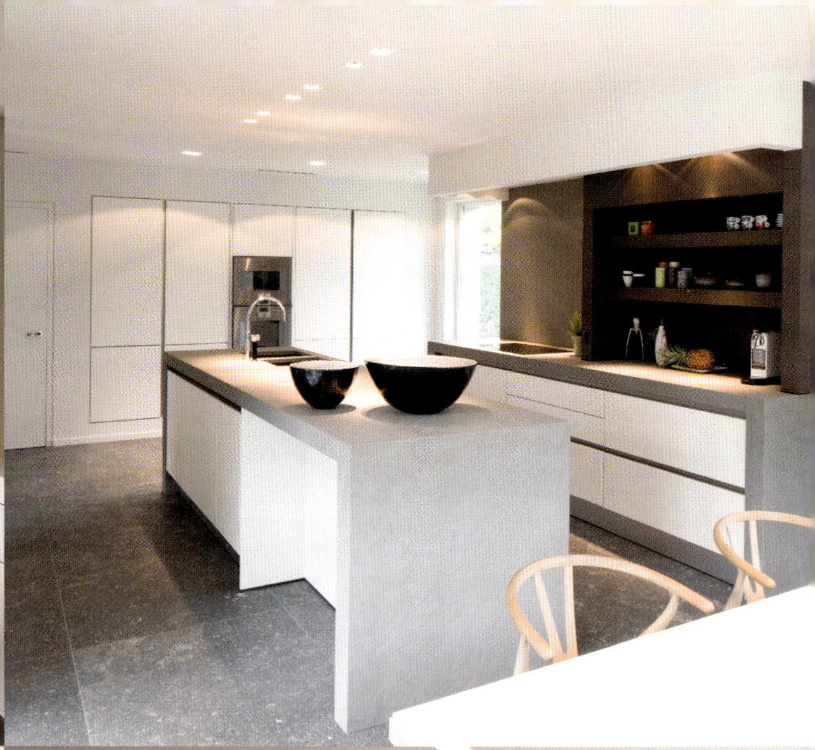
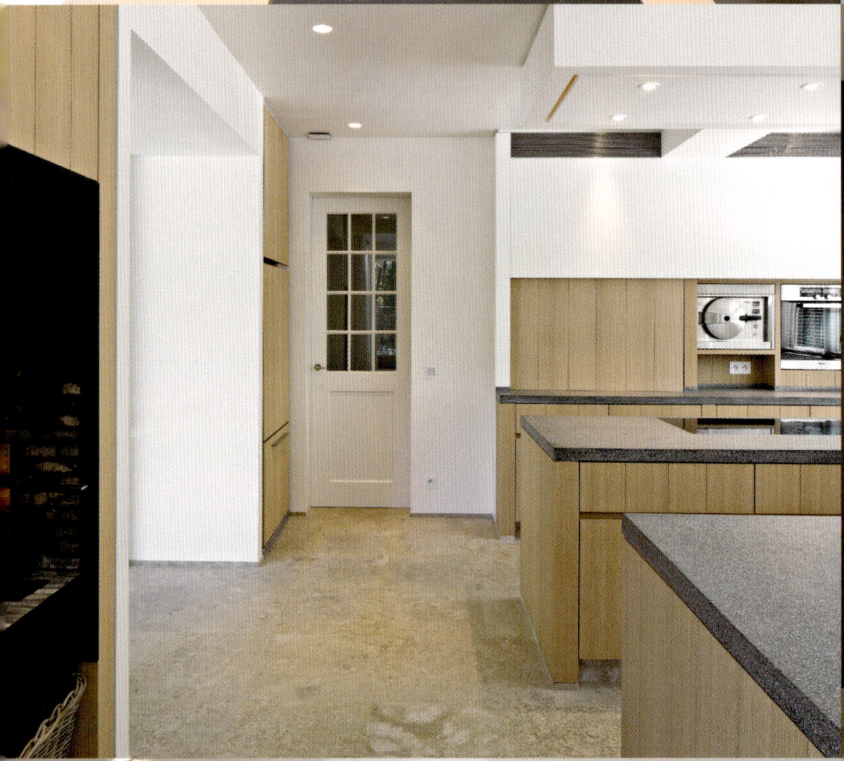
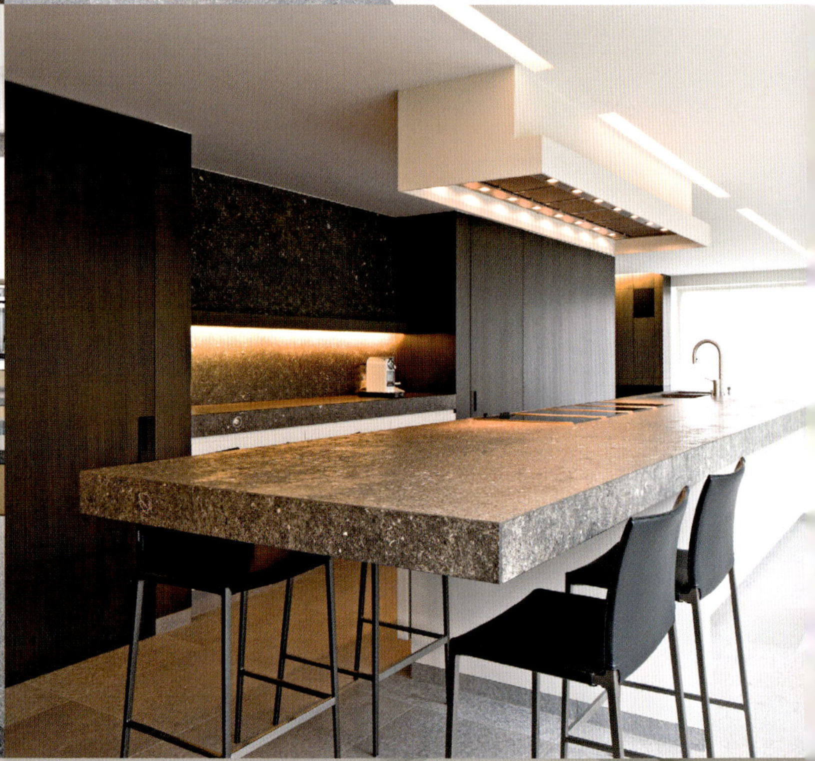
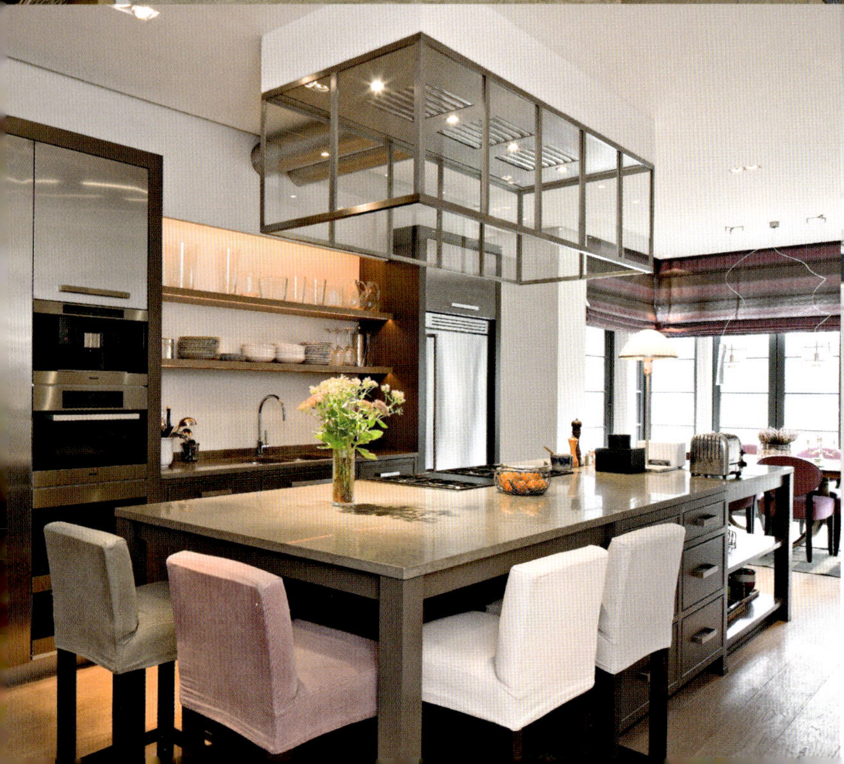
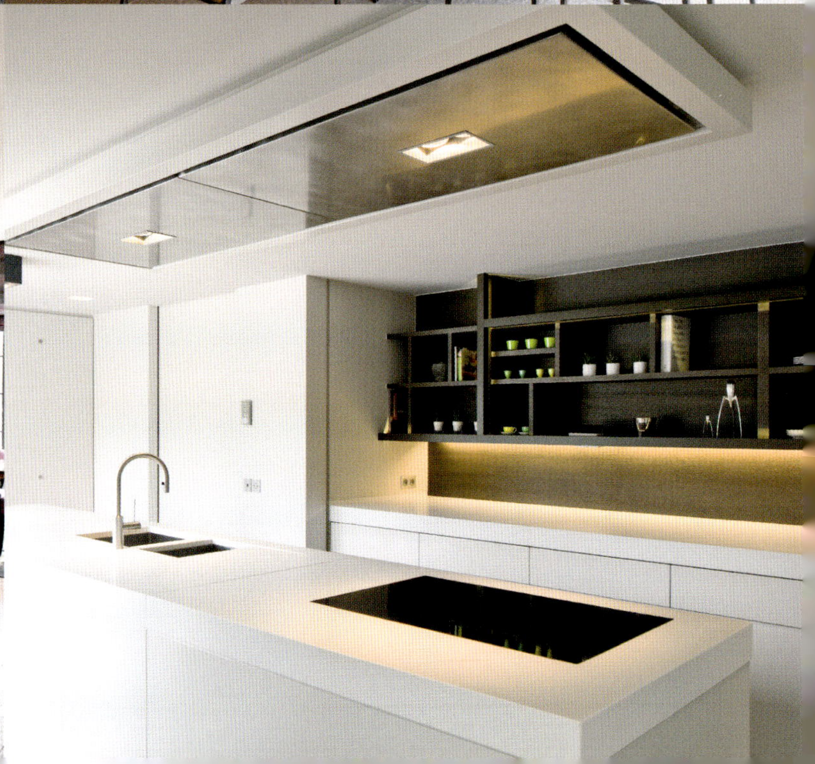

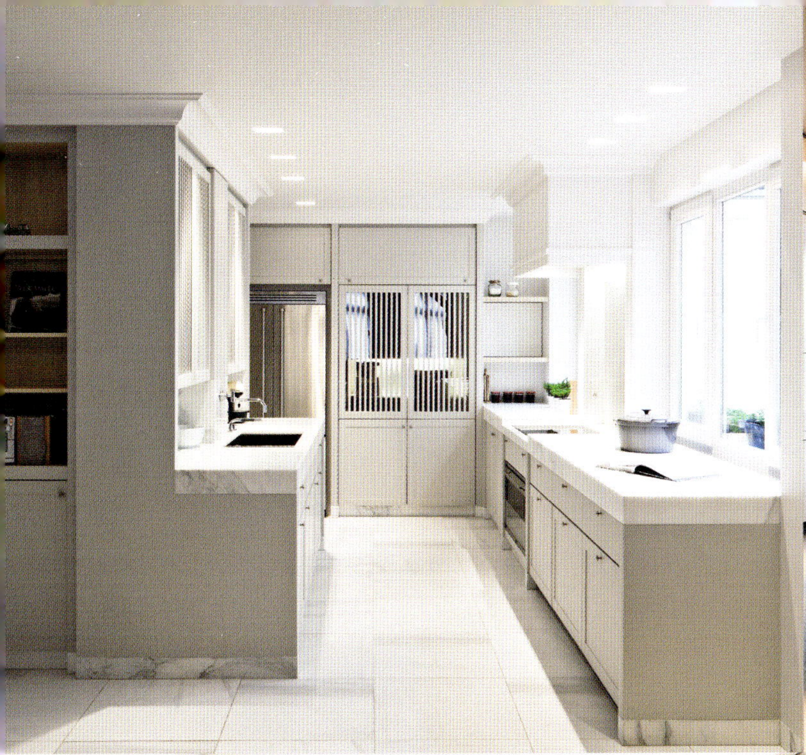
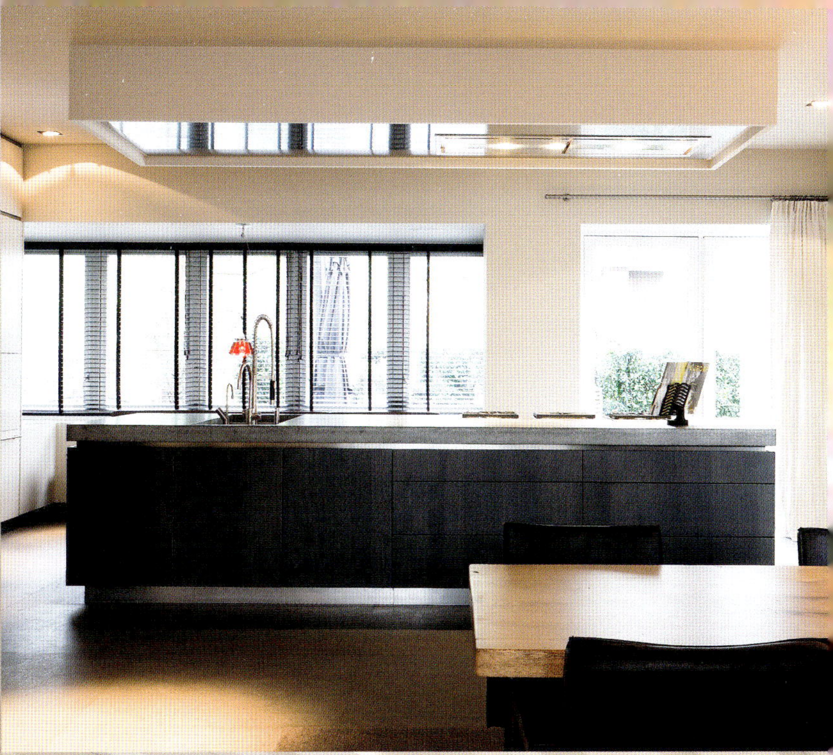
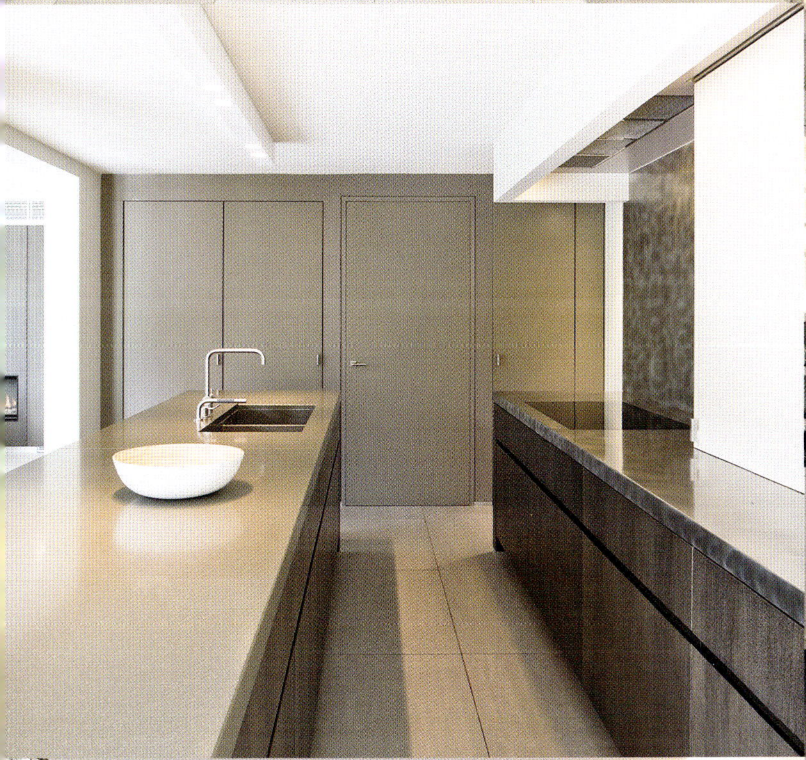
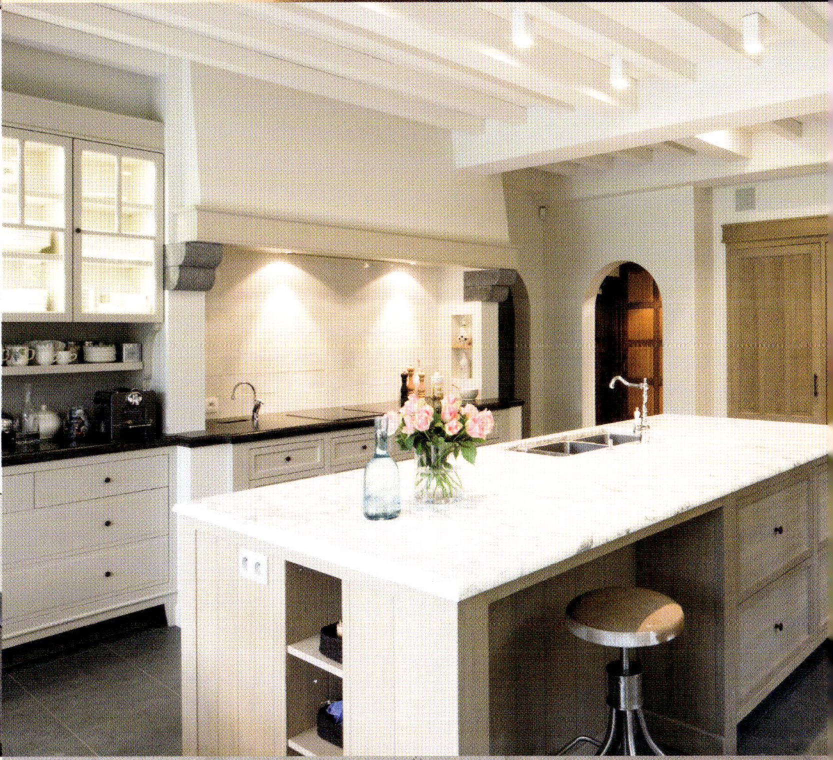
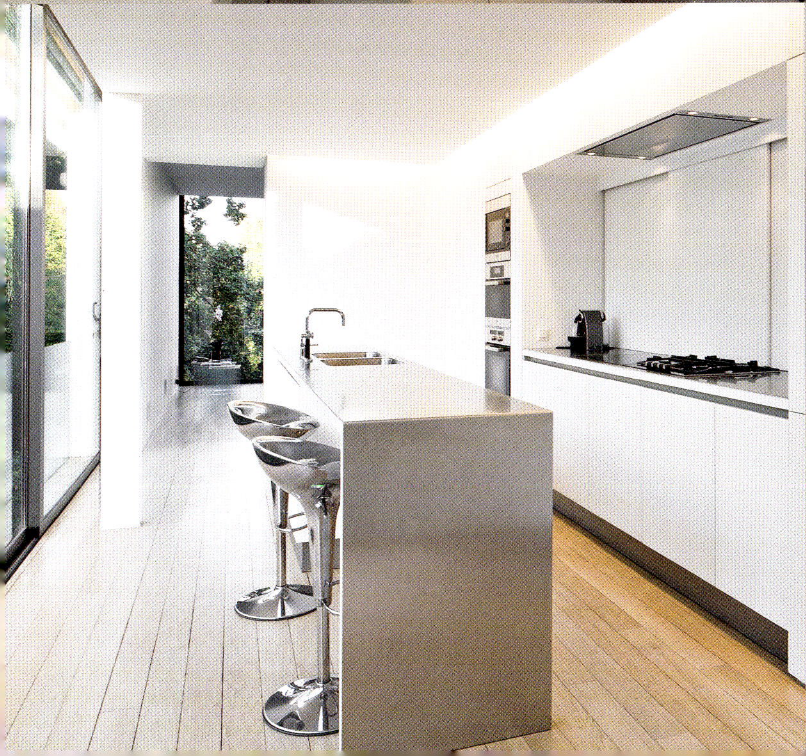
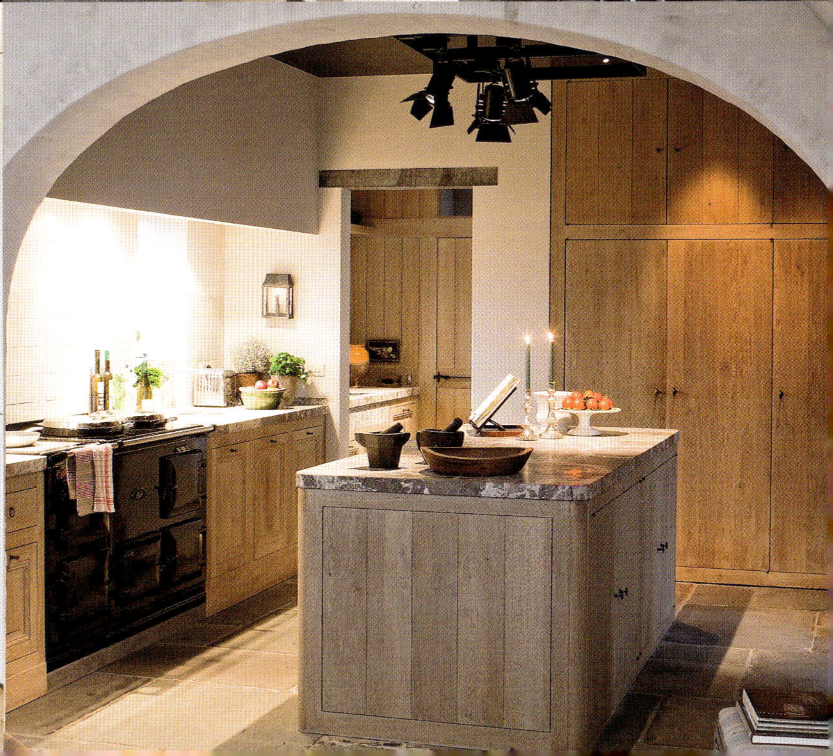

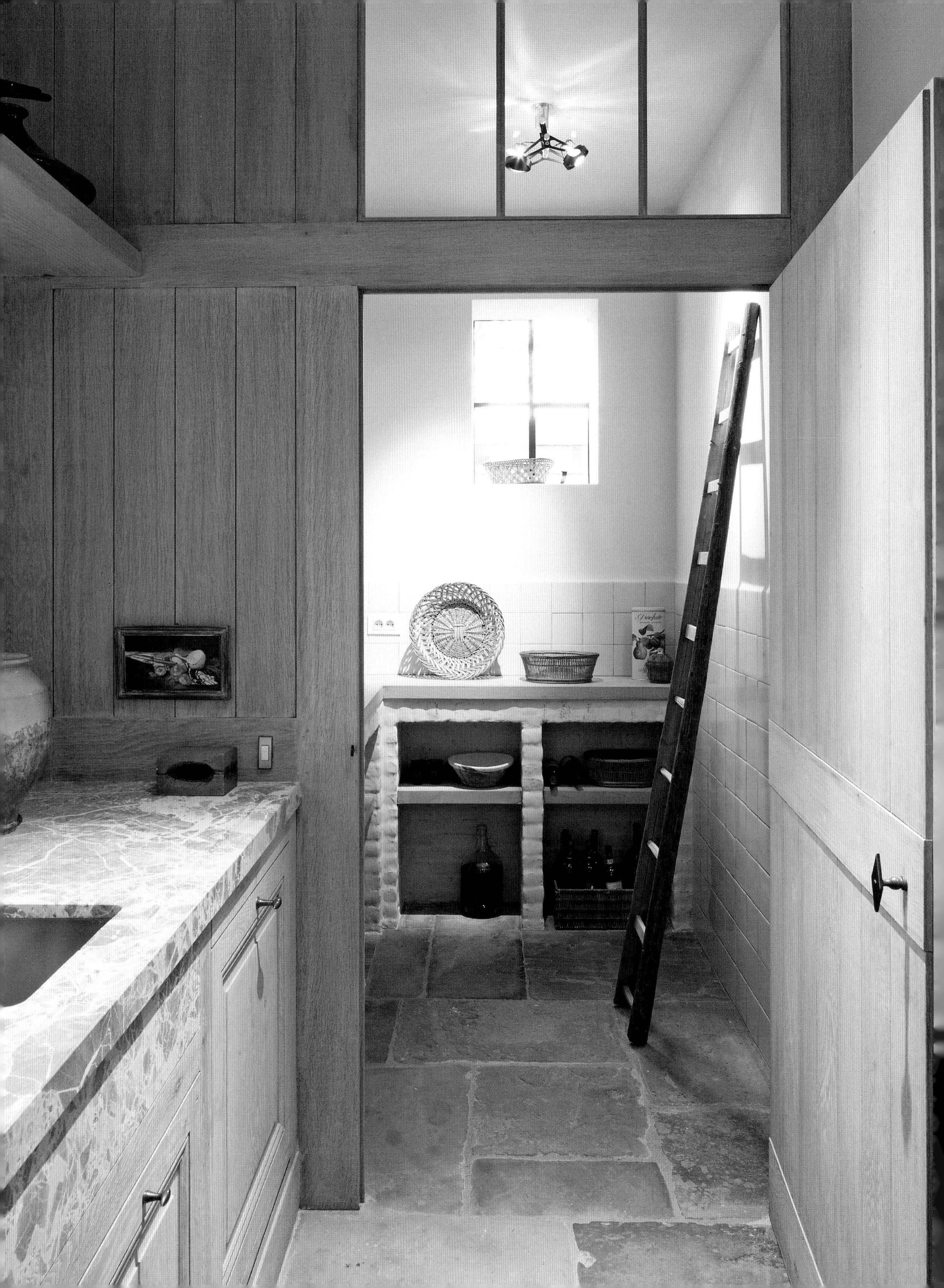

# [ FOREWORD ]

This new seventh edition (2011-2012) presents 30 previously unseen photographs of kitchens by renowned interior architects and kitchen designers.

The range is nothing if not diverse, from classic country kitchens to resolutely contemporary and minimalist designs.

This reference book includes hundreds of fascinating photographs for each kitchen specialist and is a source of inspiration for anyone intending to redesign their kitchen or to do a makeover in line with the latest trends, with the most recently developed materials, high-quality kitchenware and furnishings.

**Wim Pauwels**
Publisher

De Menagerie creation based on a design by the firm of architects Moors-Mestdagh.

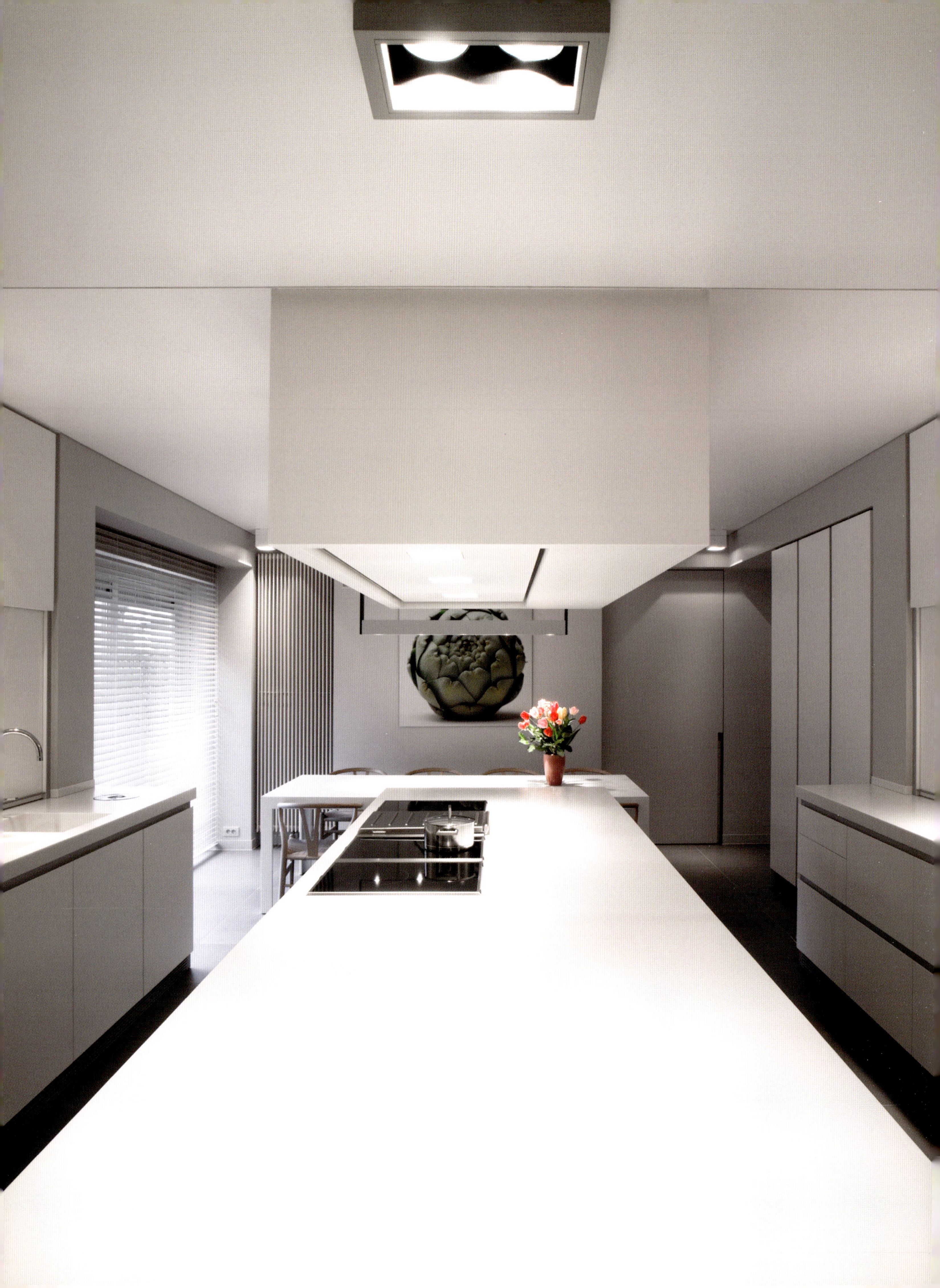

# [ A KITCHEN FIT
# FOR A KING - OR A QUEEN

This spacious kitchen designed for living and working by interior architect Filip Vanryckeghem (ixtra) constitutes the second phase of renovation of a splendid residential complex in Kortrijk.

The owners were anxious to create a real living kitchen, and this was achieved by simply removing a wall.

Let us first take a look at the central working area: the cooking island with its seating area. To the left we see the sink unit under a sliding cabinet for storing tableware and tall units housing the oven with a 76 cm warming drawer by Wolf (SubZero). There is also a pull-out larder cupboard.

On the right there is a similar working area with a sliding cabinet, in which there are three additional integrated Miele appliances and a static area for other standalone appliances. The adjacent tall units have sufficient space for a large refrigerator and freezer by Gaggenau.

In addition to the Vario appliances by Gaggenau, the island offers plenty of room as an additional work area and as a serving area for the dining area.
The wide, serene table area has been given pride of place by the new terrace window leading to the living room.

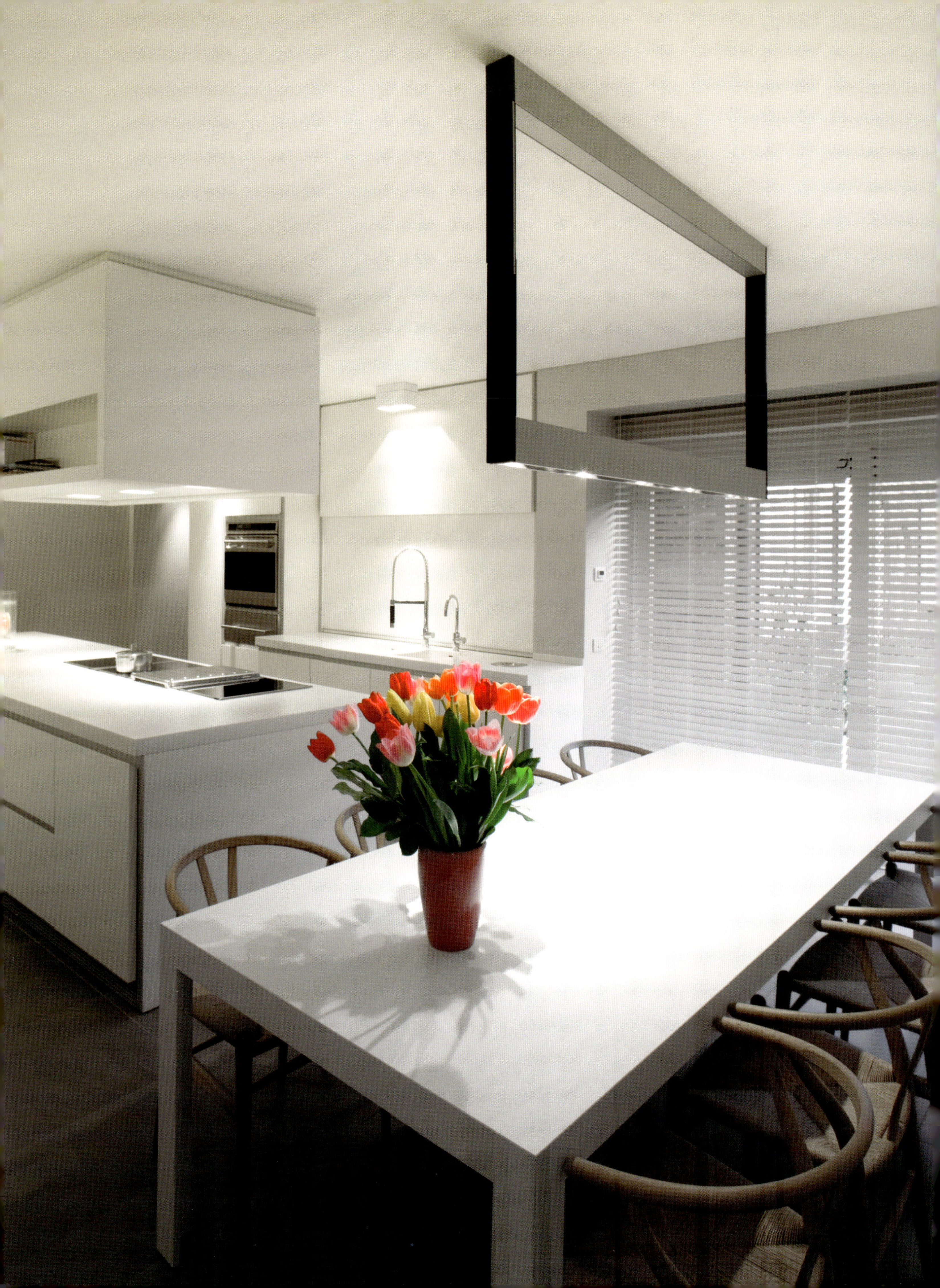

Chairs by Hans J. Wegner in natural oak around a standard table by Bulthaup. Table lamp by Kreon. Sink fittings by Dornbracht.

The kitchen is fully fitted with 28 mm thick front panels, finished with scratch-resistant textured paint.
All the recessed grooves and decorative strips are made with solid 3 mm aluminium.
Aluminium ventilated skirting boards by Häfele.
In the background on the right, bar stools designed by Bataille & Ibens for Obumex.

Worktops (including the two sinks) are made of Corian.

Surface-mounted waste system by Eisinger/Franke.

Between the Gaggenau knobs, socket by Niko (Mysterious model).

[ **iXtra Interior architecture**
Vanryckeghem Filip
Ieperstraat 18
B - 8930 Menen
+32 (0)474 311974
info@ixtra.be
www.ixtra.be

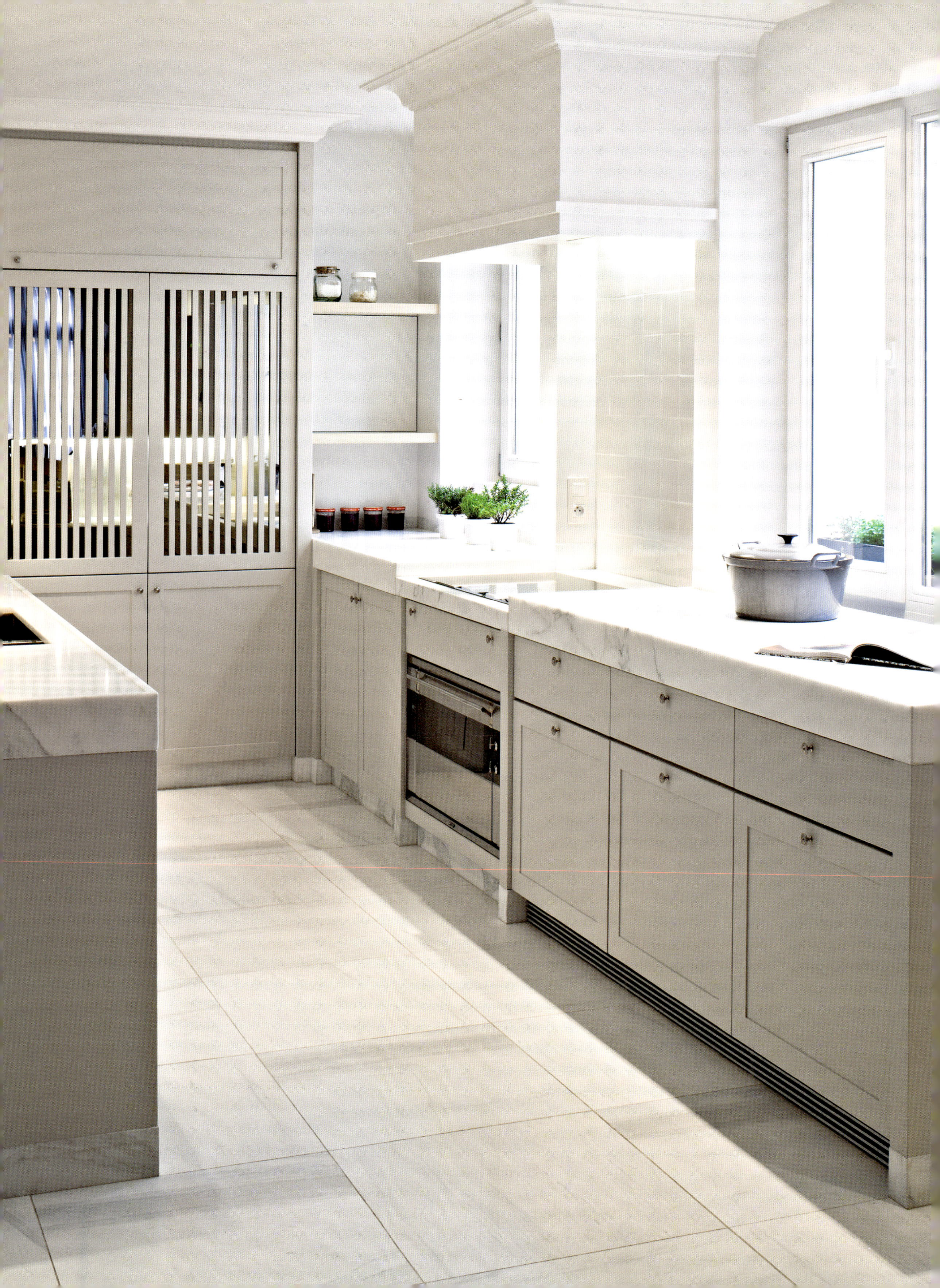

# [ CONTEMPORARY CLASSIC IN THE HEART OF BRUGES

This kitchen, created by Filip Vanryckeghem (the firm of interior architects iXtra), is in a typical Bruges dwelling house in the throbbing heart of this historic city.

This location inspired the design of this kitchen, both in the details and in the style elements.

The cooking area offers a pleasant view of the typical inner courtyard.
Ceramic floor tiles in imitation marble (Carrara) by Porcelanosa.
Worktops and cupboard skirting boards clad with Calacatta natural stone. The kitchen wall is coated with traditional Dutch white tiles.
Kitchen appliances by Smeg.
The profiled cabinet doors are fitted with special mirror glass (Antelio bronze type).

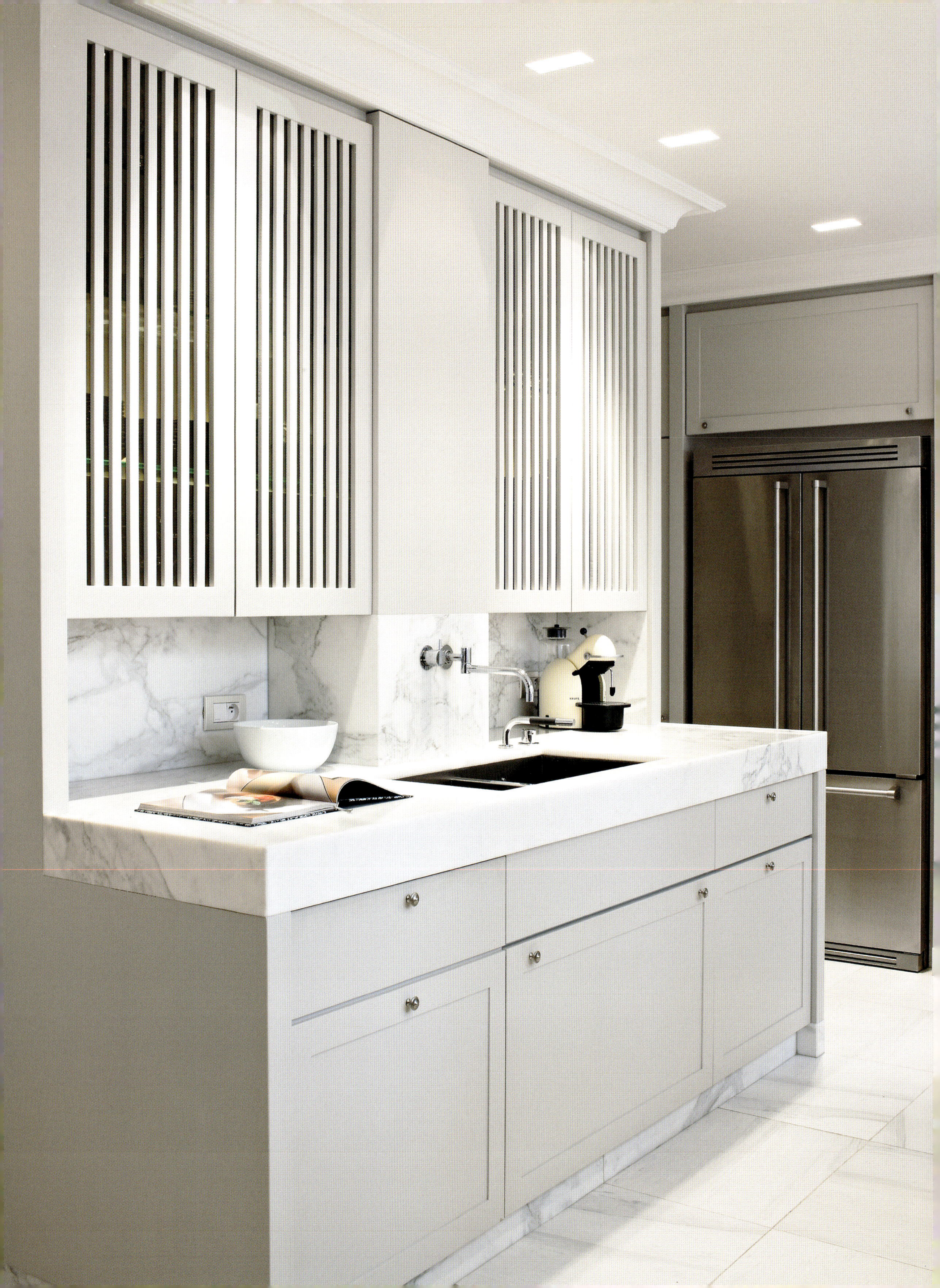

**20**
The sink unit with incorporated storage area (including a dishwasher) offers some extra space for tableware in the profiled wall units.
Refrigerator by Amana. A double sink unit by Franke, sink fittings by Vola and mounted handles by Peter Van Cronenburg. Lighting by Kreon.

[ **iXtra Interior architecture**
Vanryckeghem Filip
Ieperstraat 18
B - 8930 Menen
T +32 (0)474 311974
info@ixtra.be
www.ixtra.be

Details of the bread and coffee cupboard with a natural stone sliding tablet, which can be locked in place thanks to two profiled pivoting/sliding door systems. This cupboard also houses the microwave oven.

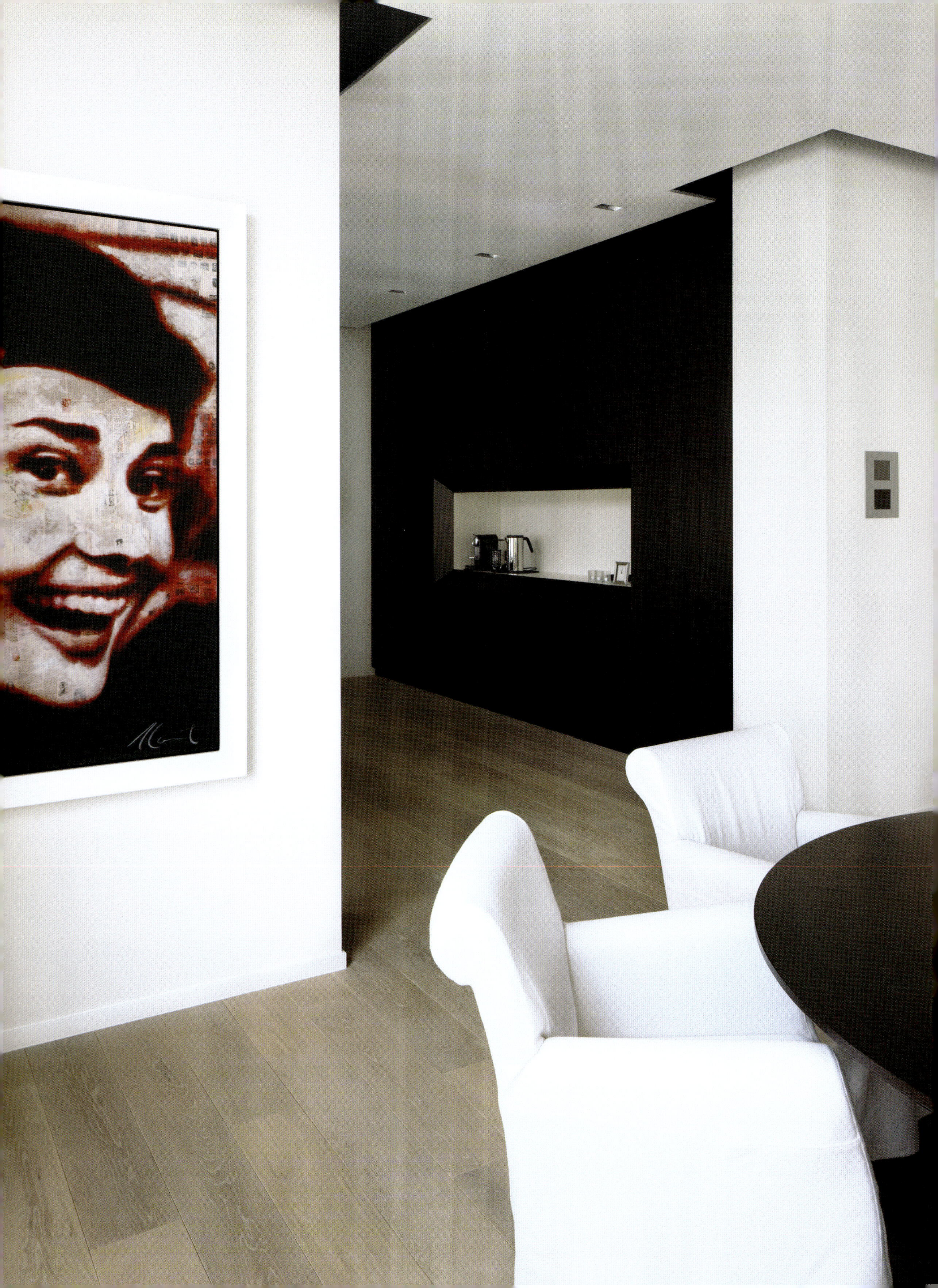

# [ CONSTANTLY STRIVING FOR PERFECTION

Obumex began designing and creating exclusive kitchens in 1960. Half a century later, this family-owned company with Geert Ostyn at the helm has developed into one of the most trendsetting producers of high-quality kitchens and total concepts, the work of a team of 100 people with a passion for excellence.

We present in these pages four very recent kitchen design projects implemented by Obumex. This is only one small sample of the company's amazing diversity, but it gives some idea of the commitment that has for 50 years been the driving force behind Obumex's desire to offer high quality products and to constantly seek design perfection.

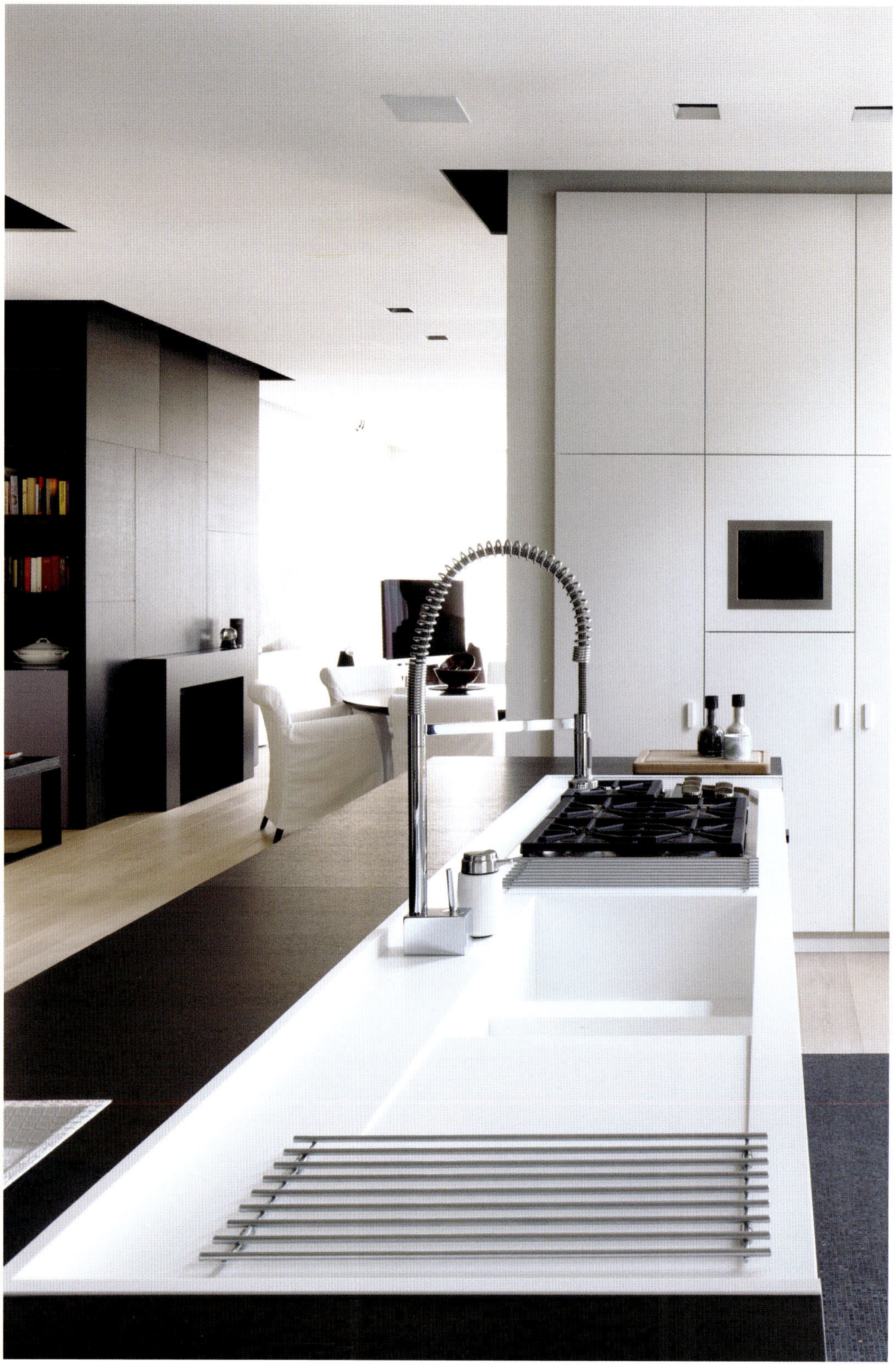

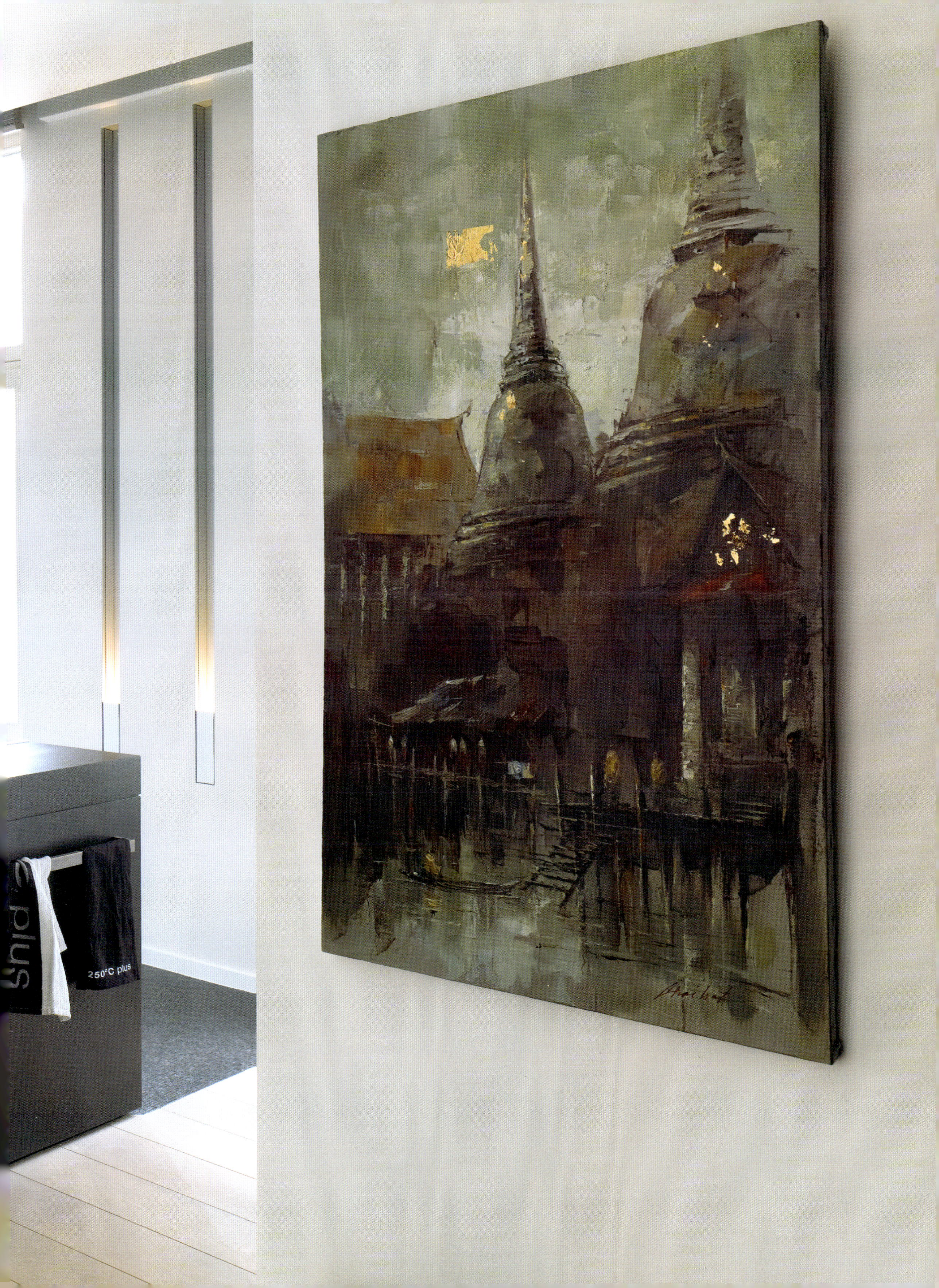
250°C plus

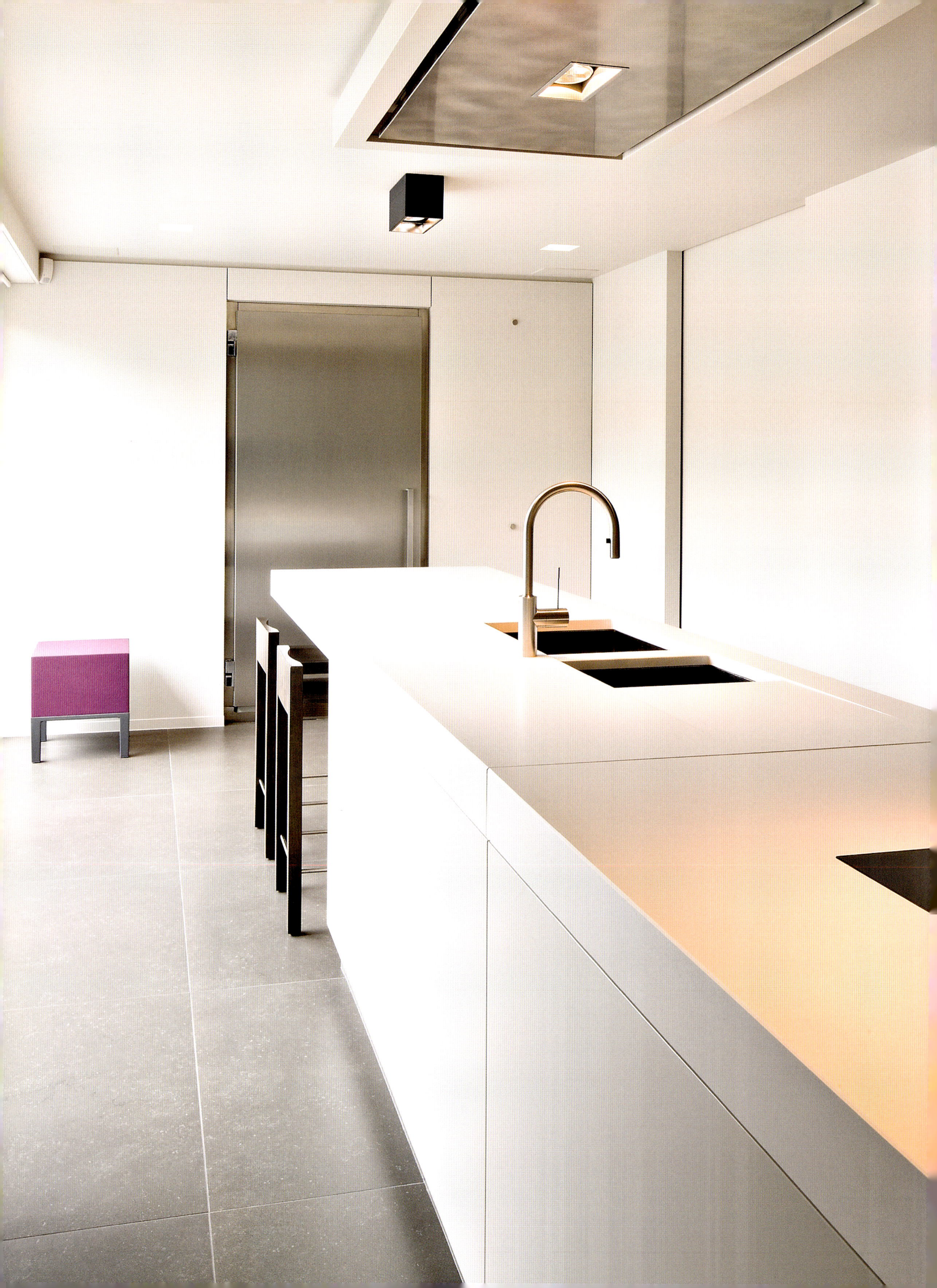

# [ KITCHEN WITH SUPERB GARDEN VIEW

This kitchen is located in an extension of the house. This space was designed as a kitchen in such a way as to give the owners a perfect view of the garden and the surrounding hilly landscape.

They opted for a rather austere living kitchen that offers the possibility of added flexibility and a rear wall with plenty of room for personal inspiration.

The design was signed by Xavier Gadeyne, an interior architect with Obumex, the company that was commissioned to coordinate and implement the work of extending the house.

The floor covering that was selected consists of 90x90 cm ceramic "grey Buxy" tiles.
The extractor hood is made of stainless steel.

The long central block, with its adjacent cooking and sink areas, offers a panoramic view of the garden.
The worktop made of white composite stone (thickened to 10 cm) extends to create a suspended table.
Half-height stools by Bataille & Ibens for Obumex.
In the background of the photograph (in the middle) there is a stainless steel feature door leading to the cold storage area.

The kitchen and dining room can be separated by a wide sliding partition. The kitchen is finished in white satin paint, with touches of sandblasted dark stained oak.

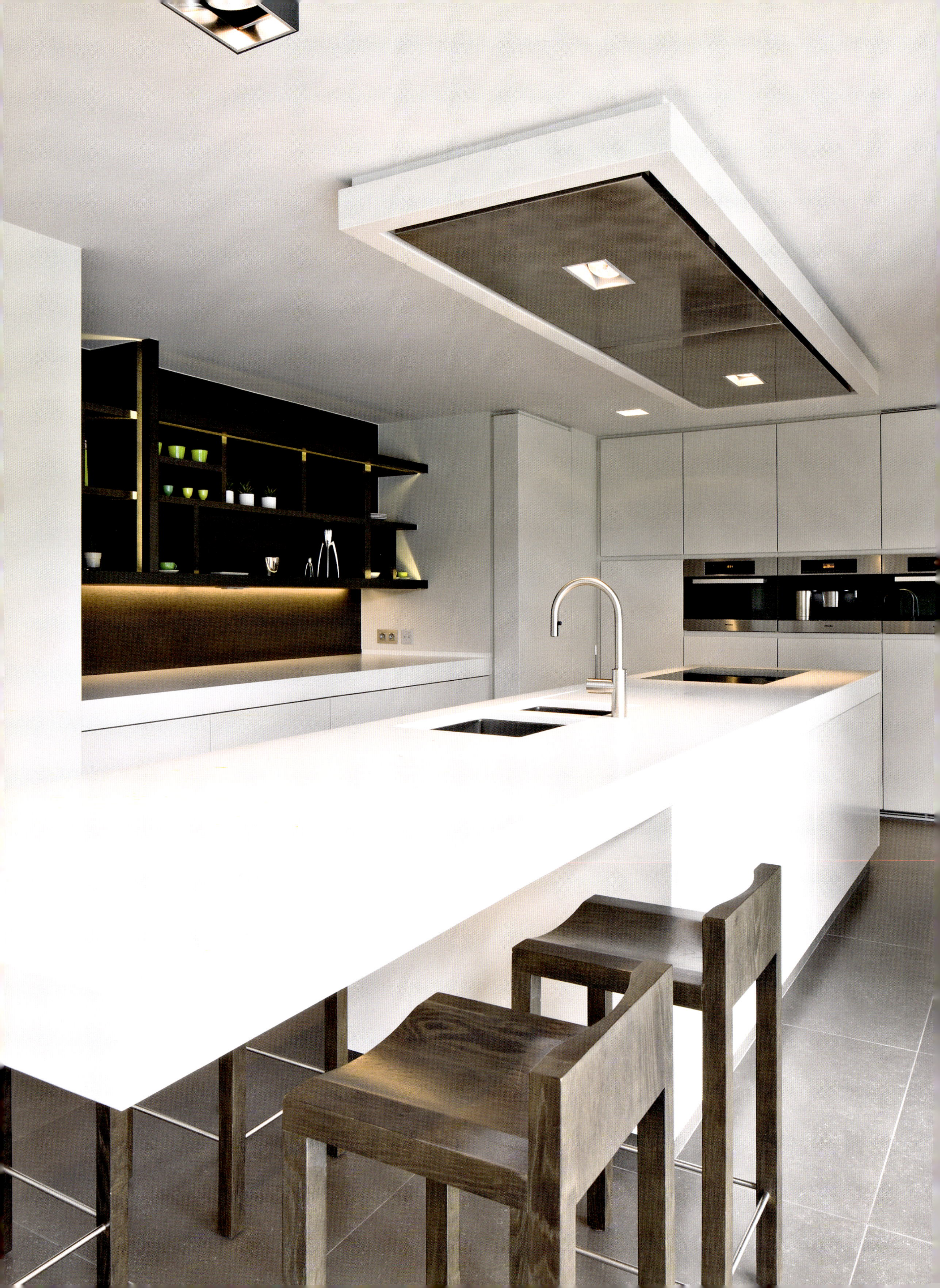

The ovens are horizontally integrated in the kitchen design at working height.

[ **Obumex nv**
Diksmuidestraat 121
B – 8840 Staden
T +32 (0)51 70 50 71
F +32 (0)51 70 50 81
www.obumex.be

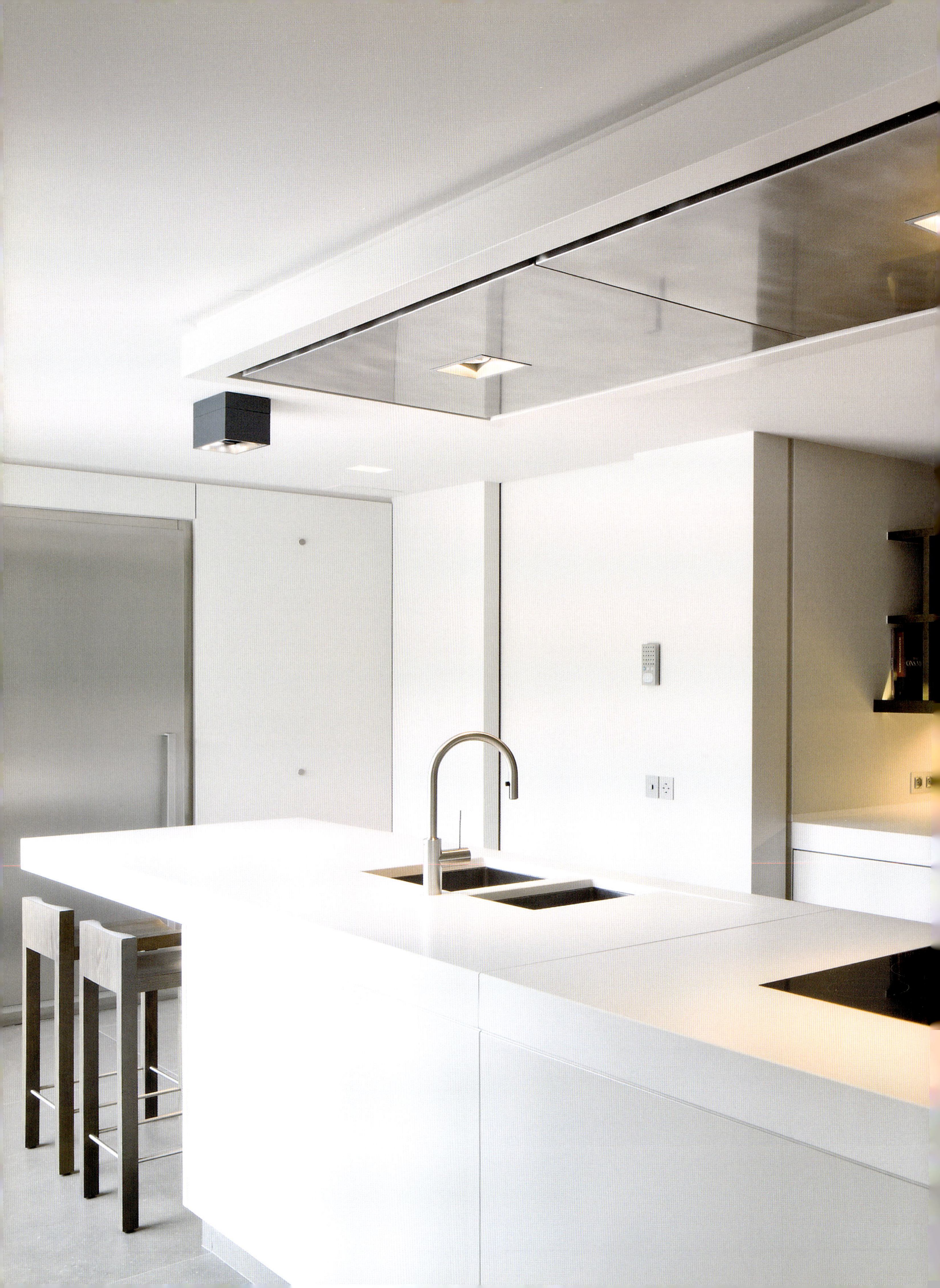

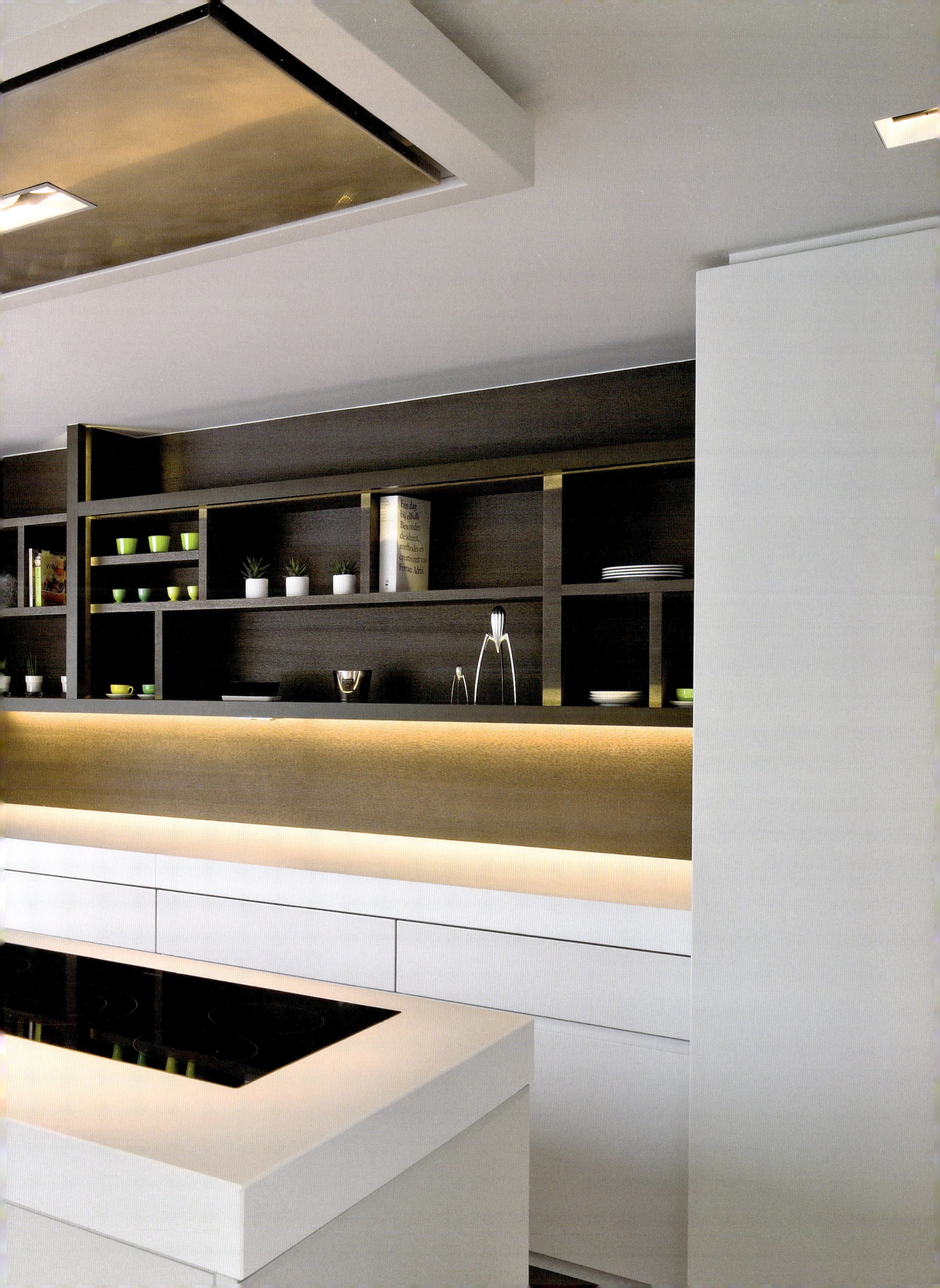
Een dag
bij elBulli
Bewonder

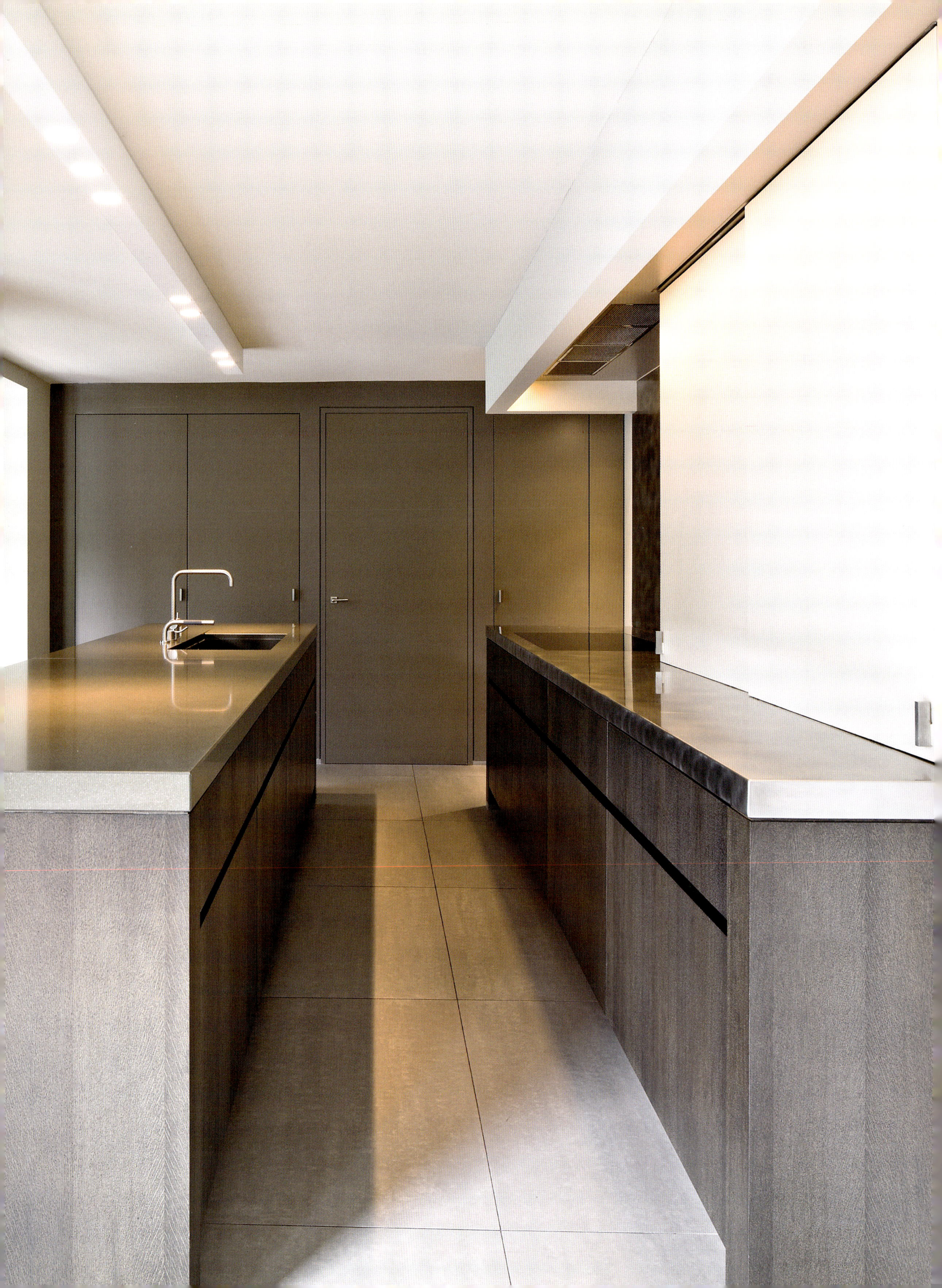

# [ A KITCHEN AND DINING ROOM COMBINED

For this design, Tom Sileghem, an interior architect working for Obumex, decided to link the separate kitchen area with the dining room by means of a fireback by using the same materials in the two areas.
This technique creates a sense of unity of the whole.

Obumex undertook the design, coordination and implementation of the two spaces.

For the floor coverings, the designers opted for 100x100 cm full ceramic tiles.
The worktops and sink units on the left are made of Silestone (Unsui Leather Touch),
while the cupboards are made of oak veneer (colour Gris Roche). Sink fittings by Vola.
The cooking area features a brushed stainless steel worktop.

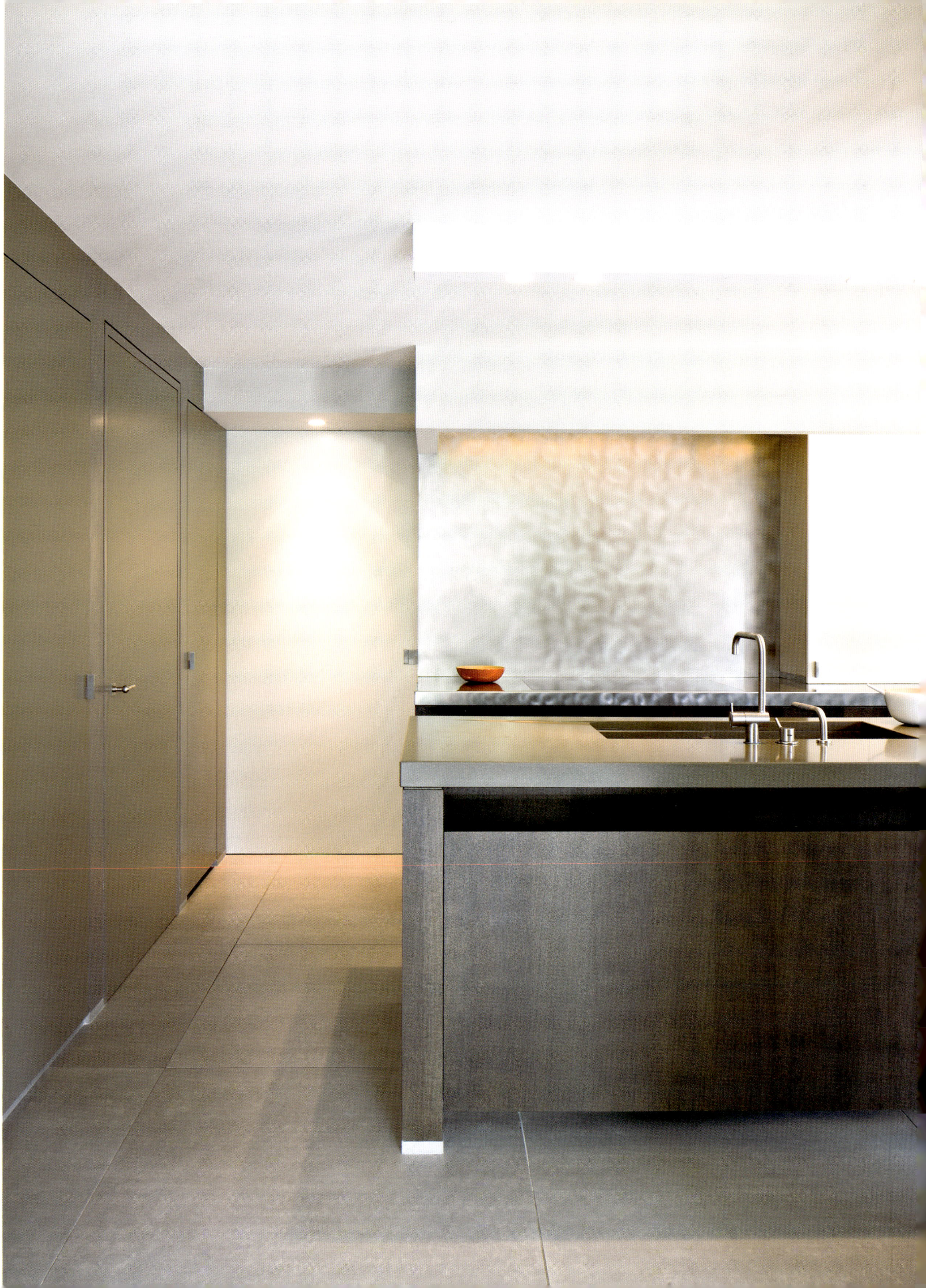

# [ A FEELING OF WARMTH

Pierre Daems, an interior architect with Obumex, designed this country living kitchen that positively exudes charm and homeliness thanks to the presence of the open fire and the use of wood.

The cupboard fronts and uprights in this kitchen were designed by Obumex in natural oak. The floor is coated with large Pietra di Medici tiles.

Chairs by Hans J. Wegner around the dining room table by Christian Liaigre. Obscura lamp above the table.

The worktop is coated with granito.

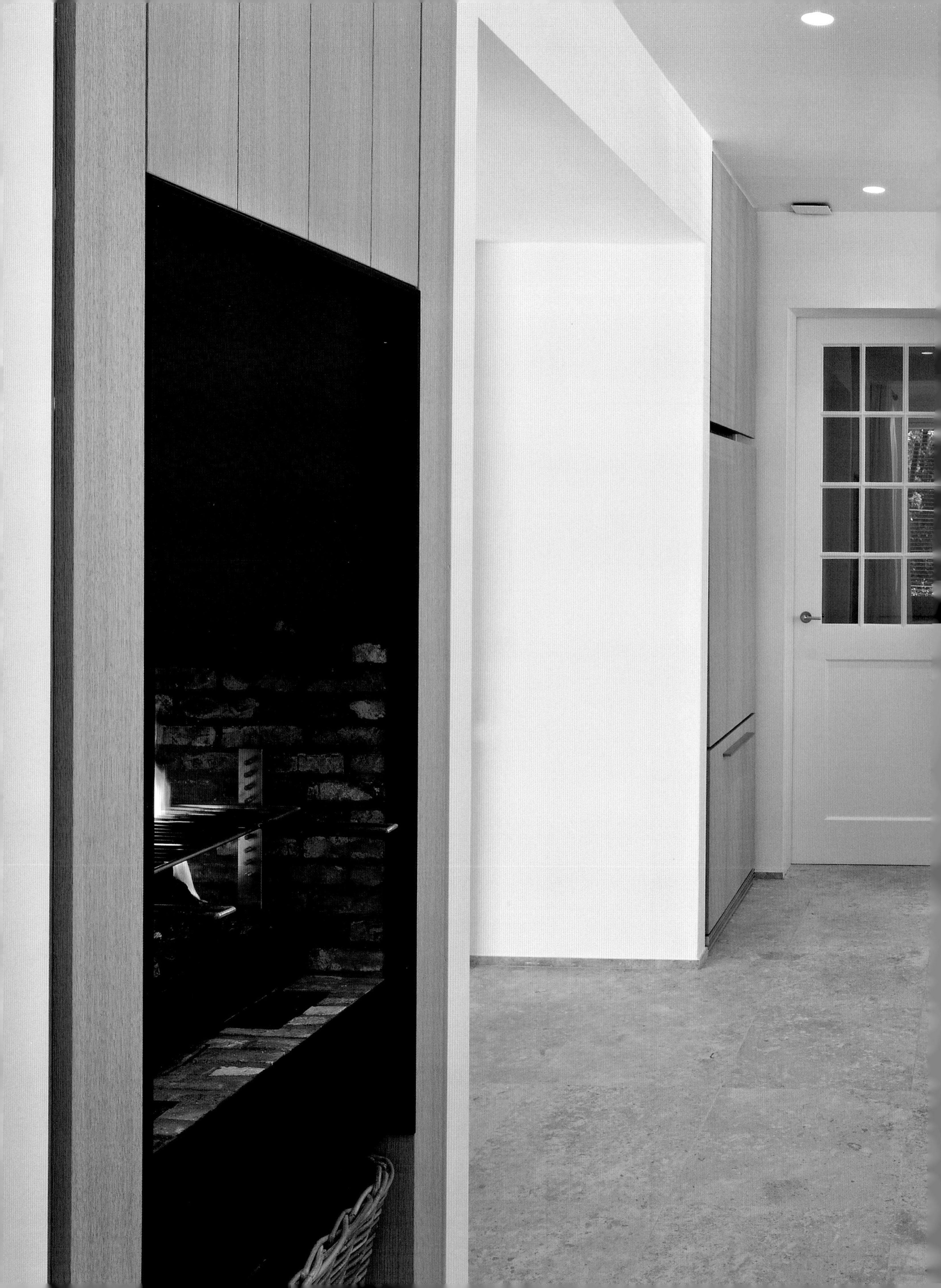

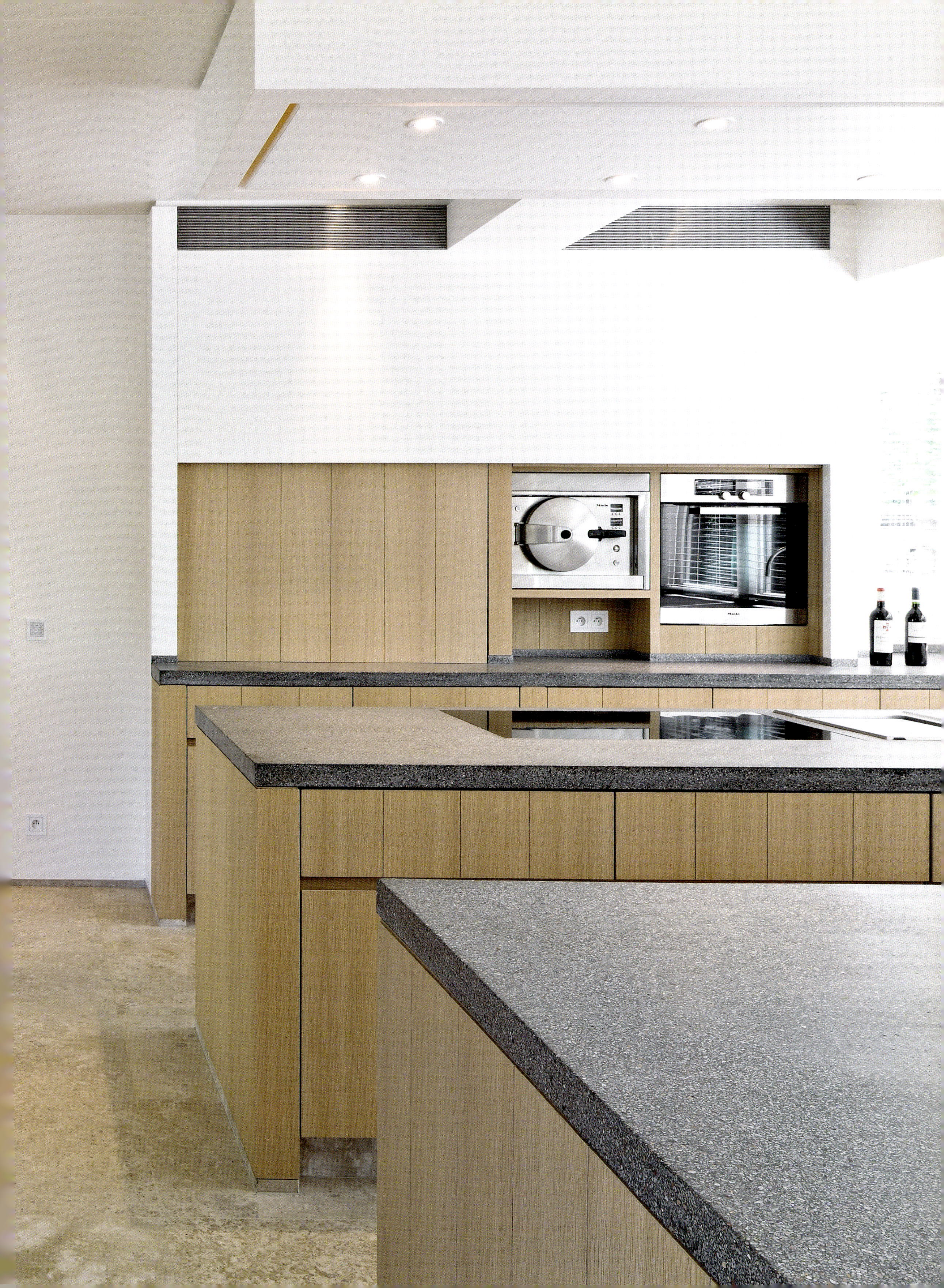

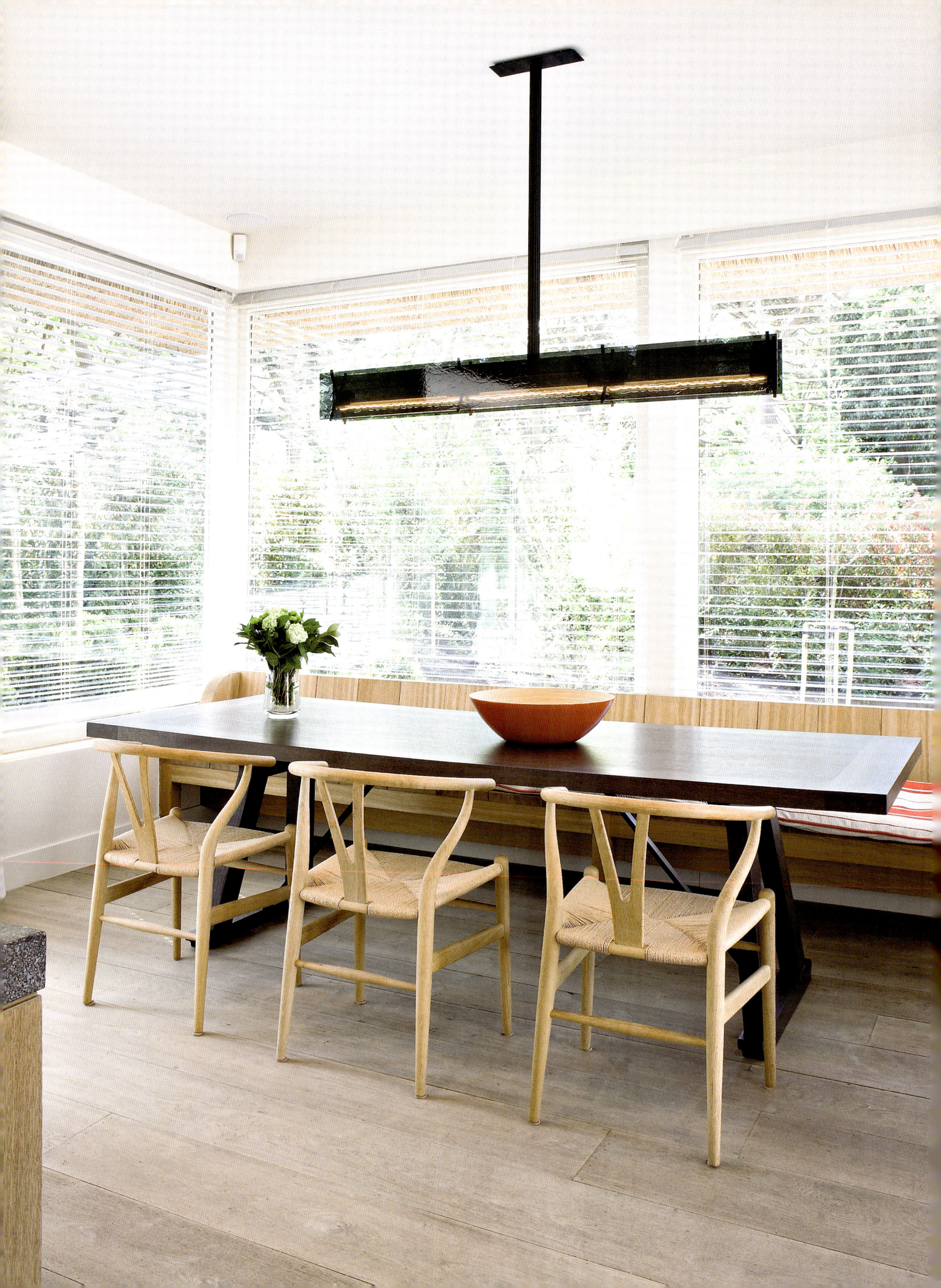

The stained oak parquet flooring creates a warm feeling in this living kitchen, in perfect harmony with the Pietra di Medici natural stone floor that defines the cooking area.

**Obumex nv**
Diksmuidestraat 121
B – 8840 Staden
T +32 (0)51  70 50 71
F +32 (0)51  70 50 81
www.obumex.be

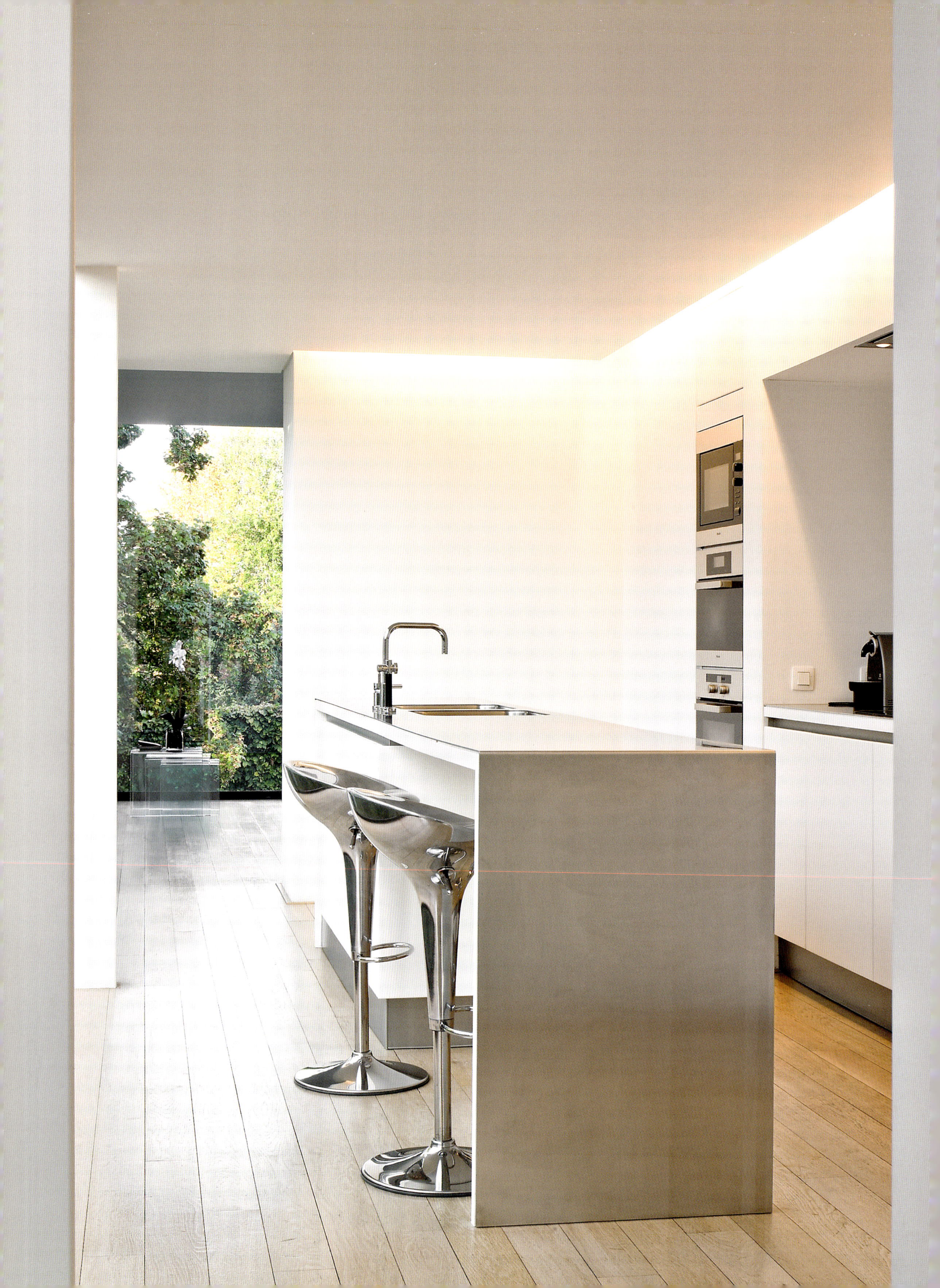

# [ KITCHENS WITH AMBIANCE

Ambiance Cuisine is a real family-owned company that was set up by a couple who are interior architects (van Havere-de Hasque). Along with their son Xavier, who has followed in their footsteps, in the past 15 years they have built up a strong reputation as designers of unique high quality kitchens that combine functionality, aesthetic appeal and character.

For Ambiance Cuisine, design is not a luxury but a way to create solutions that make kitchens not only stylish but also practical.
When Ambiance Cuisine designs a kitchen, to make sure every detail is according to plan they call on the services of experienced fitters.

Ambiance Cuisine is a recognised dealer for Poggenpohl, which is one of the top names in contemporary design kitchens offering the legendary robustness of German craftsmanship. Moreover, Ambiance Cuisine's "Provence" range of kitchens has been highly successful in recent years (see pages 54-57).
In addition, in this first article Ambiance Cuisine presents a design kitchen that is destined for success: the Schüller range.

A Schüller kitchen in a house designed by the architect Bruno Erpicum (the "Next Line" model finished in white textured paint).

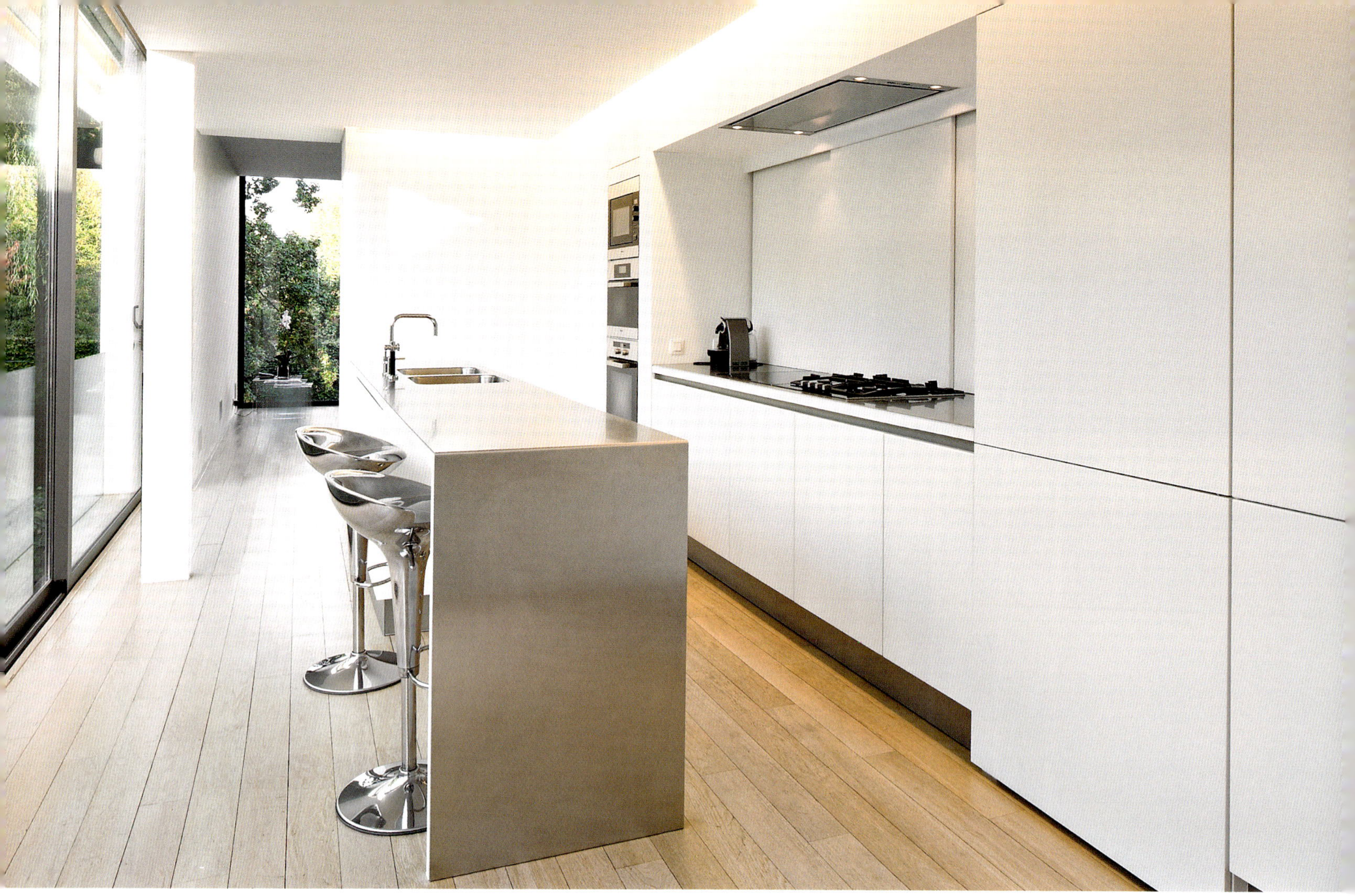

Sink fittings by Dornbracht, oven, steam oven, warming drawer and microwave by Miele and extractor hood by Novy. Sliding doors with textured paint.

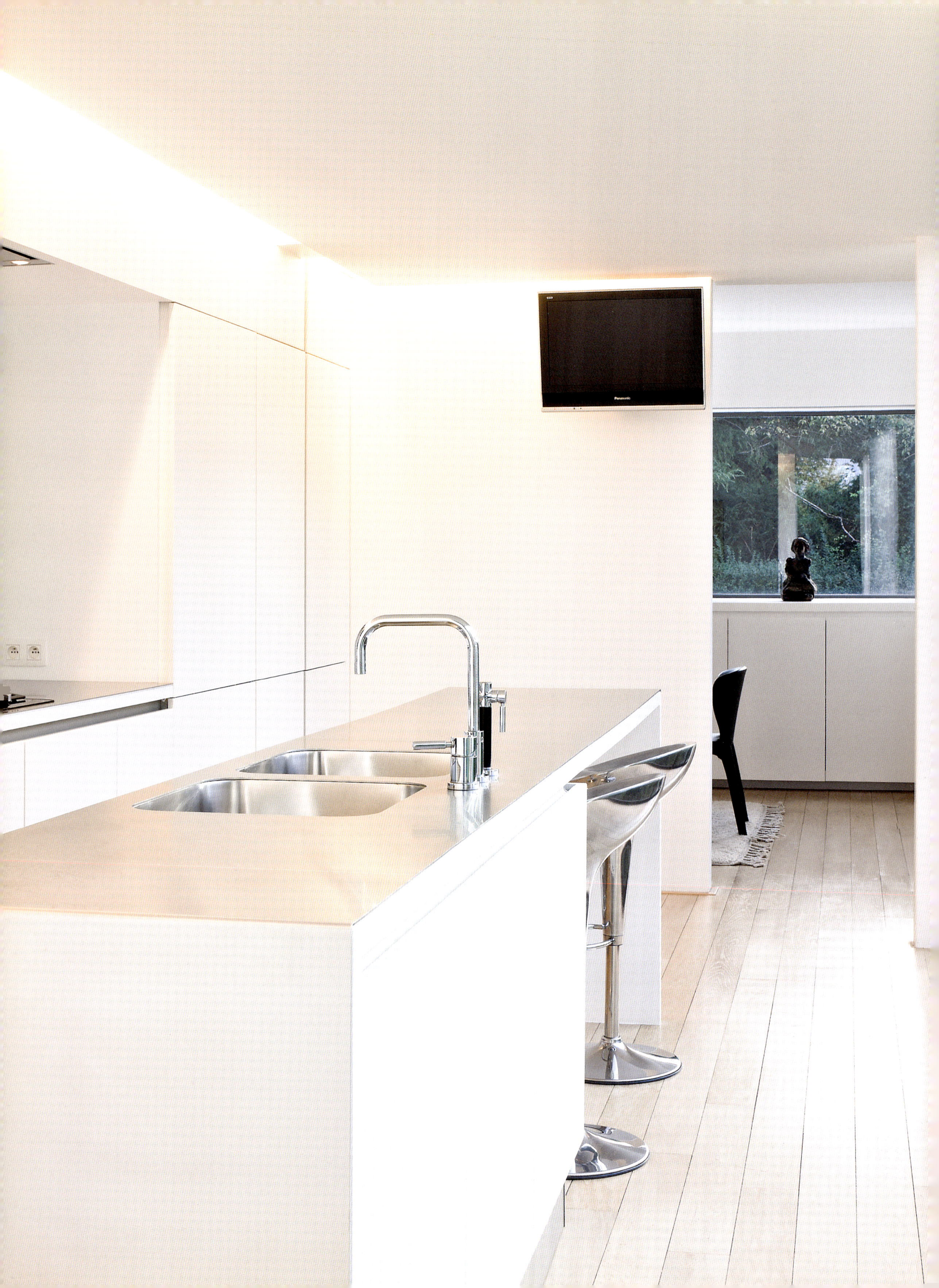

The worktop is made of Blanco stainless steel with a welded sink. Hob by Siemens.

[ **Ambiance Cuisine**
Chaussée de Waterloo 1138
B – 1180 Uccle
T +32 (0)2 375 24 36
Ambiance Poggenpohl
Avenue Reine Astrid 479-481
B – 1950 Kraainem
T +32 (0)2 767 12 17
www.ambiancecuisine.com

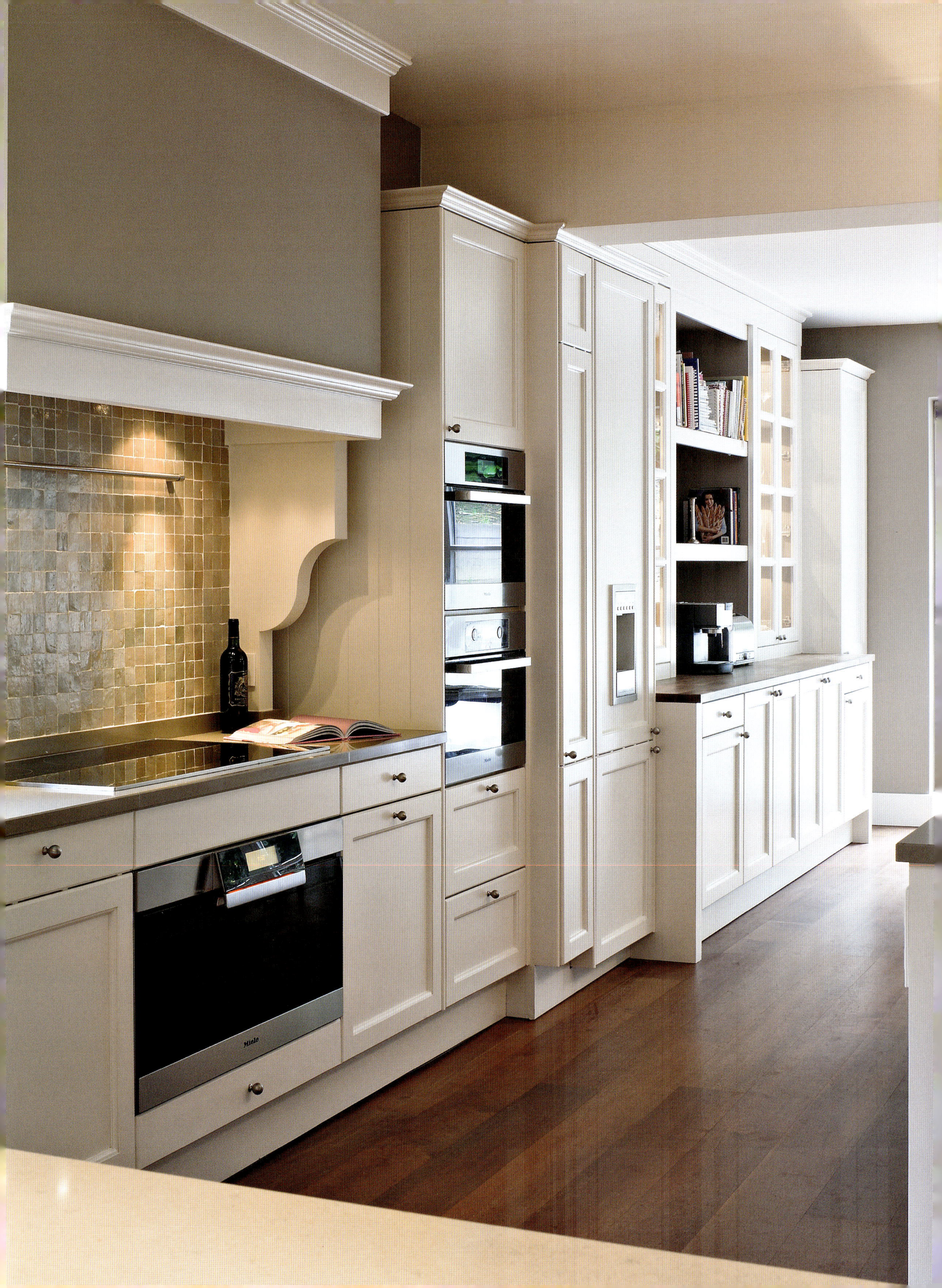
Miele

[ A BLEND OF PROVENCE
AND OLD ENGLAND

This second kitchen by Ambiance Cuisine (the first is featured on p. 48-53) has a very particular style and atmosphere that is more akin to sunny Provence, but has touches of the cosiness of Olde England.
The Provence model is a traditionally designed kitchen, full of quaint charm but with every imaginable modern convenience.

This kitchen was created by lovers of traditional country kitchens: cosy, warm and intimate.

This "Provence" kitchen by Ambiance Cuisine made of
MDF was lovingly patinated by Corinne de Hasque.

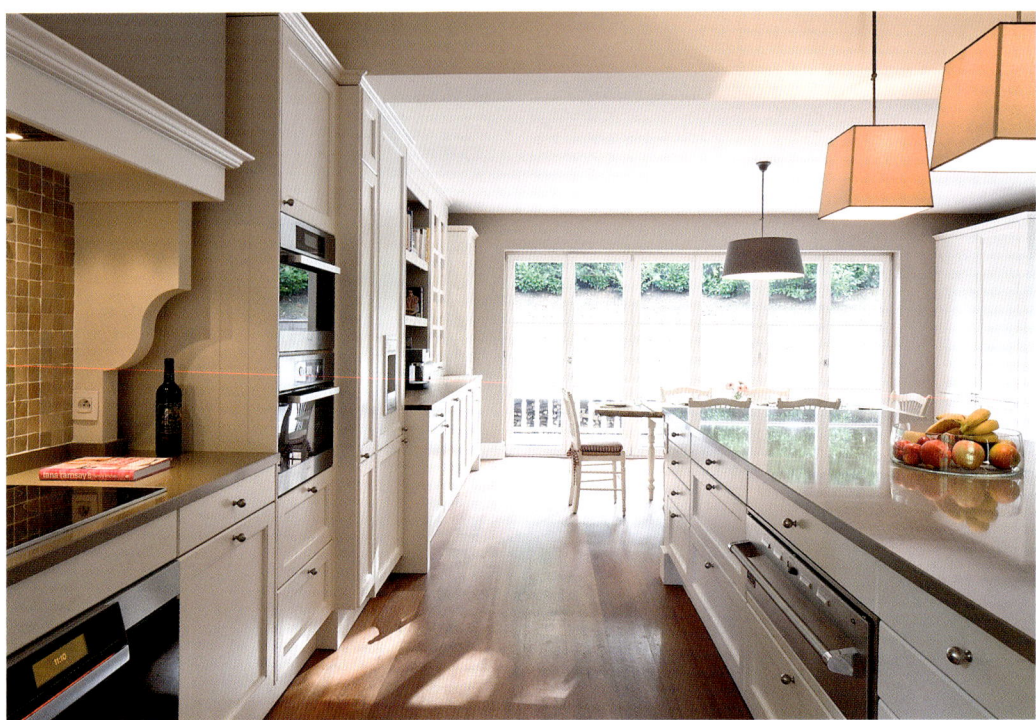

The worktops are coated with Caesarstone. Miele appliances, refrigerators and wine storage racks by Gaggenau, warming drawers by Viking.

[ **Ambiance Cuisine**
Chaussée de Waterloo 1138
B – 1180 Uccle
T +32 (0)2 375 24 36
Ambiance Poggenpohl
Avenue Reine Astrid 479-481
B – 1950 Kraainem
T +32 (0)2 767 12 17
www.ambiancecuisine.com

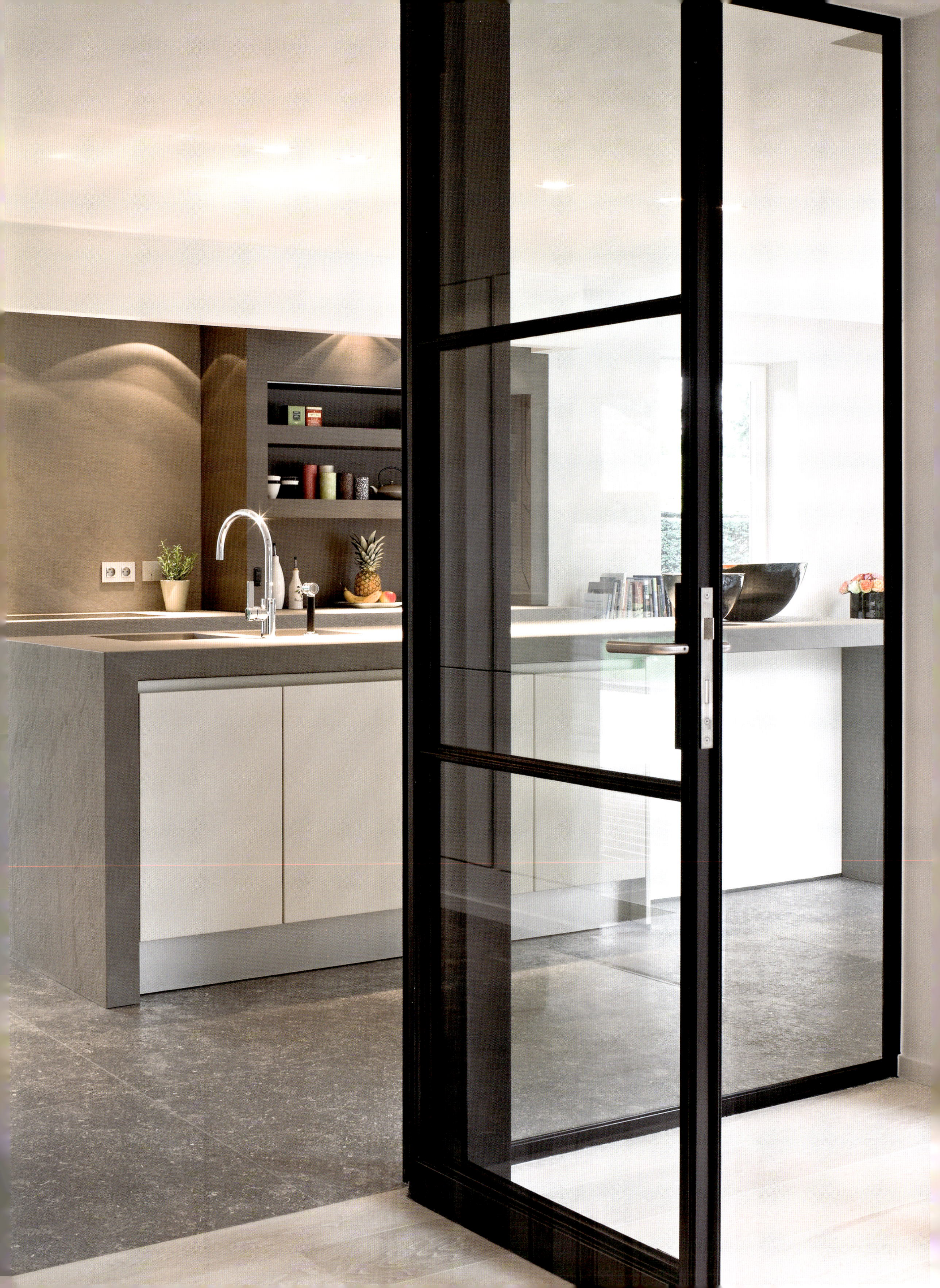

# A UNIQUE SPECIALISATION : KITCHEN WORKTOPS

Louis Culot is one of the few companies that specialises completely in the production and fitting of kitchen worktops made of natural stone or composite materials.

Since the company moved four years ago to much larger premises in the town of Puurs, Louis Culot and its team have forged an even more solid reputation for quality. The warehouse and workshop are now combined in one large area, which means that the different processes (transportation, sawing and polishing) can be carried out even more quickly and more efficiently. And thanks to CNC machinery, perfect finishing is now routine.

In addition to kitchen manufacturers, including a number of large companies, Louis Culot's 400m² showroom attracts a host of retailers and fitters as well as architects and private clients.

The following articles present two very different kitchens with worktops signed by Louis Culot. Noteworthy is the combination of several different trends, ranging from resolutely modern, austere and contemporary designs (p. 58-63) to timeless country kitchens (p. 64-69).

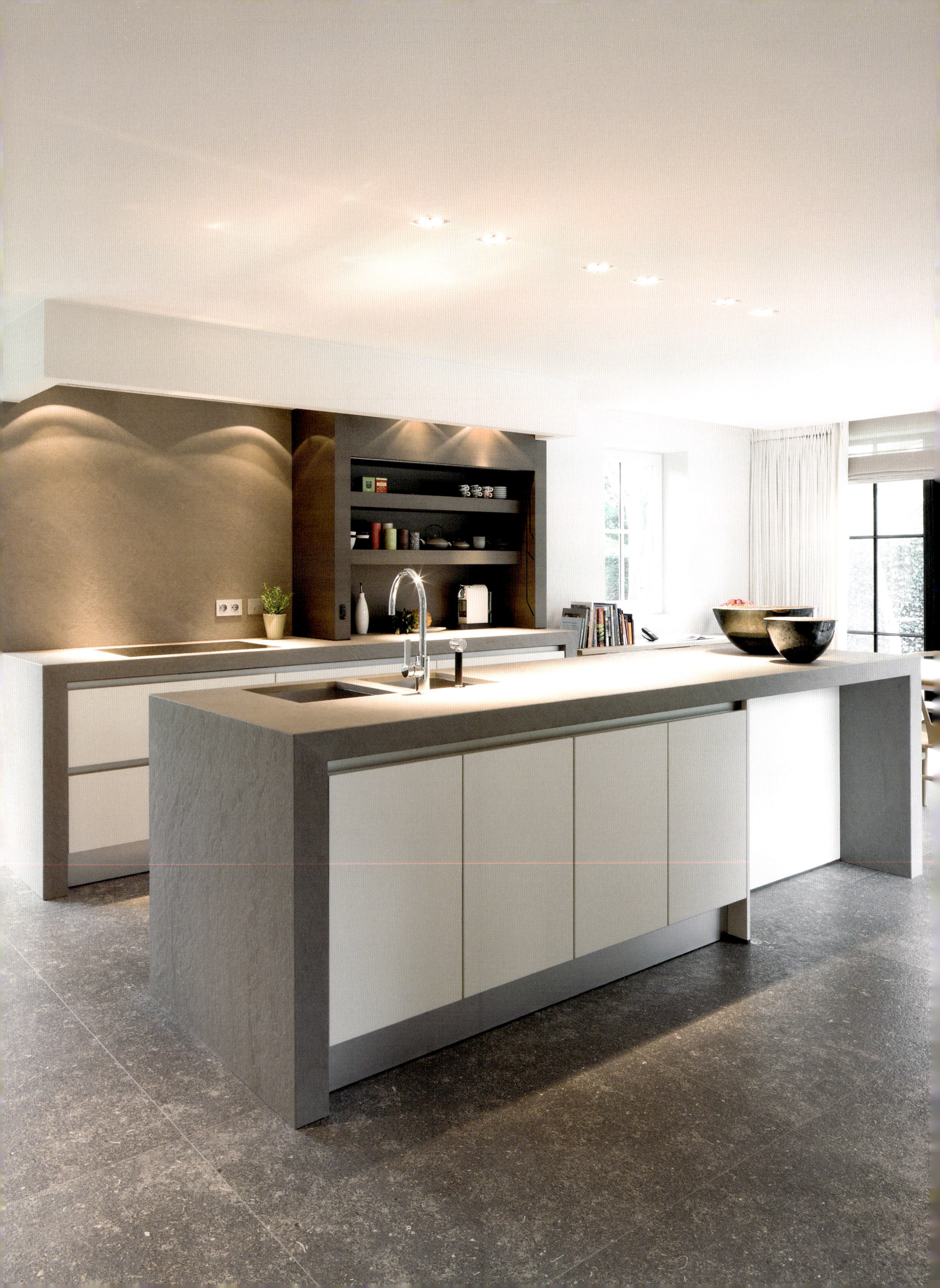

These kitchen worktops were made by Louis Culot in Grigio Quartzite (flamed finishing). The panels are 3 cm thick and are thickened to 8 cm in oblique sections.
The lateral supports are a continuation of the worktop. In addition, there are two built-in sink units and a flush-fitted hob.
The rear wall of the cooking area is also made of flamed Grigio Quartzite (2 cm thick).

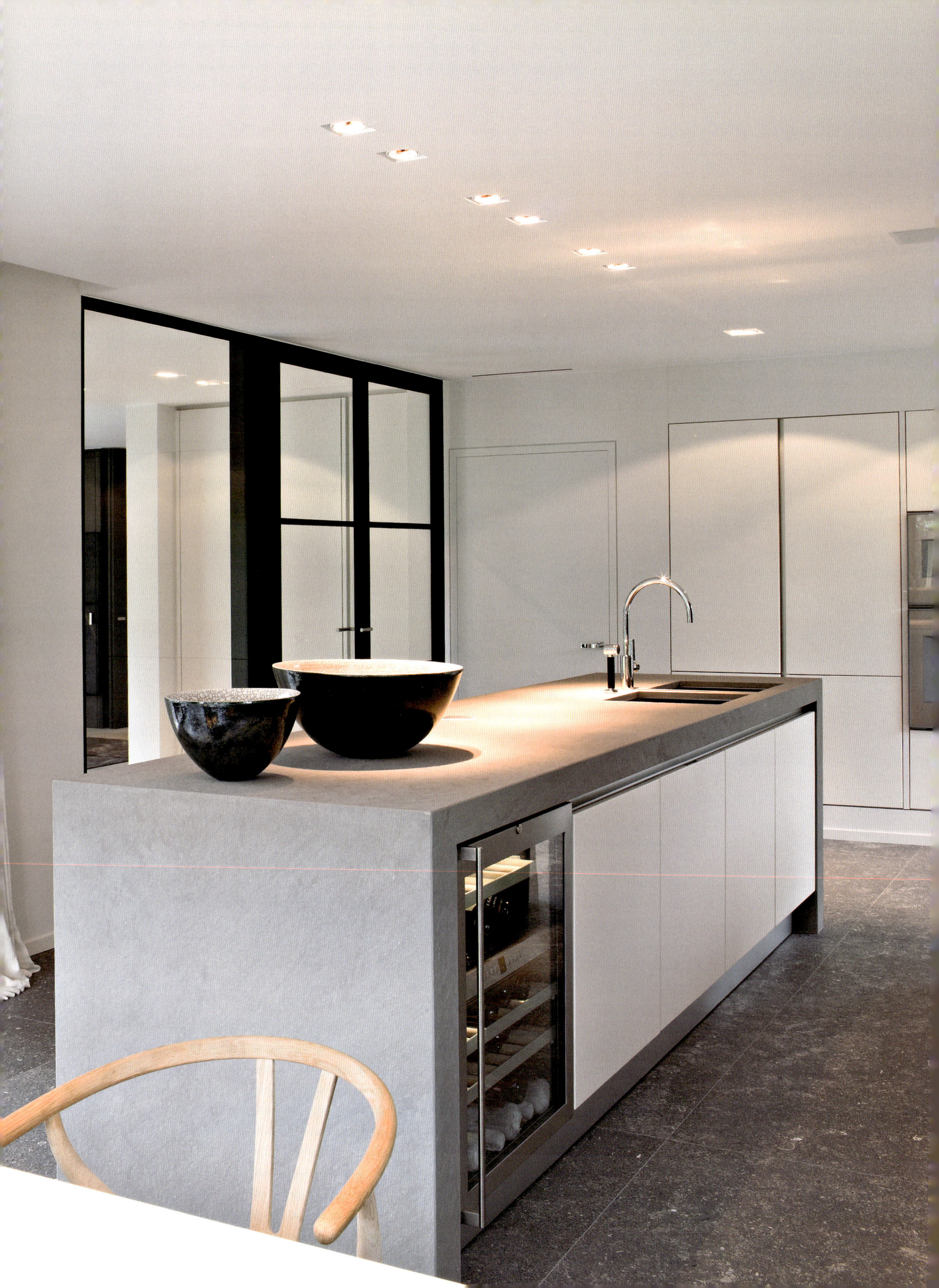

[ **Louis Culot**
**Kitchen worktops in natural stone and composite materials**
Industriezone Puurs 550
Schoonmansveld 7
B – 2870 Puurs
T +32 (0)3 860 70 70
www.culot.be

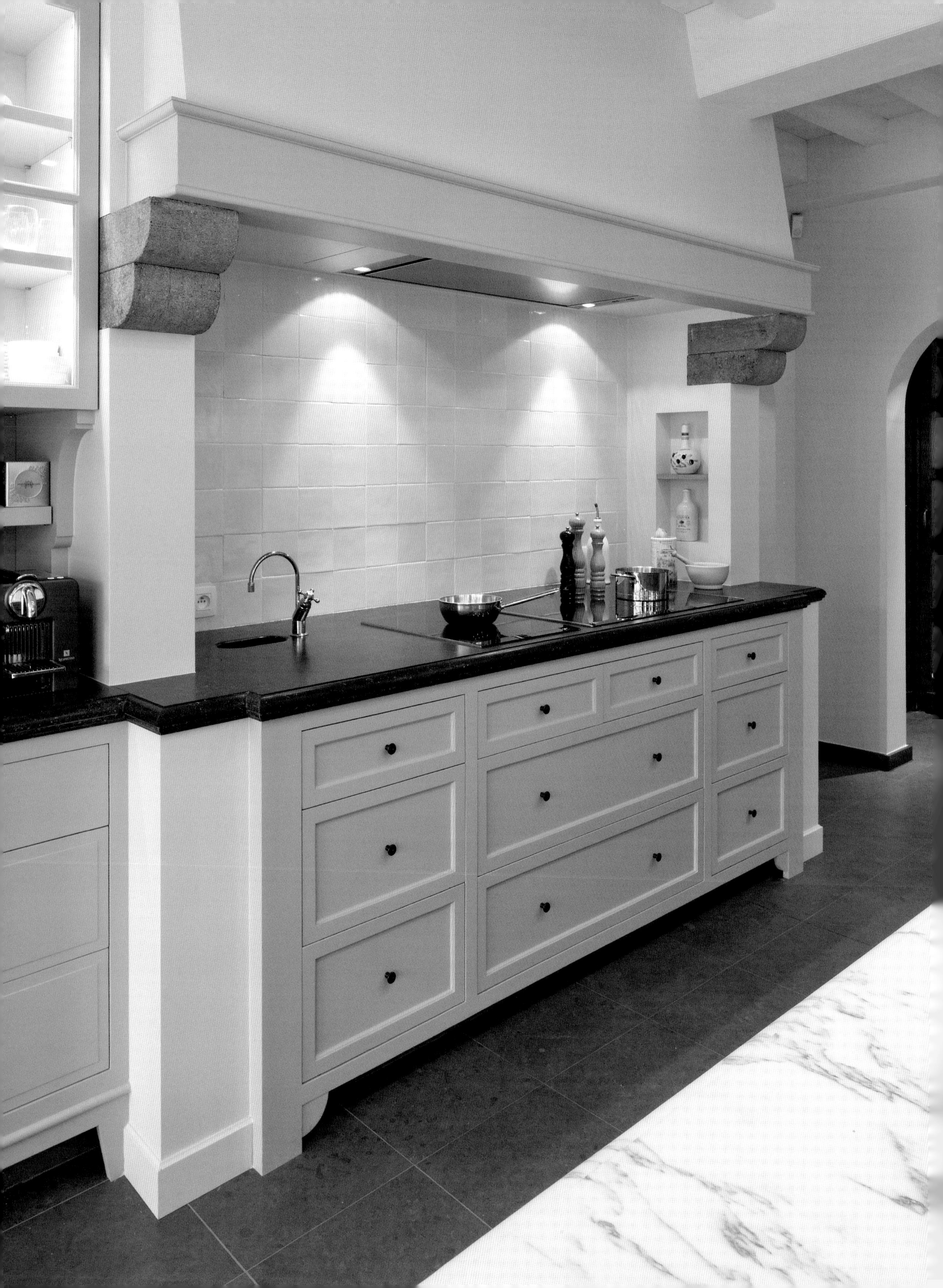

# [ A PASSION FOR PERFECTION

In this second article (see also p. 58-63), Louis Culot, *the* specialist in exclusive kitchen worktops made of natural stone and composite materials, presents a design that is decidedly different.

In spite of the considerable difference in style compared with the previous design, this kitchen still bears the two hallmarks of a masterpiece by Louis Culot: high-quality finishing and a passion for perfection.

The central island features a worktop in Arabescato honed marble, 3 cm thick with a bevelled edge.
Built-in sink unit with grooves. The island is in two parts according to an "open book" configuration.
The worktops to the left and right of the island are made of Belgian blue hardstone, with honed finish, 3 cm thick with a bevelled edge and bonded strip with 90° beading. The bevelled edge corners were painstakingly moulded by craftsmen commissioned by Louis Culot. Surface mounted hobs and built-in secondary sink.

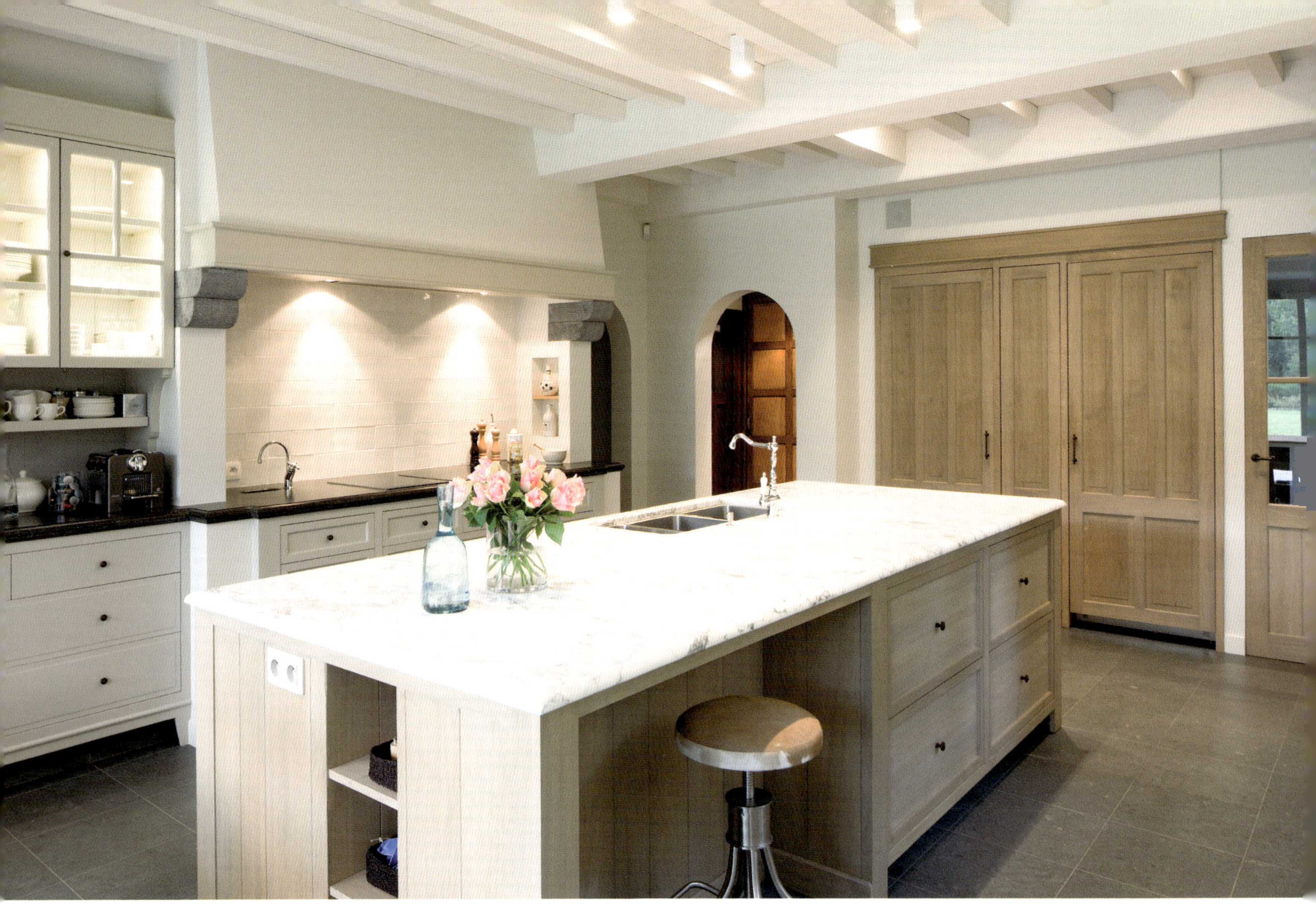

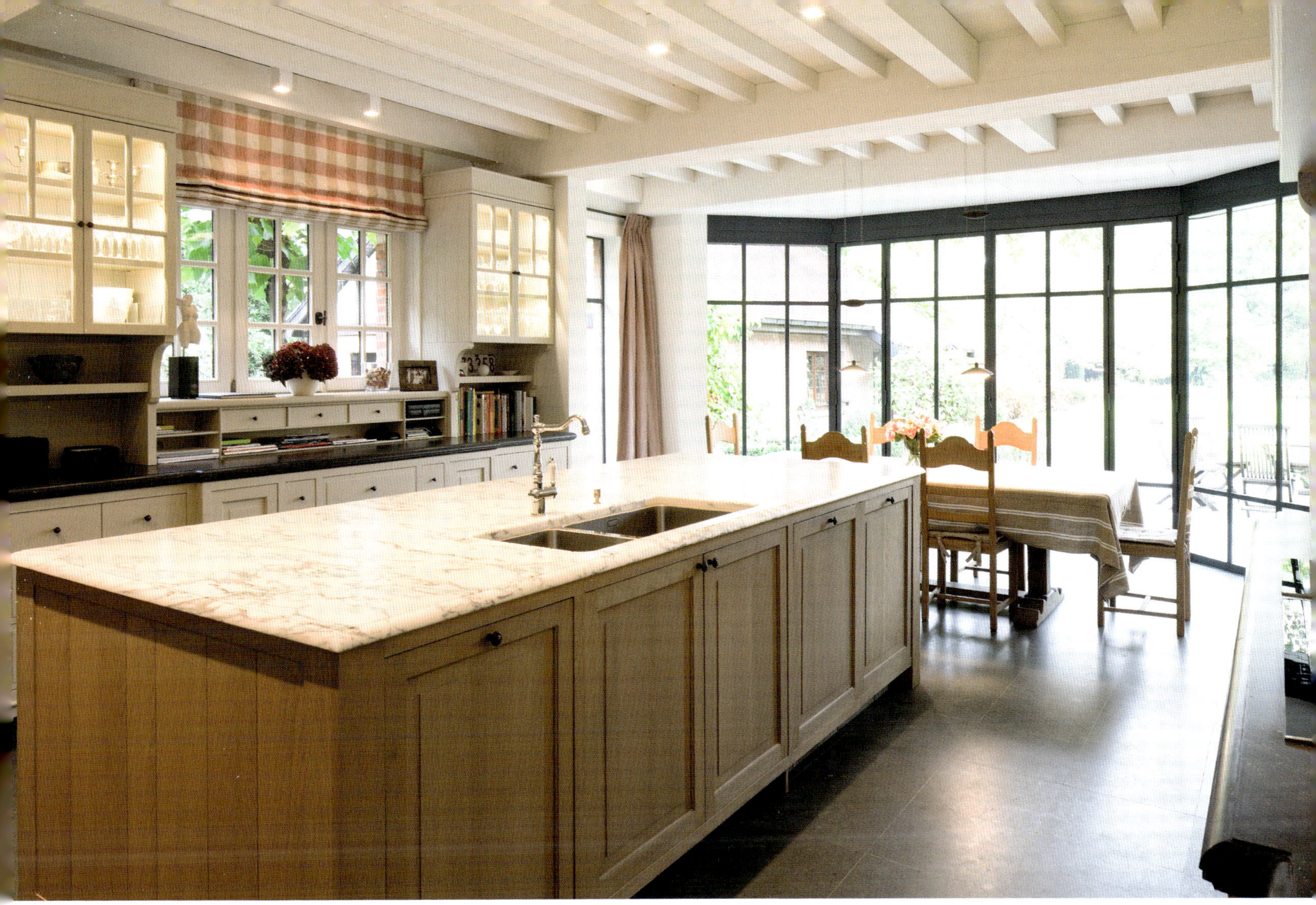

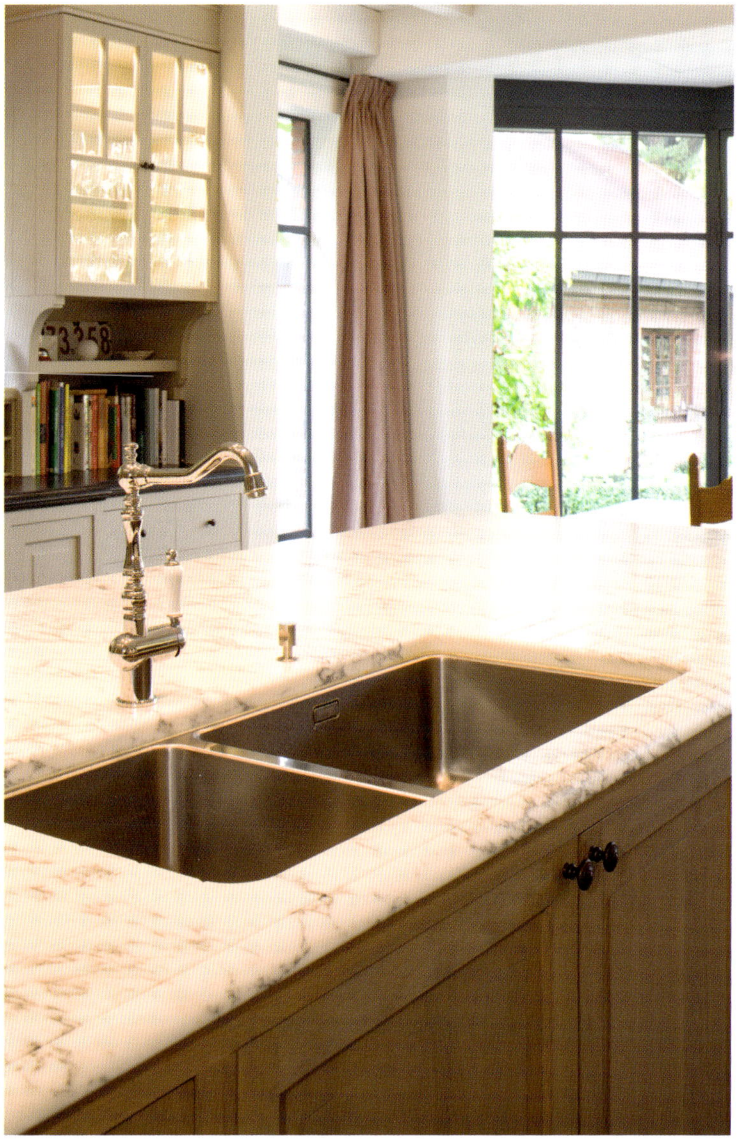

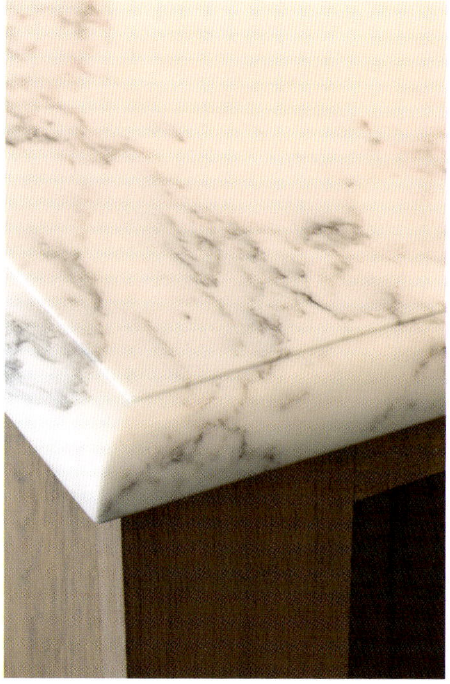

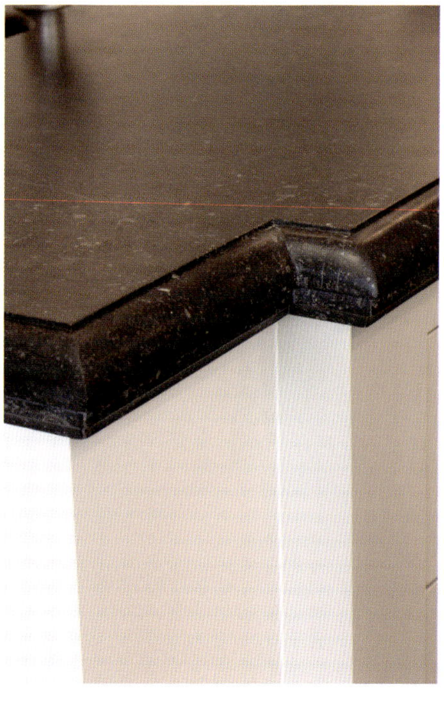

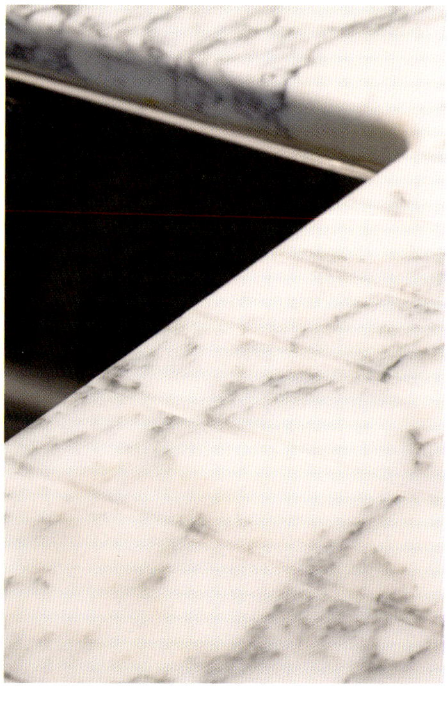

The scullery also has a worktop made of honed Belgian blue hardstone with a running splashback.

In the laundry room, Louis Culot has placed a composite worktop in honed Divinity White (Diresco) with splashback. Sink unit built in under the worktop with grooved draining surface.

**Louis Culot**
**Kitchen worktops in natural stone and composite materials**
Industriezone Puurs 550
Schoonmansveld 7
B – 2870  Puurs
T +32 (0)3  860 70 70
www.culot.be

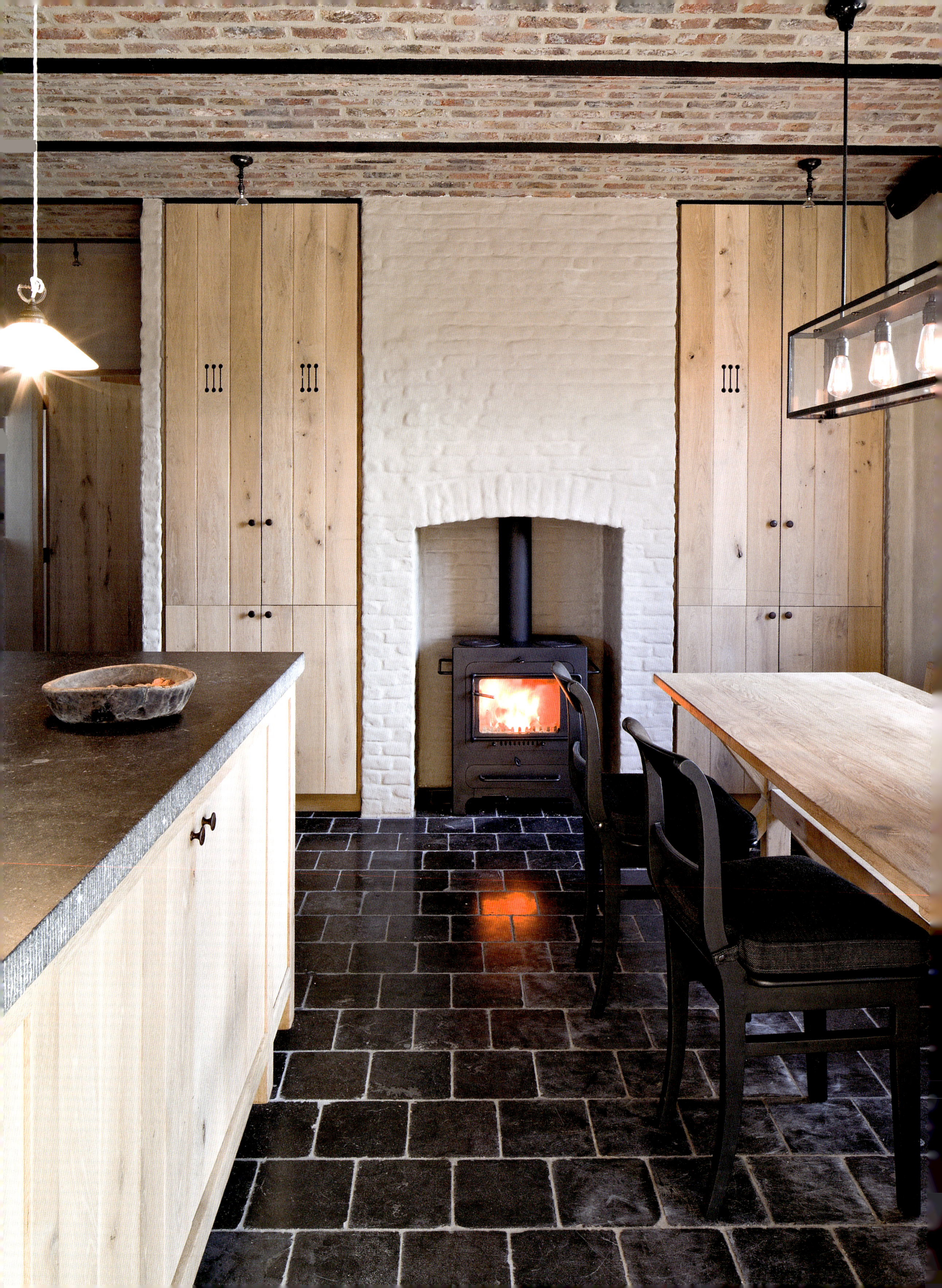

[ # PASSIONATE AND POETIC, YET EXTREMELY PROFESSIONAL

Dirk Cousaert is a very special cabinetmaker: enthusiastic about quality to the point of being iconoclastic, but also poetic, creative and artistic.

What was for Cousaert an irrepressible passion for furniture spurred him on to develop his own traditional cabinetmaking workshop that has grown into a fully-fledged specialised furniture business.
Cousaert certainly knows his job: not only is he a master in the old trades, but he is also quite at home with innovative techniques. He has a feel for materials such as wood, iron and stone, but he uses them in quite original ways to create the most beautiful tables, kitchen and bathroom furniture, doors, staircases, bookcases, etc.

Inspiration and professionalism: the key to Dirk Cousaert's philosophy of life.
His team of craftsmen draws its creative power from rough and ready - and often time-honoured and weathered - materials. Based on simple concepts and sleek designs, the company creates the most beautiful interiors.

The kitchen featured in this article epitomise Dirk Cousaert's mission: to create a living environment that has a touch of nostalgia but is nonetheless future-oriented and technically up to date.

This old courtyard farmhouse was given a contemporary makeover by Dirk Cousaert, creating a successful mix of old materials within a modern design concept.
The kitchen is in the former stables, where the original vaulting has been retained.
The chimney was built with bricks and then whitewashed. On either side of the chimney, two storage cupboards have been created, of which the upper part has ventilation grooves.
For the floor, the interior designers opted for blue hardstone tiles.

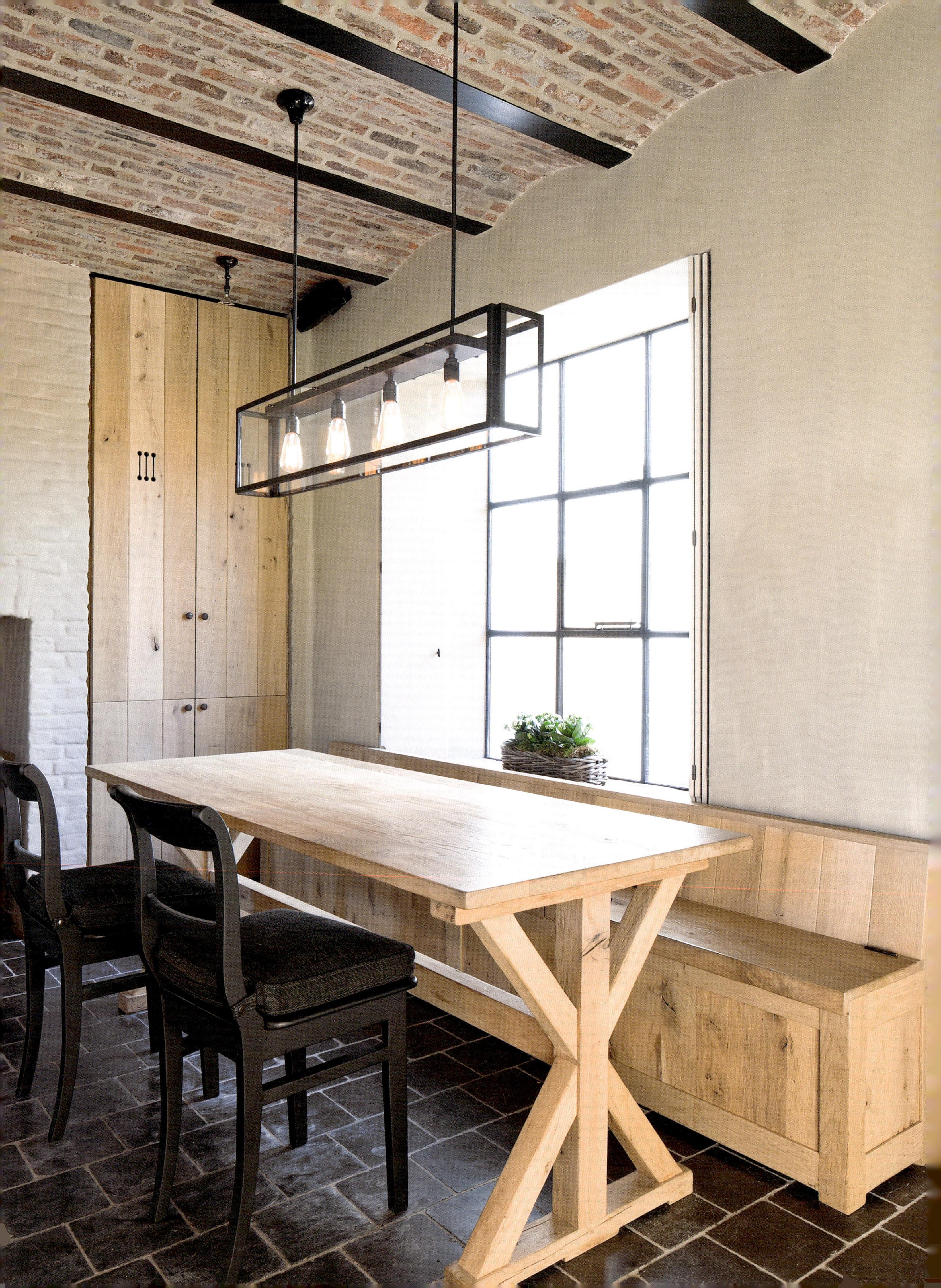

The kitchen was created by Dirk Cousaert in weathered oak. The range is by Lacanche.

**72**
The solid oak table was made according to the old trestle system. Behind the table there is a matching storage trunk-cum-bench.

[ **Dirk Cousaert**
Stationsstraat 160
B – 9690 Kluisbergen
T +32 (0)55 38 70 53
F +32 (0)55 38 60 39
www.dirkcousaert.be
info@dirkcousaert.be

The high pivoting inside door was made according to the old gate-type system. It features a tailor-made wrought iron handle.

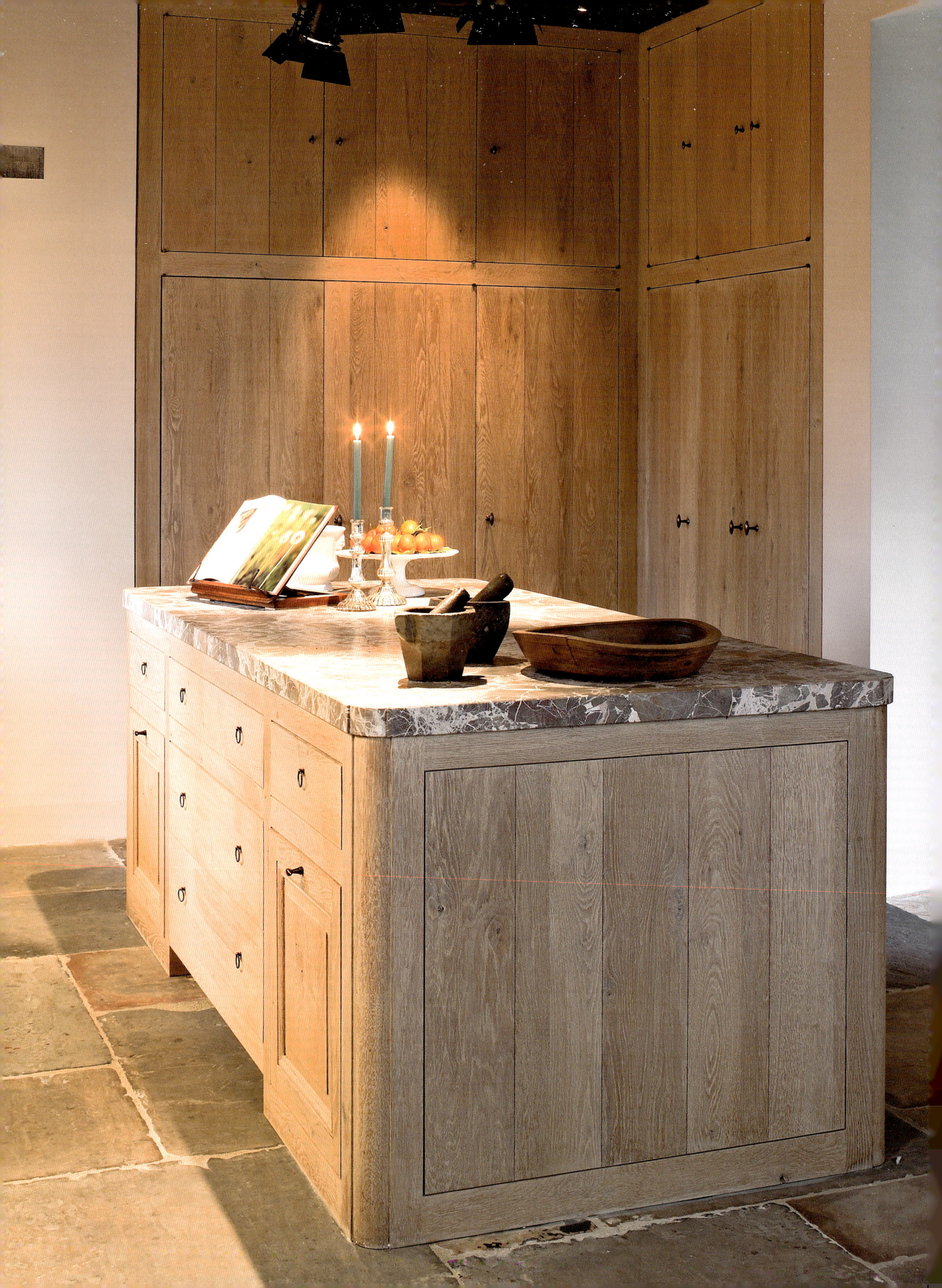

[ # TRADITIONAL CRAFTSMANSHIP COUPLED WITH PRACTICAL CONTEMPORARY DESIGN

De Menagerie, which was set up in 1997, specialises in the design and creation of exclusive high-quality kitchens.
Over the years, this company from the town of Aalst has forged an enviable reputation for quality and for excellence in traditional workmanship down to the most minute details.

For the company's founder and its driving force, Luc Lormans, and his team of creative and passionate professionals, every order they receive is a new and exciting challenge.

When it comes to design, De Menagerie's priorities are: the use of the very best materials (preferably warm, natural materials), sobriety of form and a sense of proportion. Each design is a unique project.

The company constantly strives to achieve optimum integration of the kitchen within the overall architectural concept, to create a sense of harmony with the adjacent volumes and to enhance the view from the outside.
Contemporary kitchen design has become a complex process. Many different factors determine the end result, and the aesthetic appeal of a kitchen and the luxury it offers have become just as important as the convenience offered by the living space.

The kitchen reflects the personality of the owner. De Menagerie is very much aware of this and therefore gives special attention to the need to monitor and organise each project.

The two kitchen design concepts featured in this article (p. 74-81 and p. 82-85) reflect the company's professional and client-oriented approach.

This kitchen was created by De Menagerie according to a design by the firm of architects bvba Architectenbureau Moors-Mestdagh from Lummen. The furniture was designed by Pascal Claes.

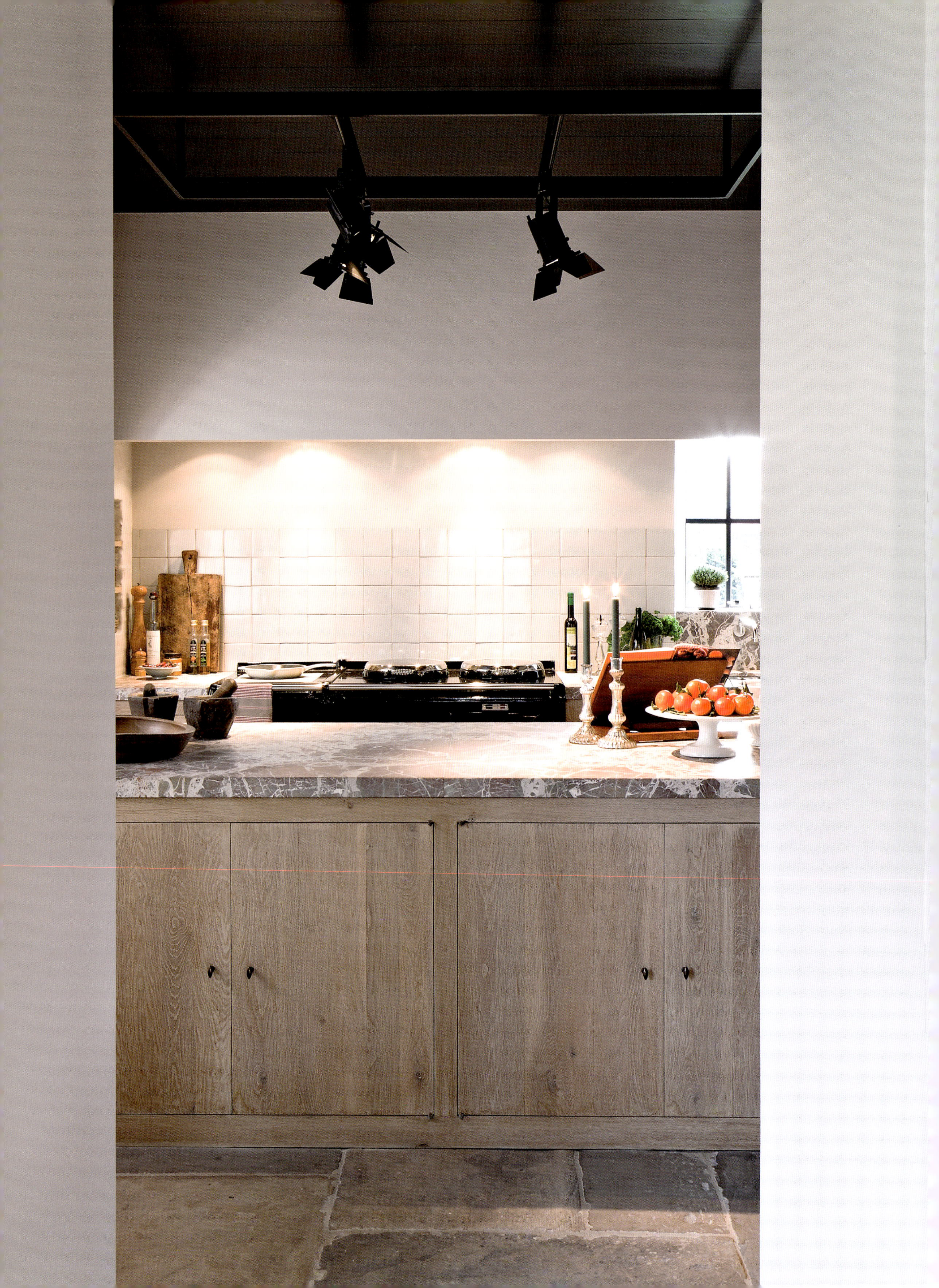

The exterior is solid oak, as is the superimposed skirting board which is interrupted in the central block and in the sink area.
The extractor hood has a base plate made of stainless steel.
The worktop is coated with a tablet in weathered Macchia Vecchia with straight edging.
The wall behind the cooking area features Dutch white tiles. External pivots with bronze fittings were selected for the plank doors.
The electric Aga range cooker has four ovens and a warming plate.

The refrigerator, microwave oven and other kitchen appliances are concealed behind the tall plank doors.
In the cooking area there is a round built-in stainless steel sink unit with a Dornbracht extendable wall mixer tap made of matt nickel.

In the sink area there are two rectangular built-in sink units and a Dornbracht single-lever mixer tap with a spray fitting, also in matt nickel finish.

The windows are made of steel. Old English tiles were selected for the floor covering.

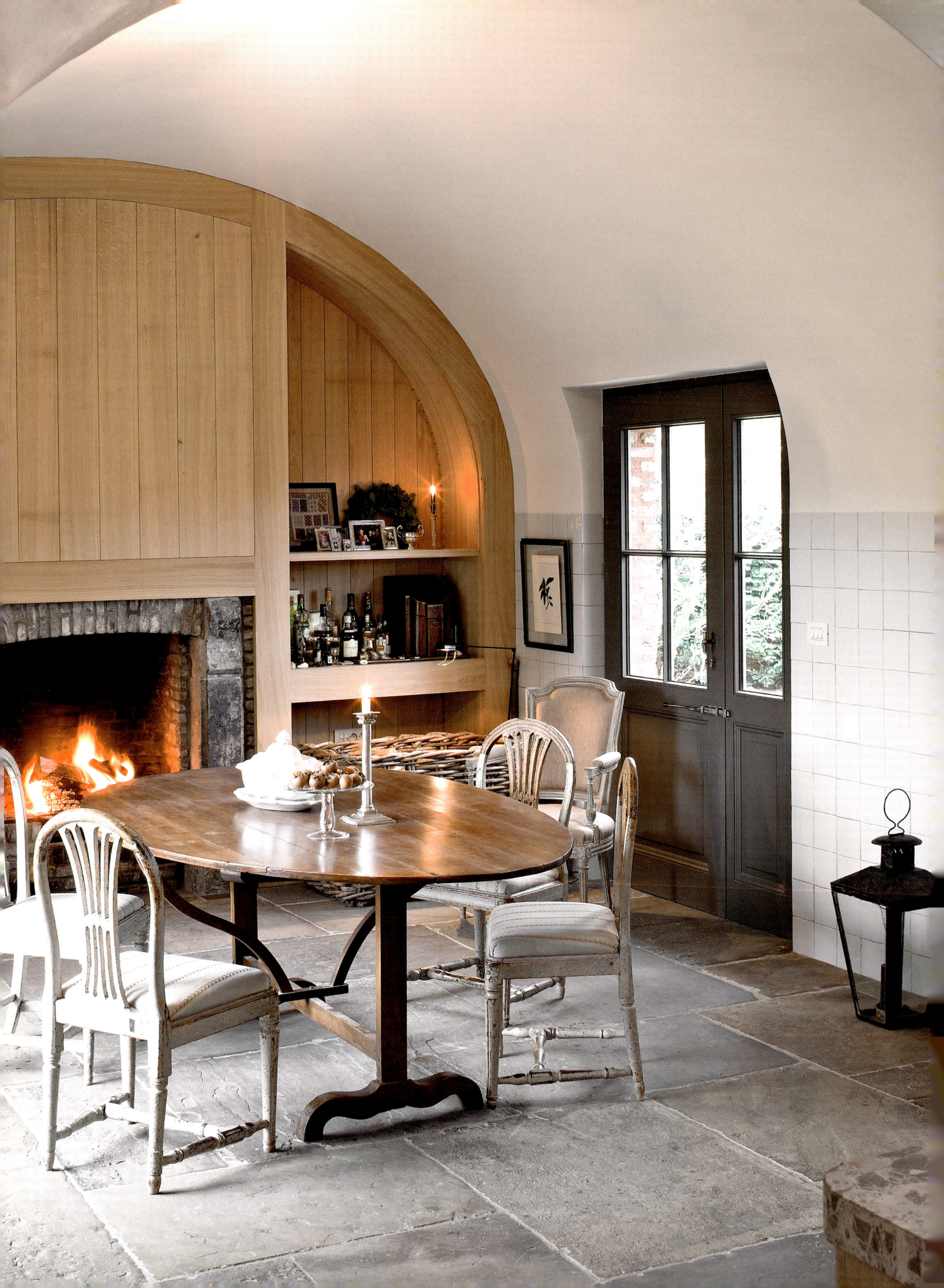

**De Menagerie**
Leo de Bethunelaan 45
B – 9300  Aalst
T +32 (0)53  78 69 39
F +32 (0)53  70 79 96
www.demenagerie.be
info@demenagerie.be

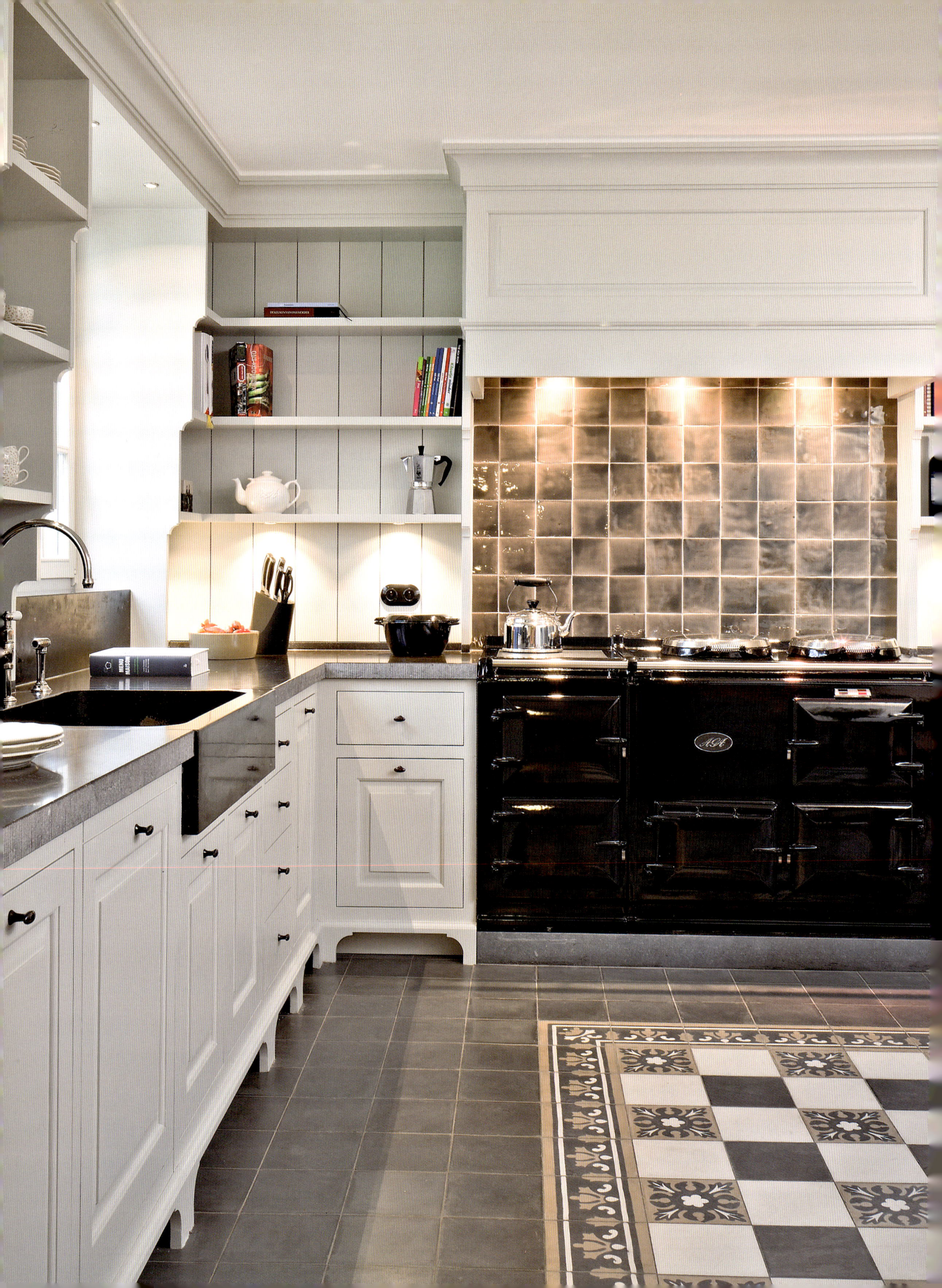

# [ COUNTRY INSPIRATION

De Menagerie specialises in exclusive kitchen design and creation. In this second design concept (see also p. 74-81), we present another fine example of the company's renowned know-how and creativity.

The exterior of this country-inspired kitchen is solid oak.
The cabinet doors have raised panels while the drawer fronts are flat.
The superimposed skirting boards are interrupted in places.
Solid oak cooker canopy with a continuous solid oak cornice.
Above the electric Aga range cooker with four ovens and a warming plate, there is a wall of hand-glazed tiles and LED lighting embedded in the canopy.

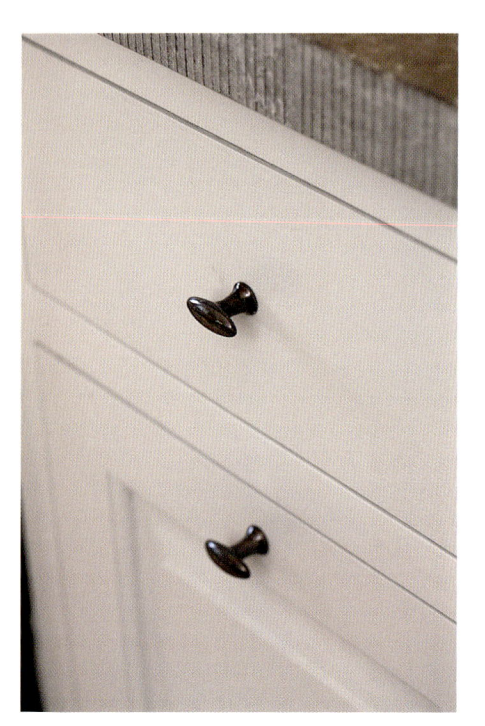

Worktop in solid blue hardstone (5 cm thick), smoothed and with hand-ribbed edging. The sink unit was carved out of solid blue hardstone.

[
**De Menagerie**
Leo de Bethunelaan 45
B – 9300  Aalst
T +32 (0)53  78 69 39
F +32 (0)53  70 79 96
www.demenagerie.be
info@demenagerie.be

The tall cabinet wall has been coated with a thick oak veneer. The furniture was painted by hand. Appliances by Gaggenau, with a built-in coffee maker and a fully integrated fridge-freezer combination which is 90 cm wide with one fridge door and one freezer drawer. The steam oven is located behind the lift-up door. For the furniture fittings, the designers opted for date-shaped knobs with bronze finishing.

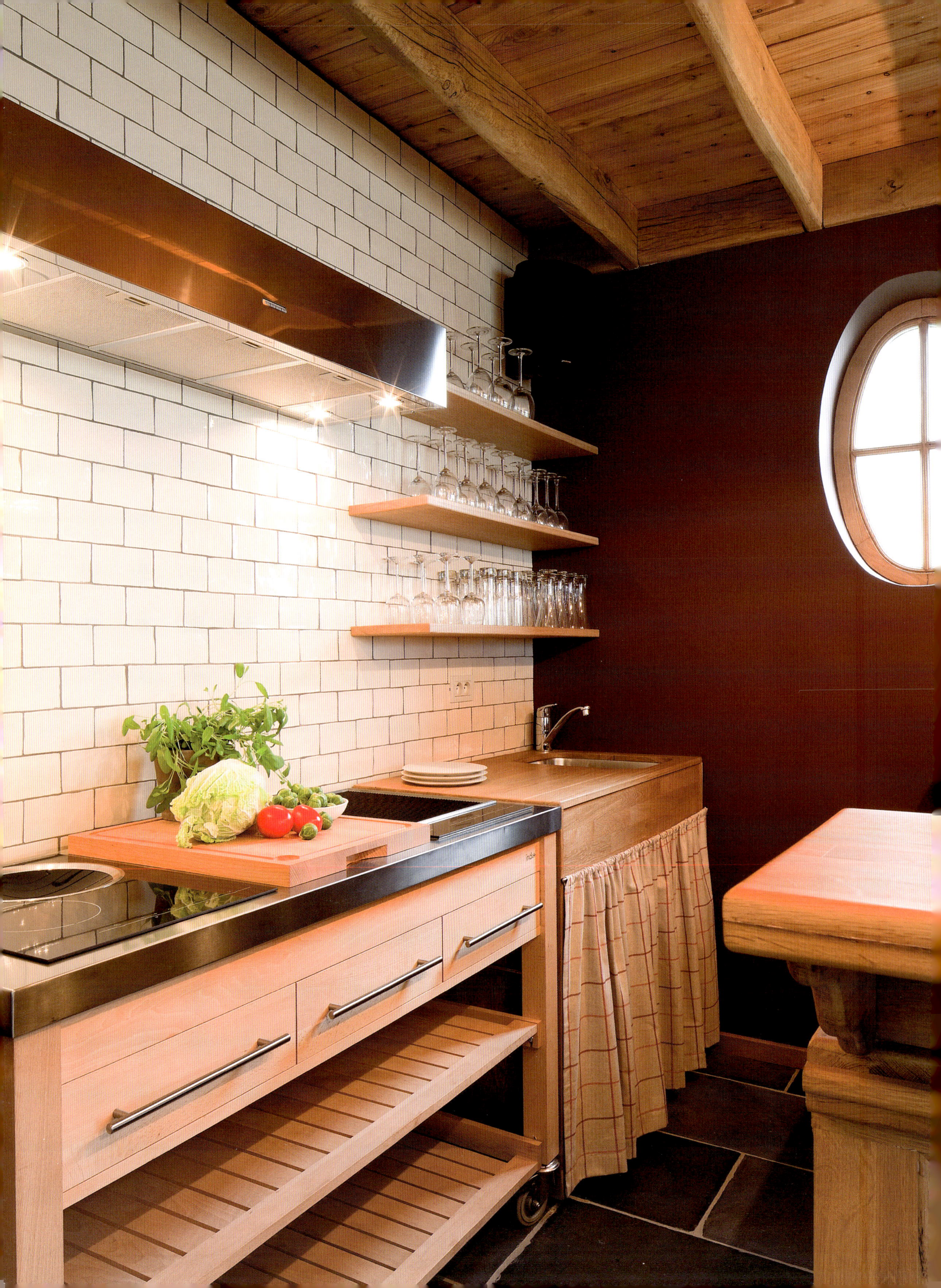

# [ A NOVEL COOKING EXPERIENCE FOR INSIDE AND OUTSIDE

indu+ introduces a brand new cooking experience.

With the robust indu+ cooker trolley, you can move your stove to wherever you like: to the kitchen, to the garden, by the pool, to the orangerie or onto the terrace. The hotplates in the trolleys are modular and easily interchangeable.
For example, the trolley can be readily adjusted to the requirements of the menu: cooking, wokking, grilling, teppanyaki or whatever takes your fancy.

With the handy chopping boards, you can create that additional working space you need: either on the side or in place of a hotplate.
And thanks to the elegant knife holders, the knives are always safe but still within easy reach. Thanks to the mobile trolley, you can cook indoors, and outdoor cooking is no longer synonymous with (gas) barbecues. Thanks to the indu+ cooker trolley, everything takes on a new dimension.

The easy way to cook, wok or grill inside or outside...

The Trolley Beechboy Ultimo combines a solid beech structure with a stainless steel worktop. Featured here with combination hotplate, chopping board and grill.

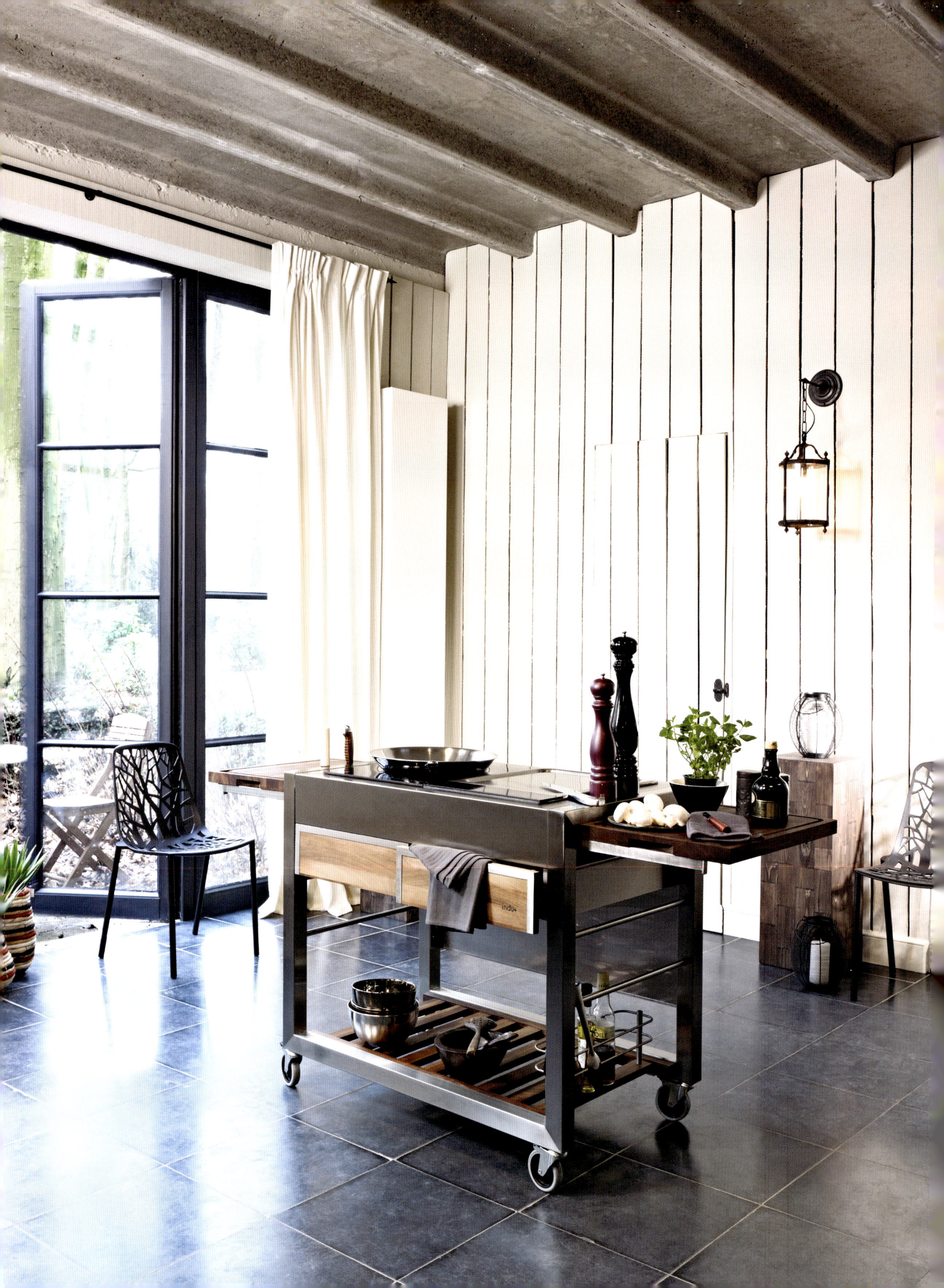

The ServeBoy Superbianco Duo in a high-quality composite material and stainless steel with walnut chopping board and induction domino hob.

The Trolley TomBoy Duo with induction wok hob and teppanyaki. Structure made of stainless steel with touches of solid walnut. Thanks to the lateral extensions, extra space can be created for chopping boards.

The ServeBoy Ultimo is a combination of a white composite material with walnut and stainless steel. The trolley features an induction domino and wok hob, chopping boards and knife holder.

The BeechBoy Solo with induction wok hob.

The TomBoy Duo with induction domino hob and infrared grill.

The hotplates can be easily interchanged at any time. A hotplate or chopping board fits into each opening. As a result, the features of the trolley can be adjusted to the chef's requirements.

Each of the 5 hotplates from the indu+ range can be placed either in the worktop in the kitchen or in a cooker trolley. The hotplates therefore have a dual function: either in the kitchen or when the weather is nice they can be put in a trolley for easy and successful outside cooking.

The ServeBoy Ultimo with Belgian blue stone cutting board, domino hob and grill.

TomBoy Duo and Ultimo

BeechBoy Duo

The TomBoy Ultimo with induction wok hob and walnut chopping board.

**Indu+**
T +32 (0)56 72 36 87
www.induplus.eu
info@induplus.eu

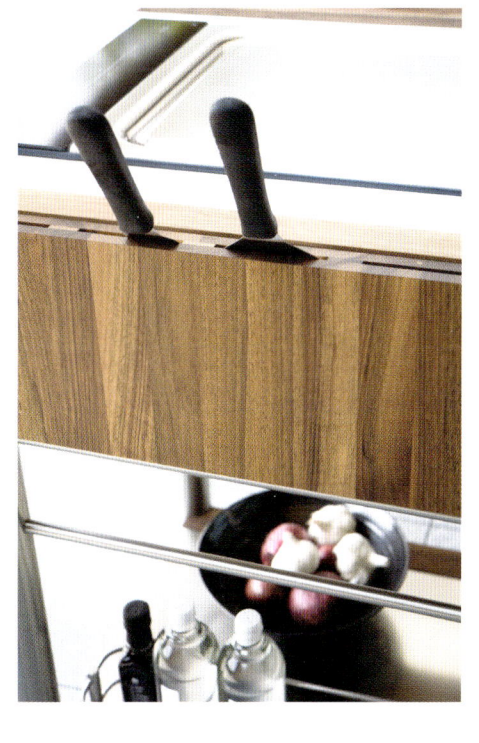

The Serveboy Solo with teppanyaki and walnut knife and spatula holder.

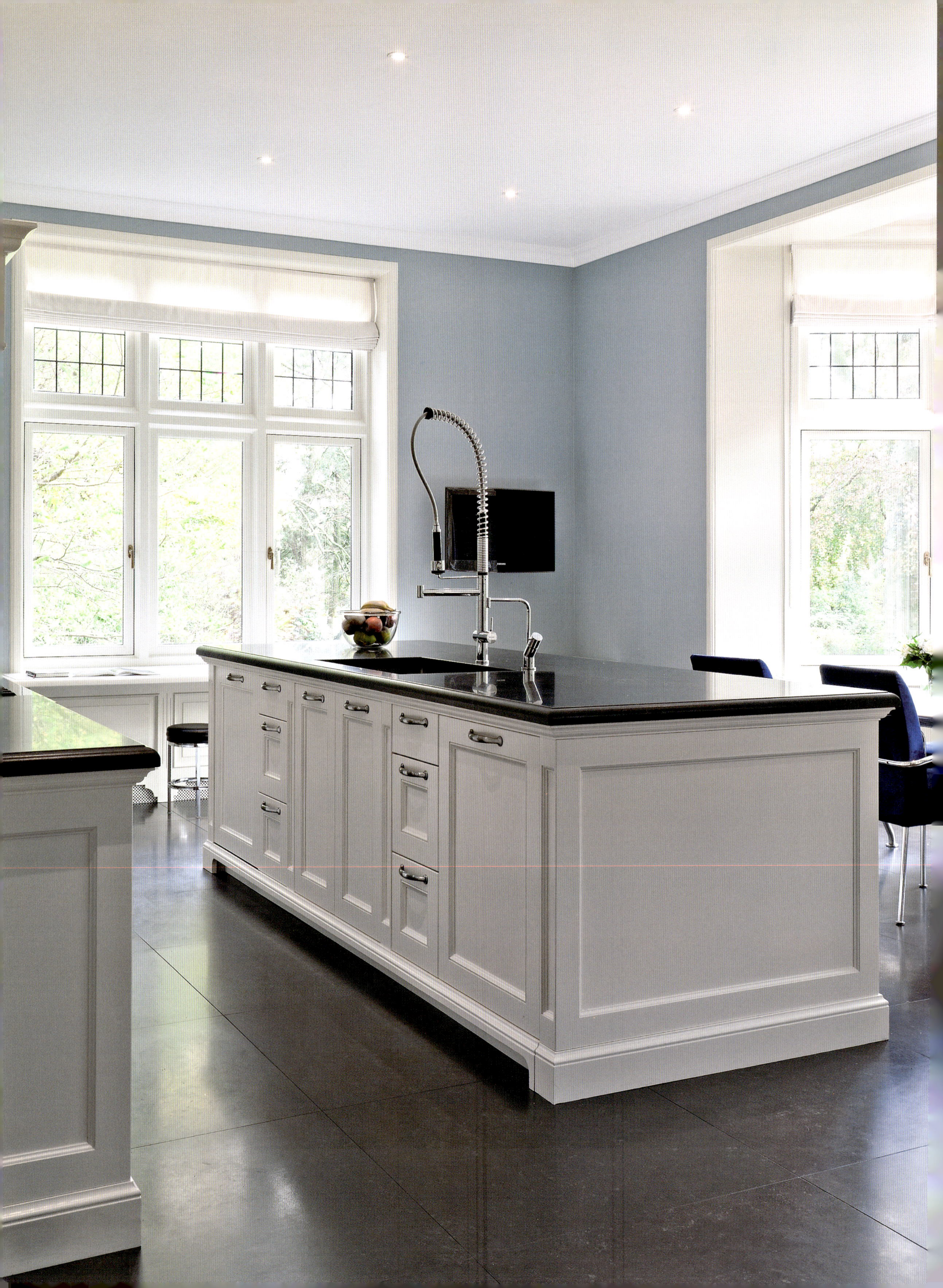

# EXCLUSIVE KITCHENS FOR CONNOISSEURS

Paul van de Kooi creates high-quality kitchens according to your requirements in the style of your choice.

Whether you prefer modern, classic or country style, Paul can provide the design concept that is best suited to your living environment.
Using the finest materials and the most skilled professionals, Paul van de Kooi creates a kitchen just for you in your home.

If you're looking for inspiration, the new showroom in Amersfoort, with its 16 exclusive kitchens on display, is the best place to start.

The articles in this book (p. 94-121) show how Paul van de Kooi can demonstrate his passion for perfection to design the ideal kitchen for any house and in any style according to the most rigorous quality standards.

In this classic kitchen, the cabinet fronts are made of solid oak. The colour is Pointing by Farrow & Ball.
The cabinet structures are made of plywood bonded with water-resistant glue.

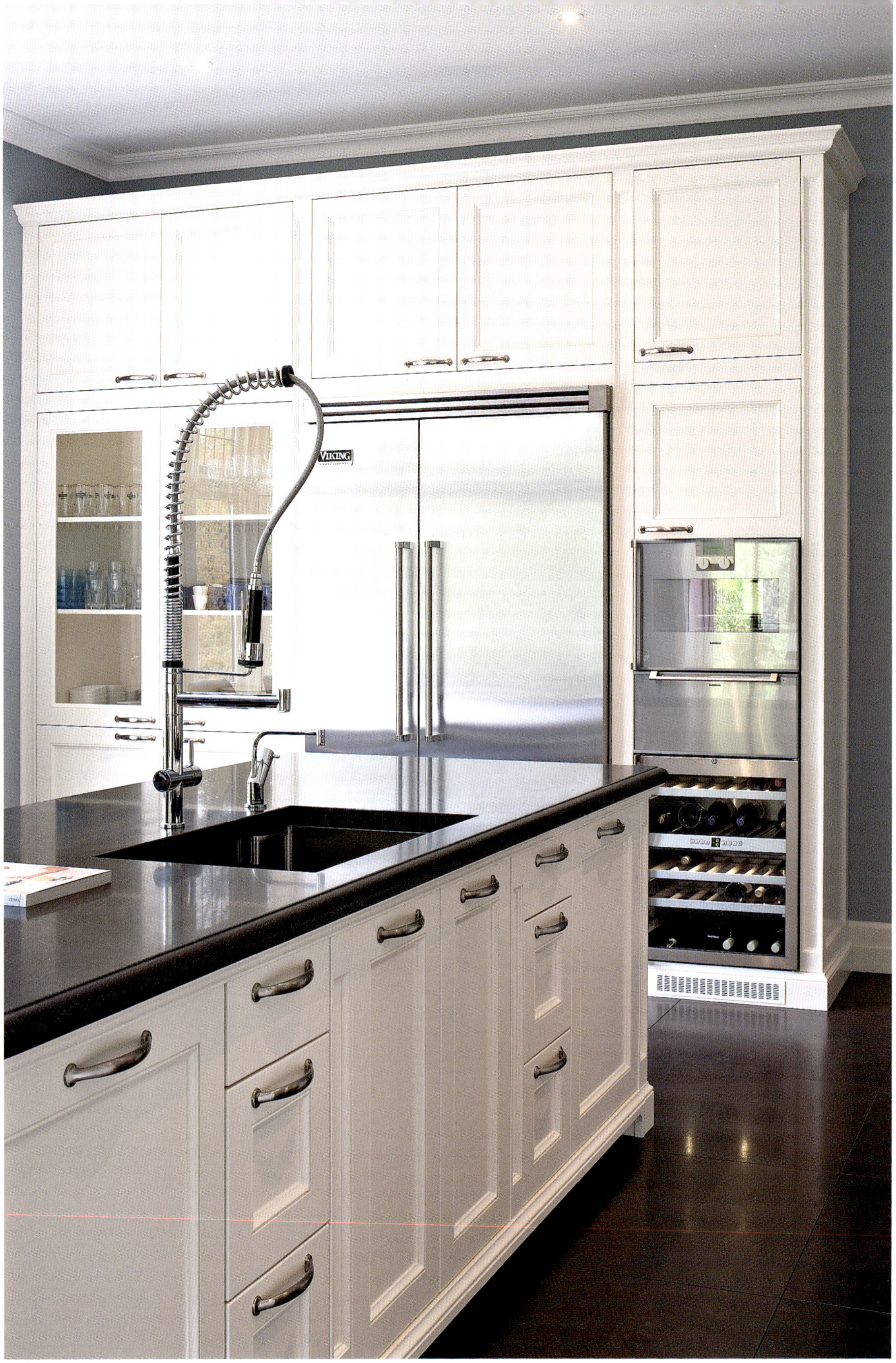
VIKING

Range cooker and refrigerator by Viking and steam oven, warming drawer and wine storage unit by Gaggenau. Tap by Gessi and worktop in granite, finished with bevelled edges.

[ **Paul van de Kooi - made-to-measure kitchens**
Nijverheidsweg Noord 74 D
NL - 3812 PM Amersfoort
T +31 (0)33 465 11 11
www.paulvandekooi.nl
info@paulvandekooi.nl

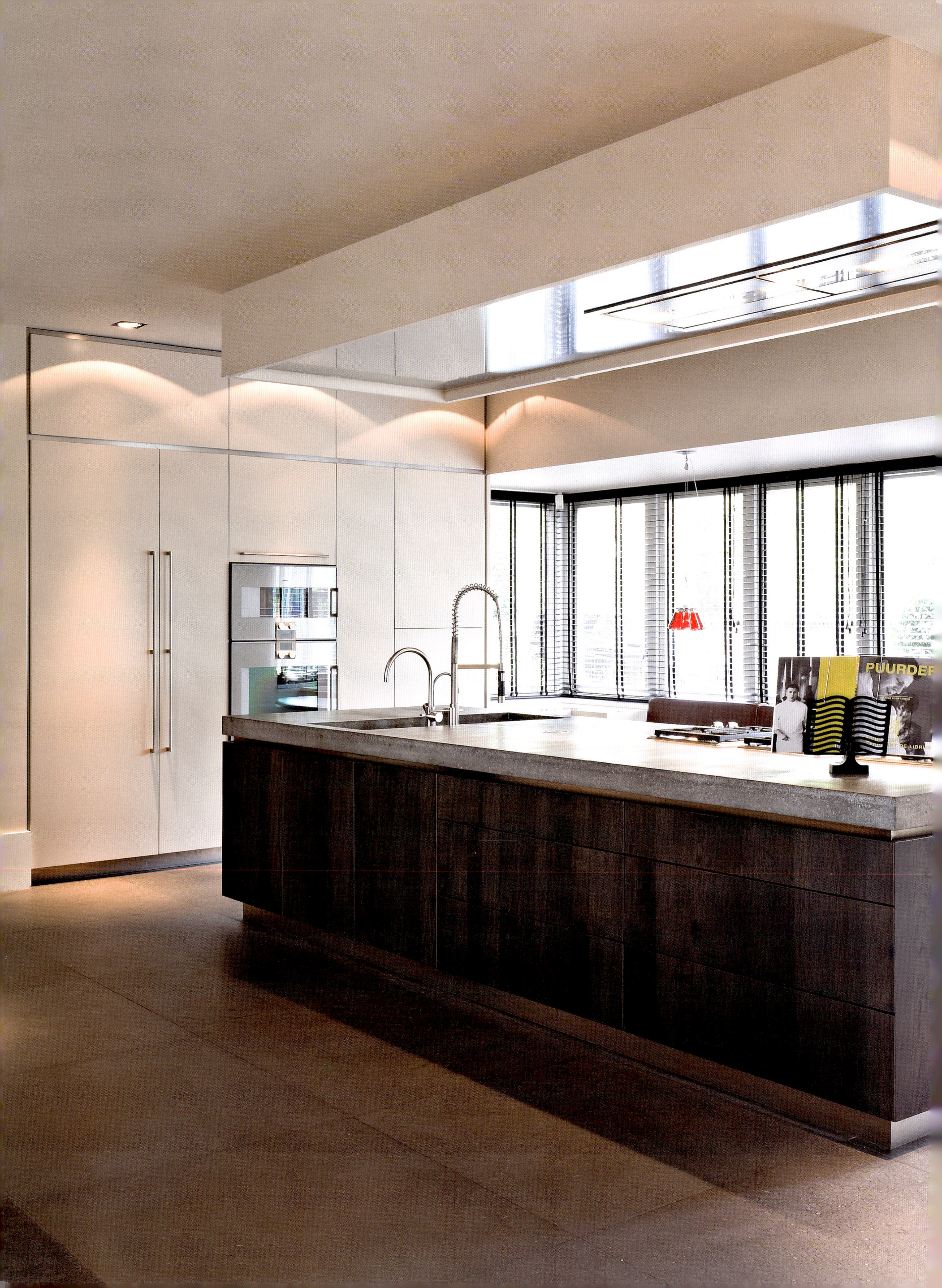

The worktop is made of in-situ cast concrete. Tap fittings by Dornbracht and hot water tap by Quooker.

[ **Paul van de Kooi - made-to-measure kitchens**
Nijverheidsweg Noord 74 D
NL - 3812 PM Amersfoort
T +31 (0)33 465 11 11
www.paulvandekooi.nl
info@paulvandekooi.nl

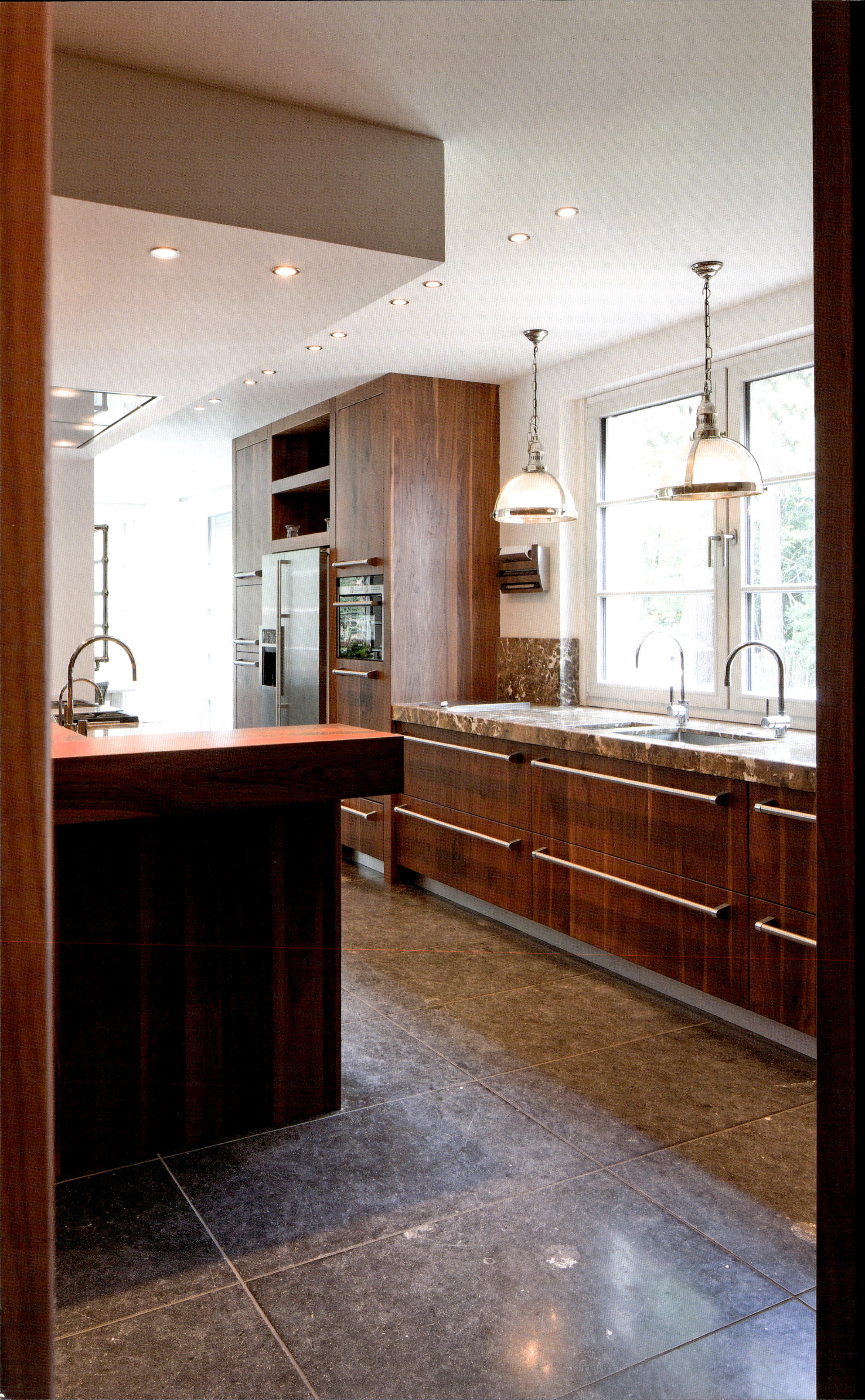

# A BLEND OF WALNUT AND MARRON EMPERADOR

In this design concept by Paul van de Kooi, the tasteful, harmonious combination of walnut and exclusive Marron Emperador natural stone (a dark brown type of marble from Spain with white-beige veins) creates a truly luxurious kitchen that exudes warmth and cosiness.

All the fronts and fixed parts of this classic country kitchen are made of stained three-layer walnut.
The cabinet structures are made of birch plywood bonded with water-resistant glue.
The worktops are coated with Marron Emperador marble.

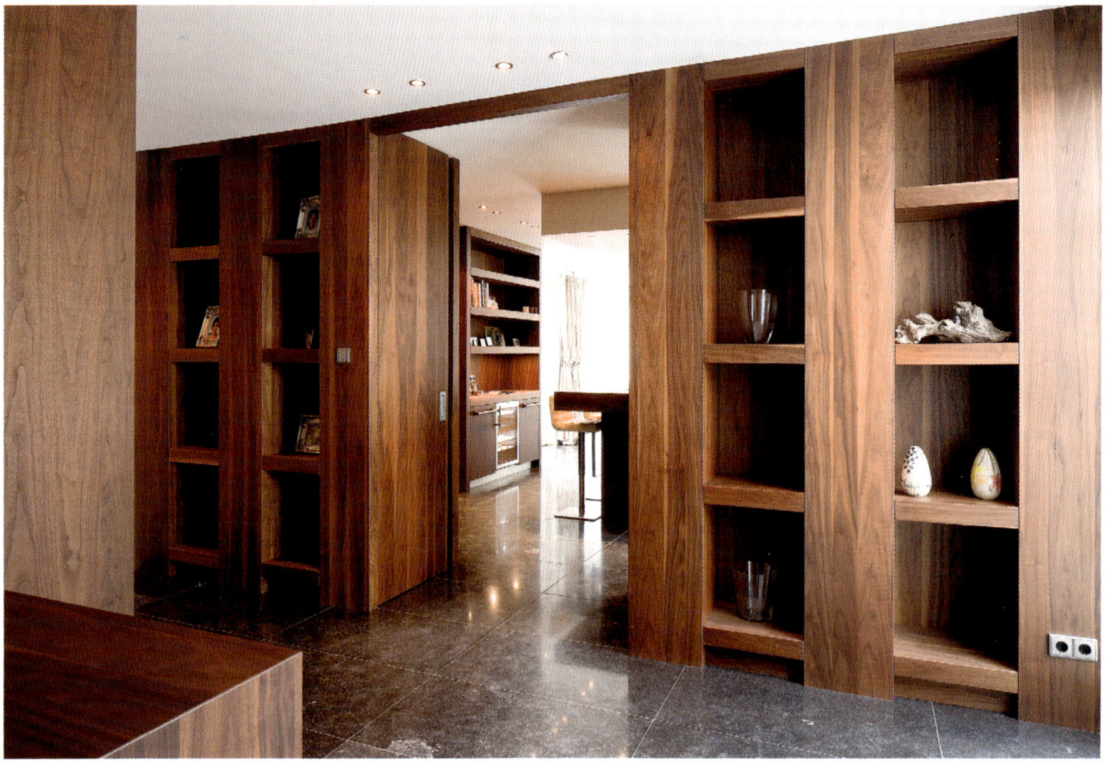

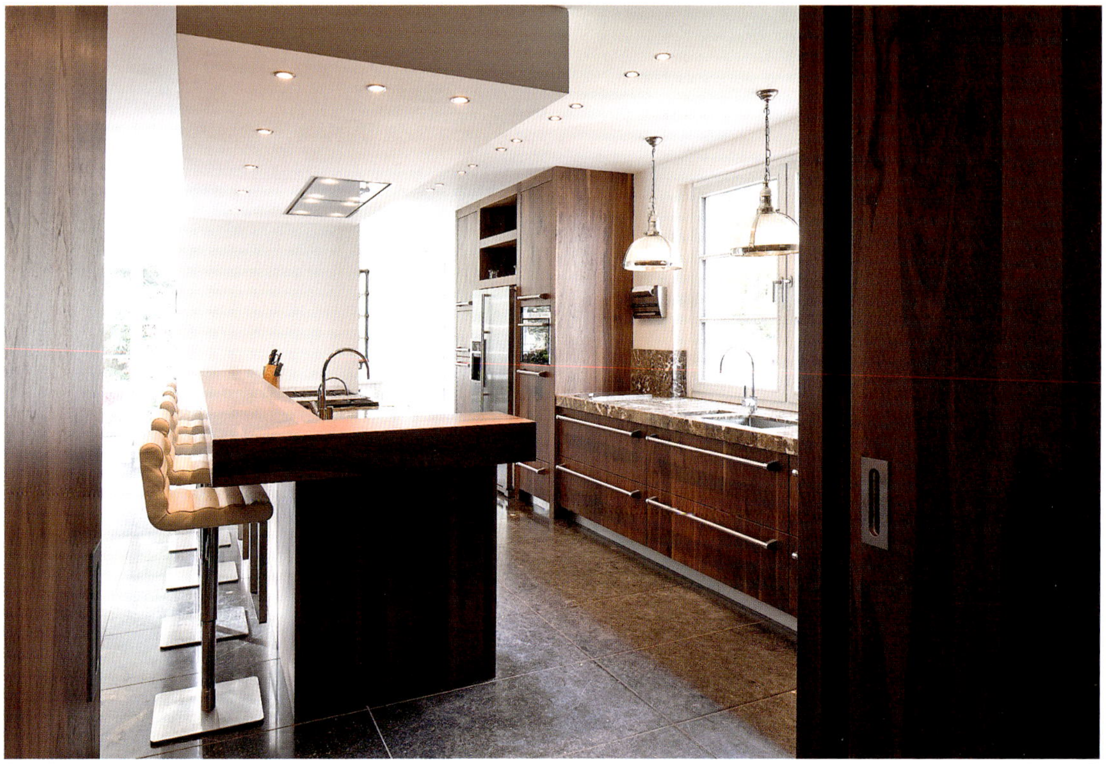

[ **Paul van de Kooi - made-to-measure kitchens**
Nijverheidsweg Noord 74 D
NL - 3812 PM Amersfoort
T +31 (0)33 465 11 11
www.paulvandekooi.nl
info@paulvandekooi.nl

Ceiling unit by Gutmann, fridge-freezer combination by Amana and combi-oven by Siemens. The Wolf range cooker is a must for genuine connoisseurs.

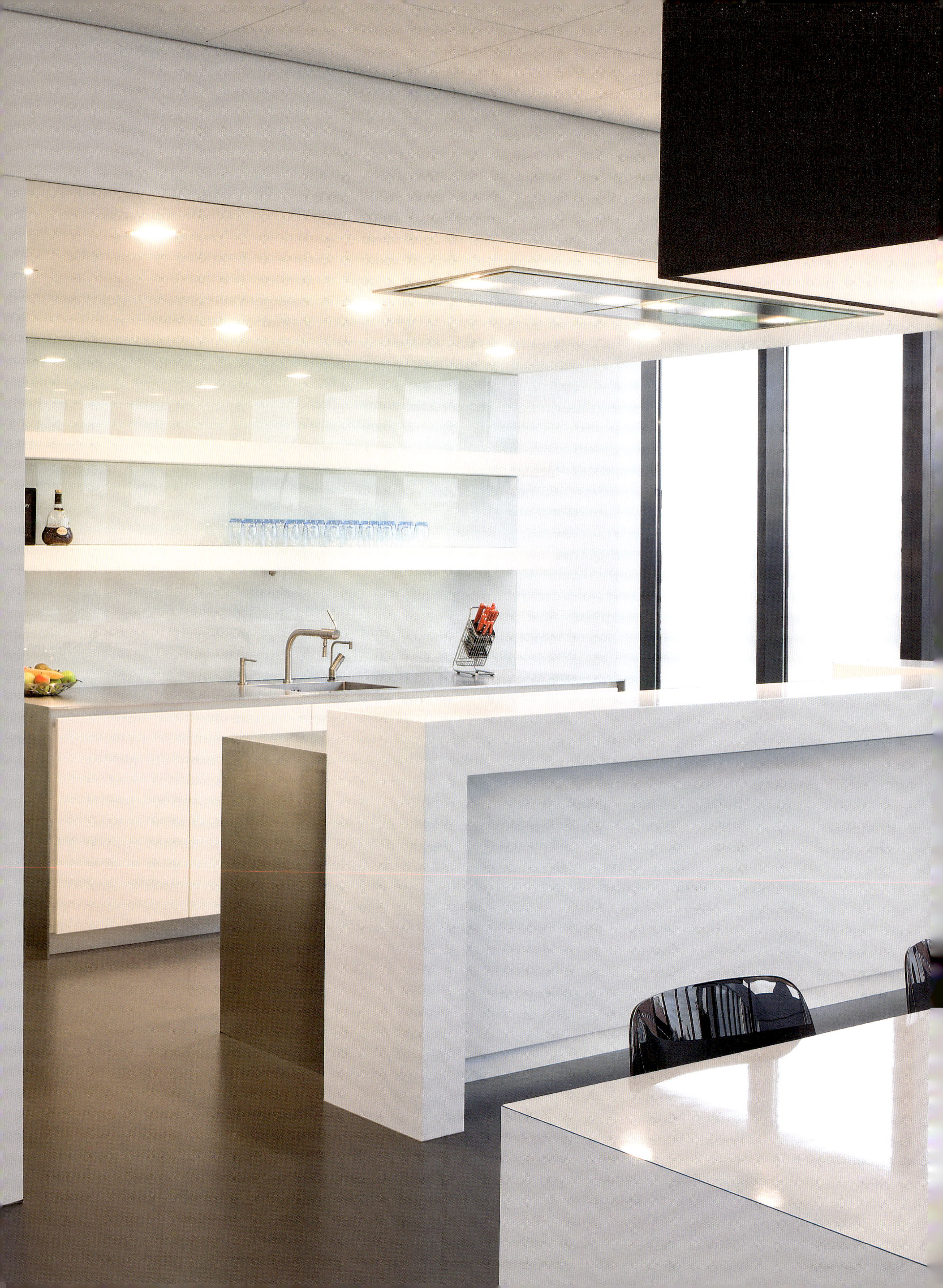

# [ MONOCHROME WHITE AND STAINLESS STEEL

In sharp contrast to the kitchen on p. 103-106, in this design project Paul van de Kooi reveals his unrivalled craftsmanship in a completely different style: a minimalist concept based on monochrome white and stainless steel, austere yet extremely modern and professional.

All the MDF cabinet fronts were sprayed.
The cabinet structures are made of birch plywood bonded with water-resistant glue.
Worktops and side panels made of stainless steel (1 cm thick).

Hob by Pitt Cooking, deep fryer and teppanyaki by Gaggenau. Wine storage unit, freezer and refrigerator also by Gaggenau.
The combi microwave, oven and combi steam oven are by Miele.
Ceiling unit with extractor by Gutmann.

**Paul van de Kooi - made-to-measure kitchens**
Nijverheidsweg Noord 74 D
NL - 3812 PM Amersfoort
T +31 (0)33 465 11 11
www.paulvandekooi.nl
info@paulvandekooi.nl

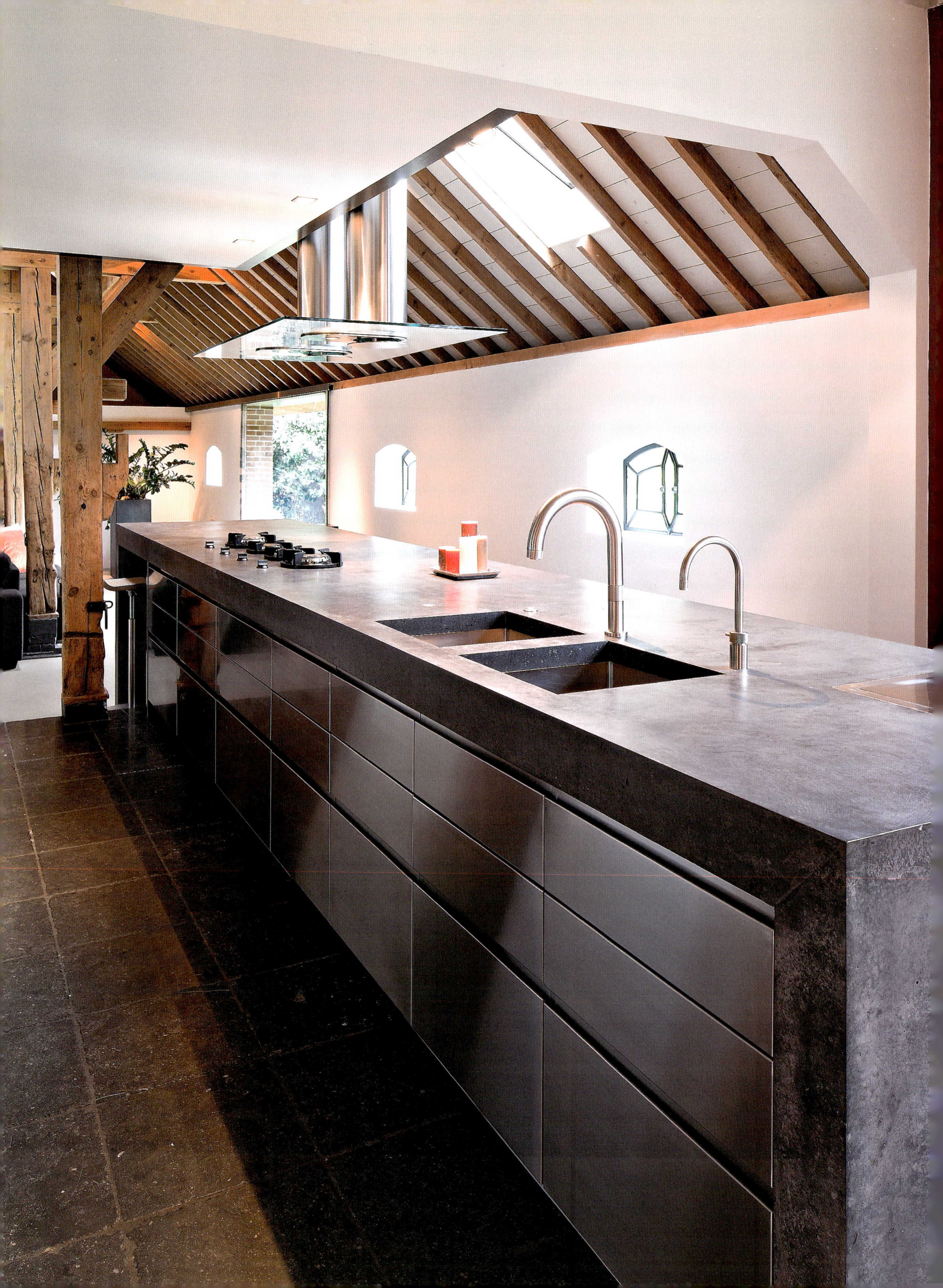

# [ AN INFINITE SOURCE OF INSPIRATION

The previous articles (p. 94-109) reveal the range of Paul van de Kooi's know-how through four special kitchens in very diverse styles.

This second series of photographs reveals that Paul van de Kooi can create the perfect kitchen for any client according to the desired specifications. These eight very different kitchen designs are a fitting illustration of what this company can do and provide a well-nigh inexhaustible source of inspiration.

The fronts of the island in this traditional country kitchen are coated with stainless steel. The side panels and the immense worktop are made of in-situ cast concrete. The cabinet structures are made of birch plywood bonded with water-resistant glue.

The spacious kitchen forms one continuous volume with the living room.
The fronts of the tall units are made of three-layer oak.

Hob by Pitt Cooking.

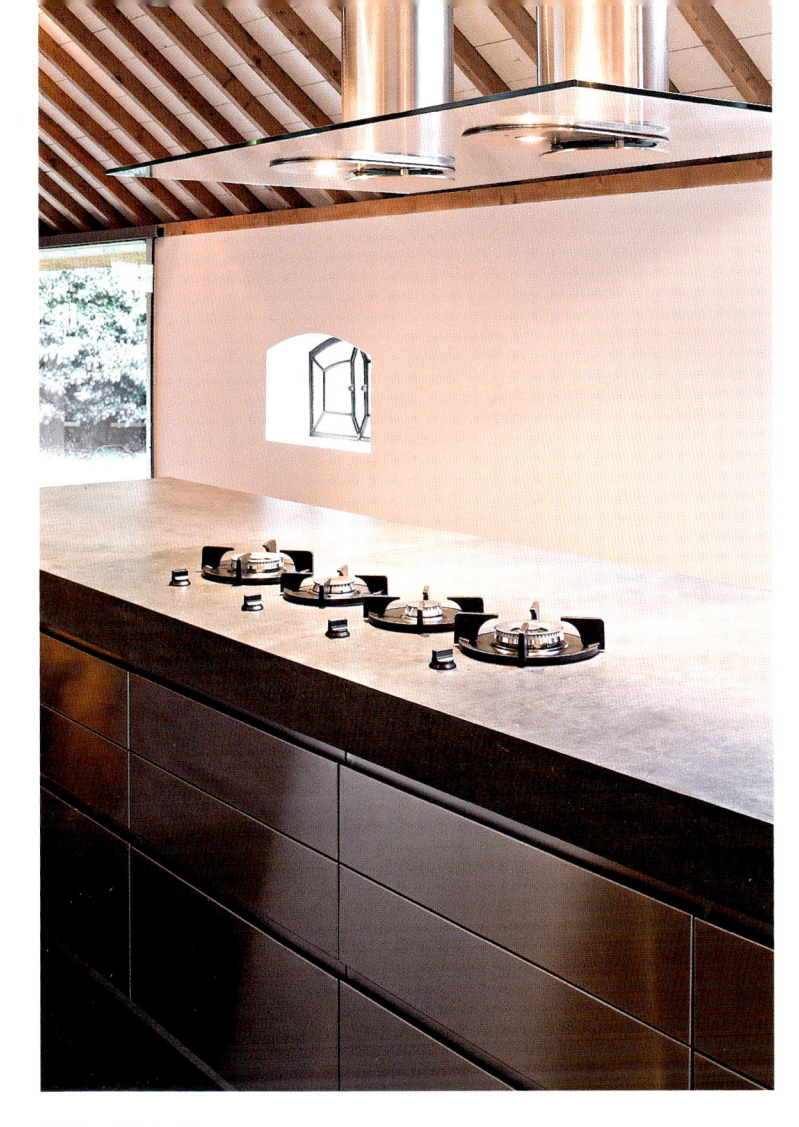

Combi microwave, combi steam oven and three warming drawers by Miele: the nec plus ultra of functionality, fully integrated within this kitchen concept.

The extractor hood was made to measure.

In this classic kitchen with its Lacanche range cooker, the cabinet fronts were made with painted solid oak panels.
The cabinet structures are made of birch plywood bonded with water-resistant glue.
The worktop and sink unit are made of Belgian blue hardstone with ribbed edgings.
Hot water tap by Quooker.

115

This country kitchen with range cooker by La Cornue features many quaint and intricate details. The cabinet structures are made of birch plywood bonded with water-resistant glue.
Fronts made of solid oak, worktops and sink unit in Belgian blue hardstone. Tap by Dornbracht, hot water tap by Quooker and coffee and combi steamer by Miele.
All the handles were specially designed and created for the client.

The worktop in this traditional yet modern country kitchen is made of in-situ cast concrete. The cabinet structures are made of birch plywood bonded with water-resistant glue. The fronts are made of stained three-layer solid oak.
Range cooker by Viking, extractor hood by Gutmann and steam oven by Gaggenau.

This traditional country kitchen with Viking range cooker features fronts made of solid three-layer oak with cabinet structures made of bonded birch plywood.
Worktop made of in-situ cast concrete.
The steam oven is by Miele, and the Gutmann extractor hood was specially reinforced and extended. The second door in the set of tall cupboards leads to the scullery.

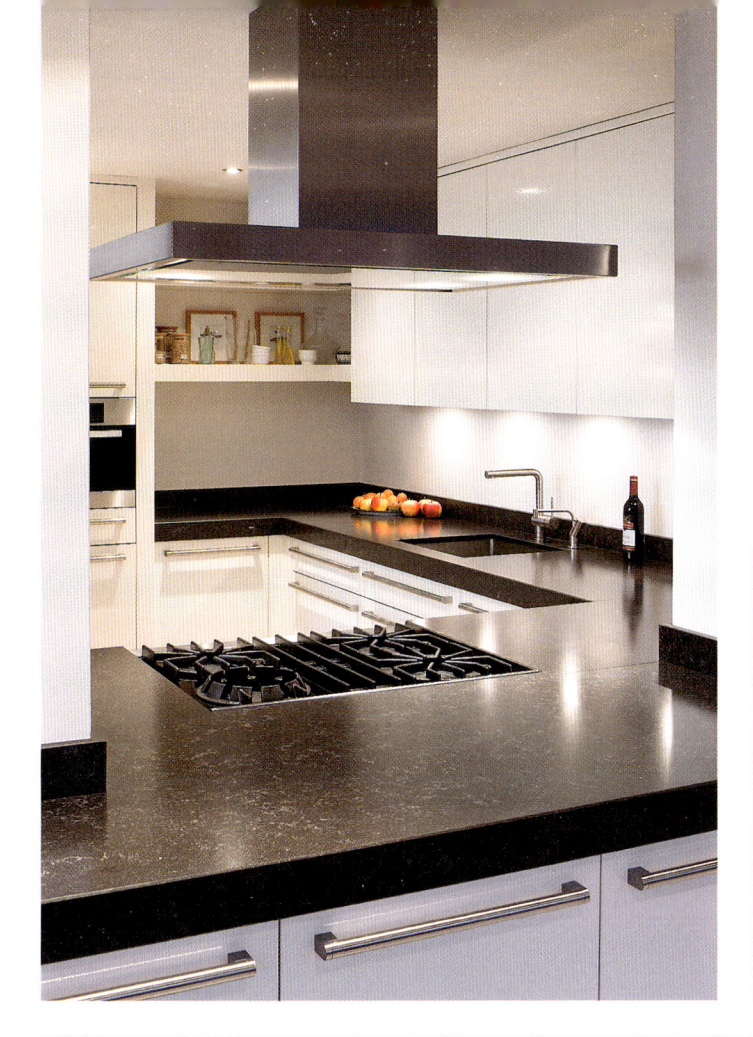

The cabinet structures of this modern kitchen by Paul van de Kooi are, as always, made of birch plywood bonded with water-resistant glue.
The fronts made of solid three-layer oak were hand-finished with high-gloss paint.
Worktop made of composite stone, range cooker by Viking, extractor hood by Gutmann and combi steam oven by Miele.

The fronts of this modern kitchen are made of three-layer solid oak, and the cabinet structures are made of birch plywood bonded with water-resistant glue.
The side panels and worktop are made of in-situ cast concrete.
In the sitting area, underfloor heating has been integrated to create a more pleasant temperature.
Hob by Pitt Cooking, combi steam oven and coffee maker by Miele.

This kitchen was created in an old classroom.
Cabinet structures made of birch plywood bonded with water-resistant glue.
The MDF fronts were sprayed with car paint and then coated with a matt finishing.
The worktop is coated with Nero Foreste granite.
Hob by Pitt Cooking and extractor hood by Gutmann.
Oven and combi steam oven by Gaggenau.
The internal drawer for Nespresso coffee capsules was made to measure.

**Paul van de Kooi - made-to-measure kitchens**
Nijverheidsweg Noord 74 D
NL - 3812 PM Amersfoort
T +31 (0)33 465 11 11
www.paulvandekooi.nl
info@paulvandekooi.nl

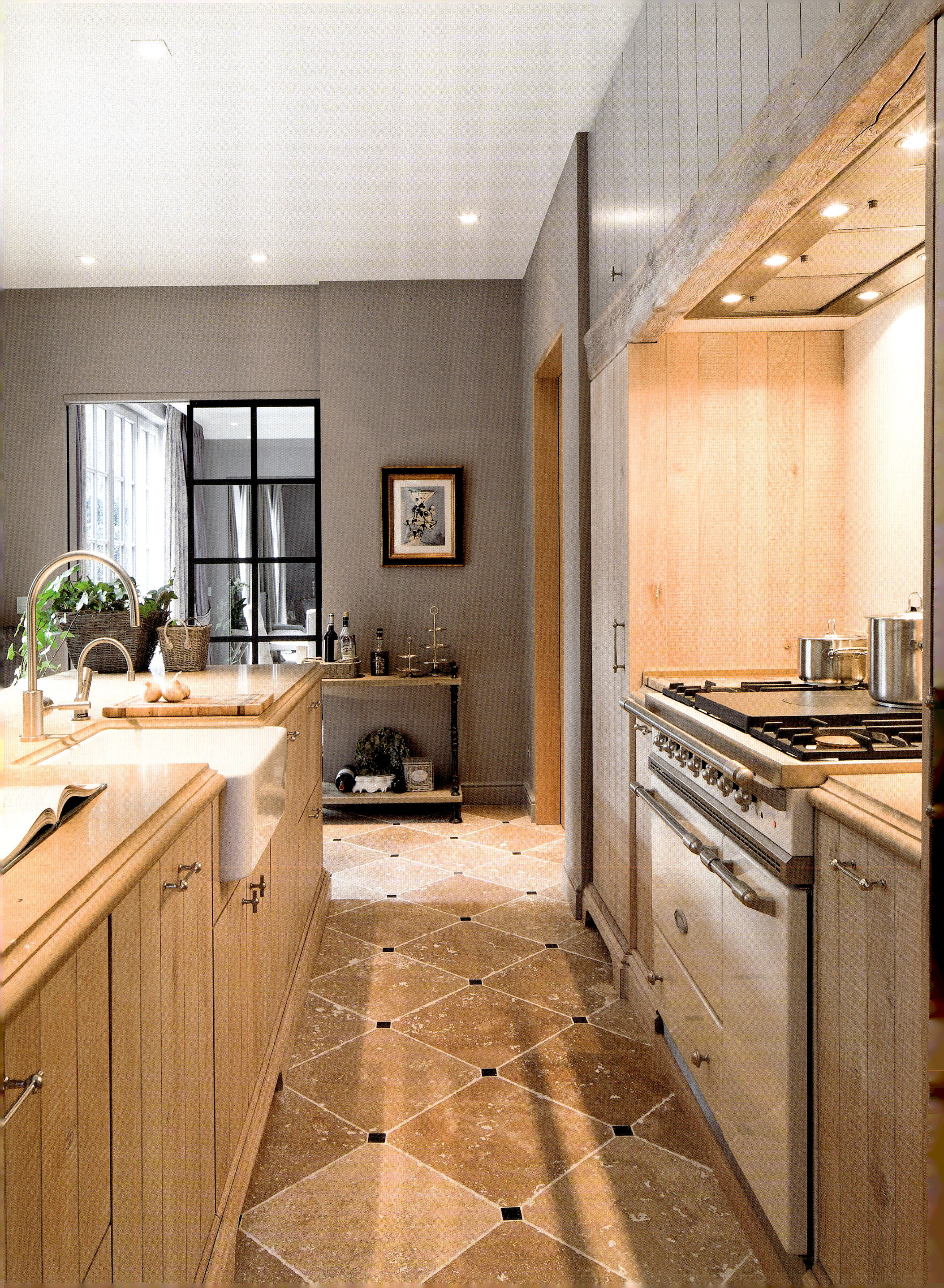

# EXCLUSIVE FURNITURE FITTINGS: THE FINISHING TOUCHES THAT MAKE A HIGH-QUALITY KITCHEN COMPLETE

Dauby is an exclusive importer and wholesaler supplied by various Italian, French and Spanish manufacturers.
For 30 years, Dauby has specialised in top-of-the-range door, window and furniture fittings in a wide variety of styles.
As an importer and distributor, Dauby attaches great importance not only to what is currently in fashion but also to future trends.
Dauby's collections feature an extensive range of design models for the modern home. In addition, there are also some examples of stylish but timeless door fittings in the old rectory, manor house and cottage styles. The materials include solid brass, solid bronze, traditional wrought iron or exclusive Britannia metal (an alloy that includes silver and tin).
These authentic fittings are cast in sand moulds and then refined by hand. Finishing is extremely important in this type of product, as the traditional production process leads to small imperfections that give the fittings a time-honoured, weathered appearance.
It is these small details that make a world of difference to your interior.
Dauby has something for everyone, from exclusive villa construction specialists to project managers or individual clients with good taste and an eye for detail.
Thanks to these unique articles, Dauby's craftsmanship is often called upon when it comes to special projects. This kitchen catalogue is a striking example.

The design features of this kitchen are truly enhanced by the furniture fittings from the Giara "Chemin de Fer" series.
The door handles of this series were designed in the late eighteenth century for the luxurious wagons of the Orient Express. The "T" model was used on the side to pull the door shut. The "L" model was placed on the other side.
This series also includes the window handles and fixed handles for the front door, as well as the full spectrum of furniture fittings ranging from knobs to all standard measurements of handles.
These products are a must for renovation projects, as existing handles can be replaced with great ease.

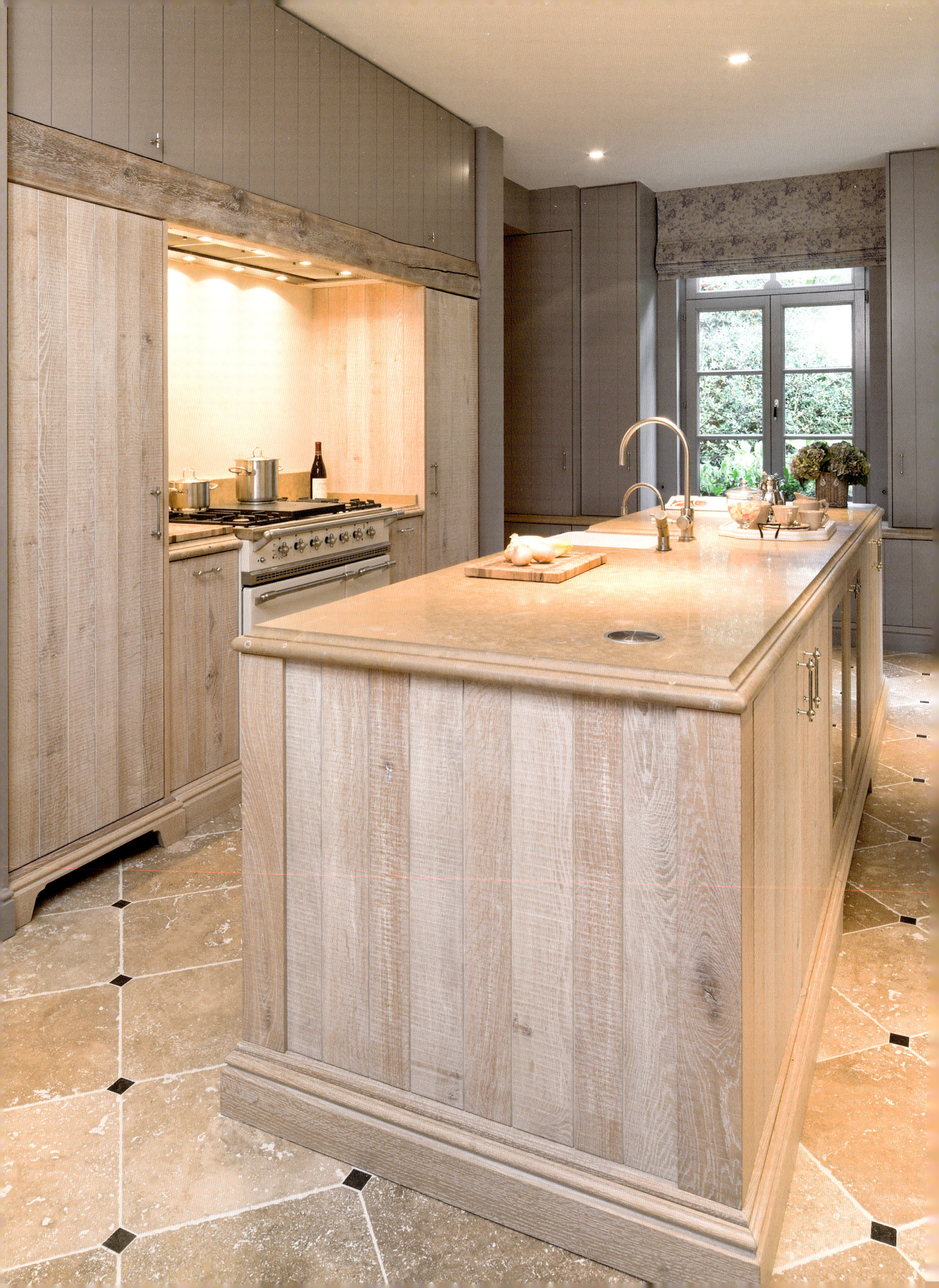

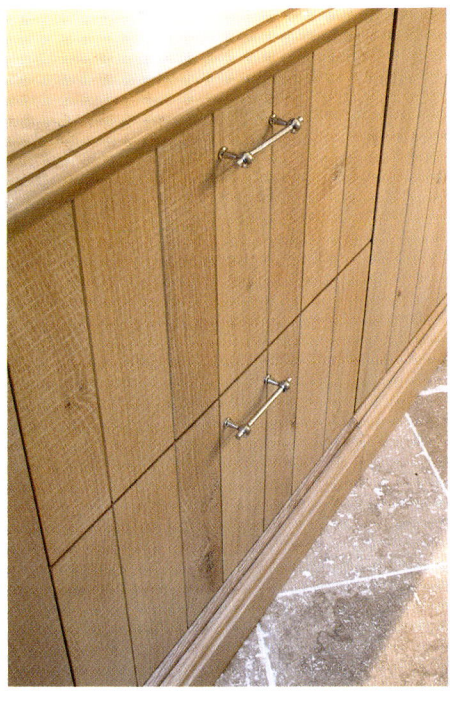

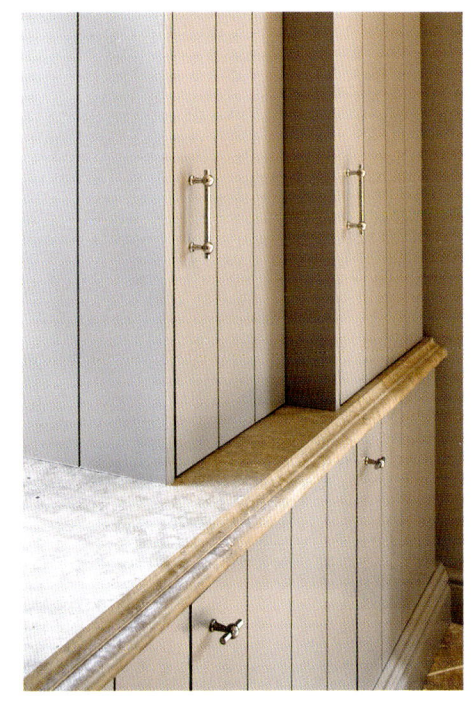

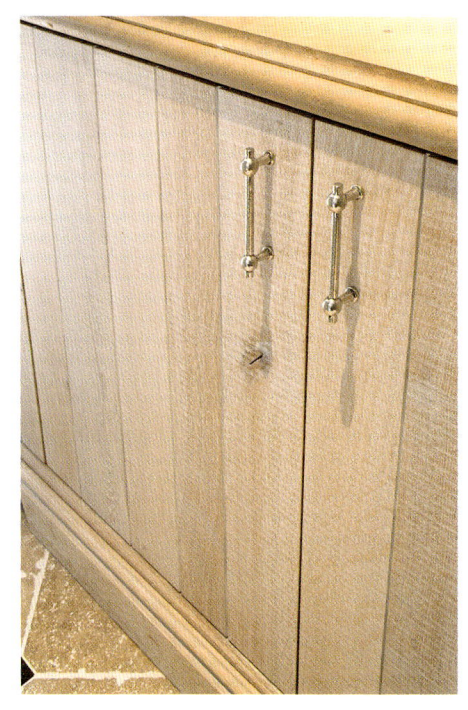

These fittings, like the other lines of Giara, are still cast using traditional craft methods in sand moulds, a technique which dates back to 3000 BC. The articles are then entirely finished by hand.
The authentic look of the product is due to the materials used by Giara in the production process: Britannia metal or bronze.
Both these materials are corrosion-resistant and they do not require a layer of varnish.
Over time and with frequent use, the fittings acquire a beautiful natural patina. A number of different finishings are available.

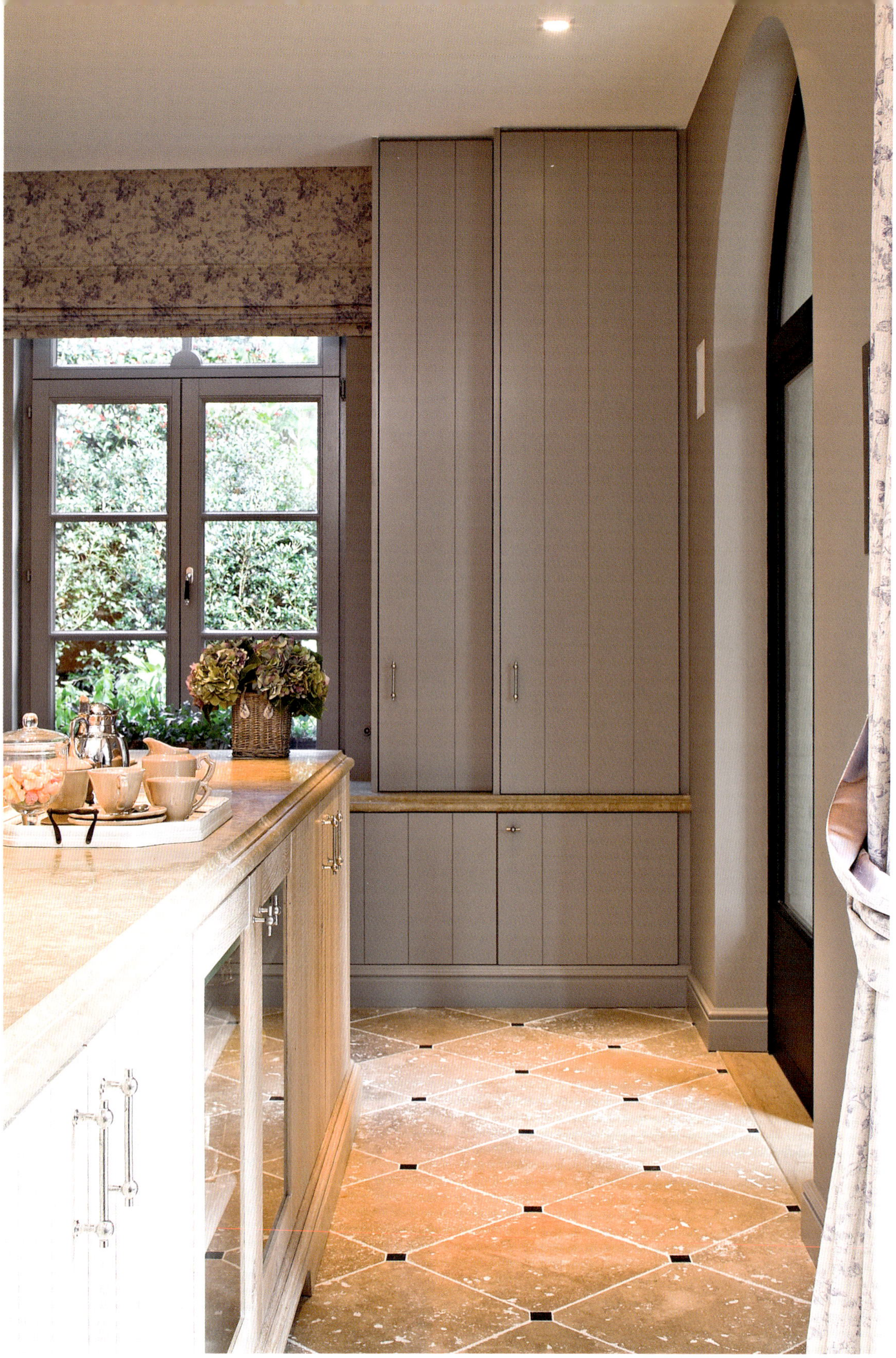

Giara has a complete range of fittings for inside and outside doors, always with matching window handles and furniture knobs or handles.

[ **Dauby nv**
Uilenbaan 86
B – 2160 Wommelgem
T +32 (0)3  354 16 86
F +32 (0)3  354 16 32
www.dauby.be
info@dauby.be

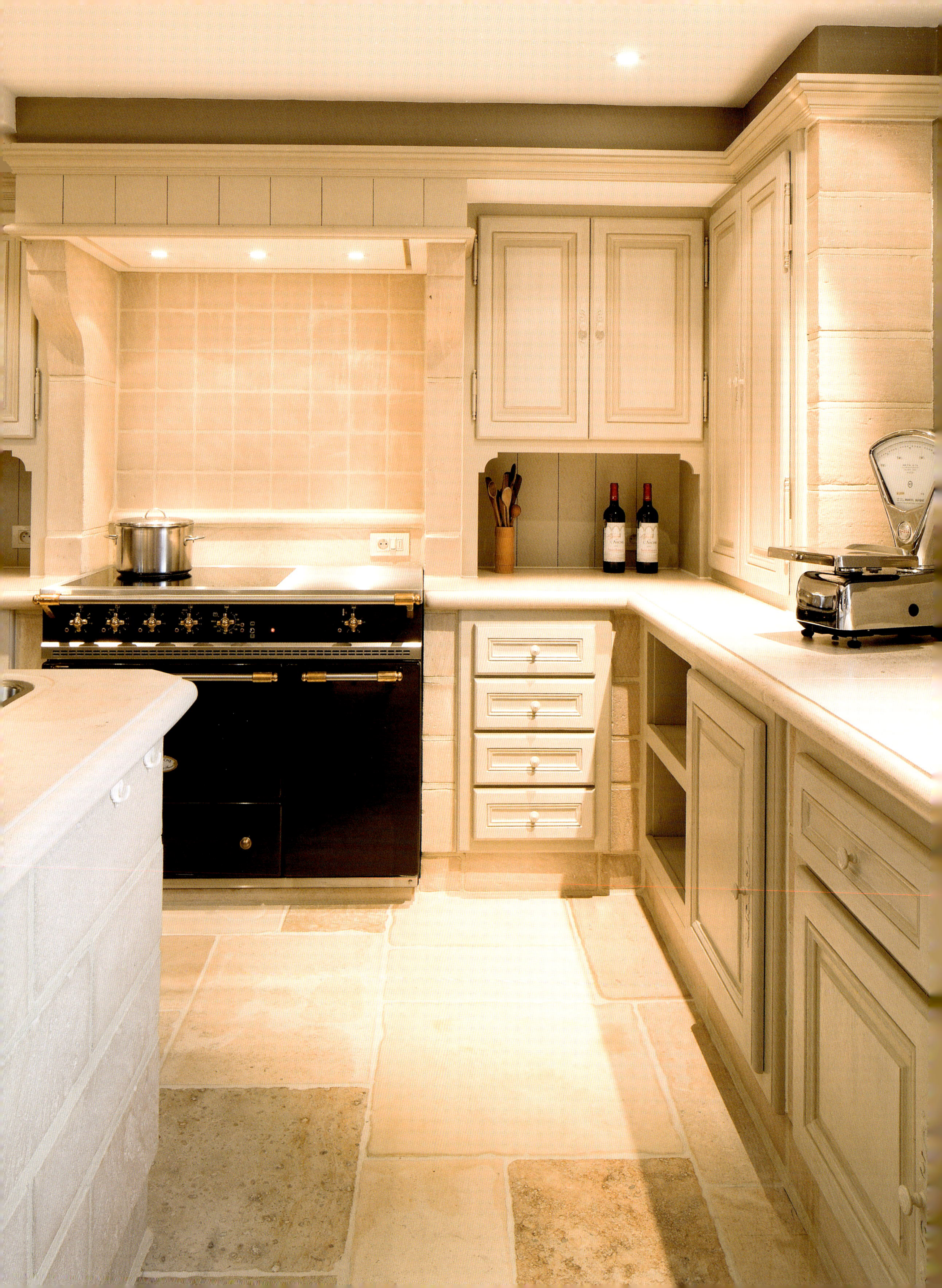

[ FUNCTIONAL AND TIMELESS
LIVING KITCHENS
WITH CHARACTER

Bourgondisch Kruis is not only one of the most reputable companies specialising in historic building materials in the Low Countries. This company from West Flanders also offers total solutions and original ways to integrate these unique materials in exclusive house design projects.

The design and traditional crafting of kitchens is one of Bourgondisch Kruis' specialities. The company has its own cabinetmaking workshop, where experienced professionals produce perfect custom-built furniture using fine materials like oak panels, and a stonemason's workshop where Burgundy limestone and blue hardstone are made into kitchen worktops, exclusive floor coverings and wall claddings, solid sinks, etc.
Customers can create their own designs or they can be assisted by Bourgondisch Kruis' own design team.

Each Bourgondisch Kruis project exudes class, functionality and timeless style. The creations featured in this article are striking examples.

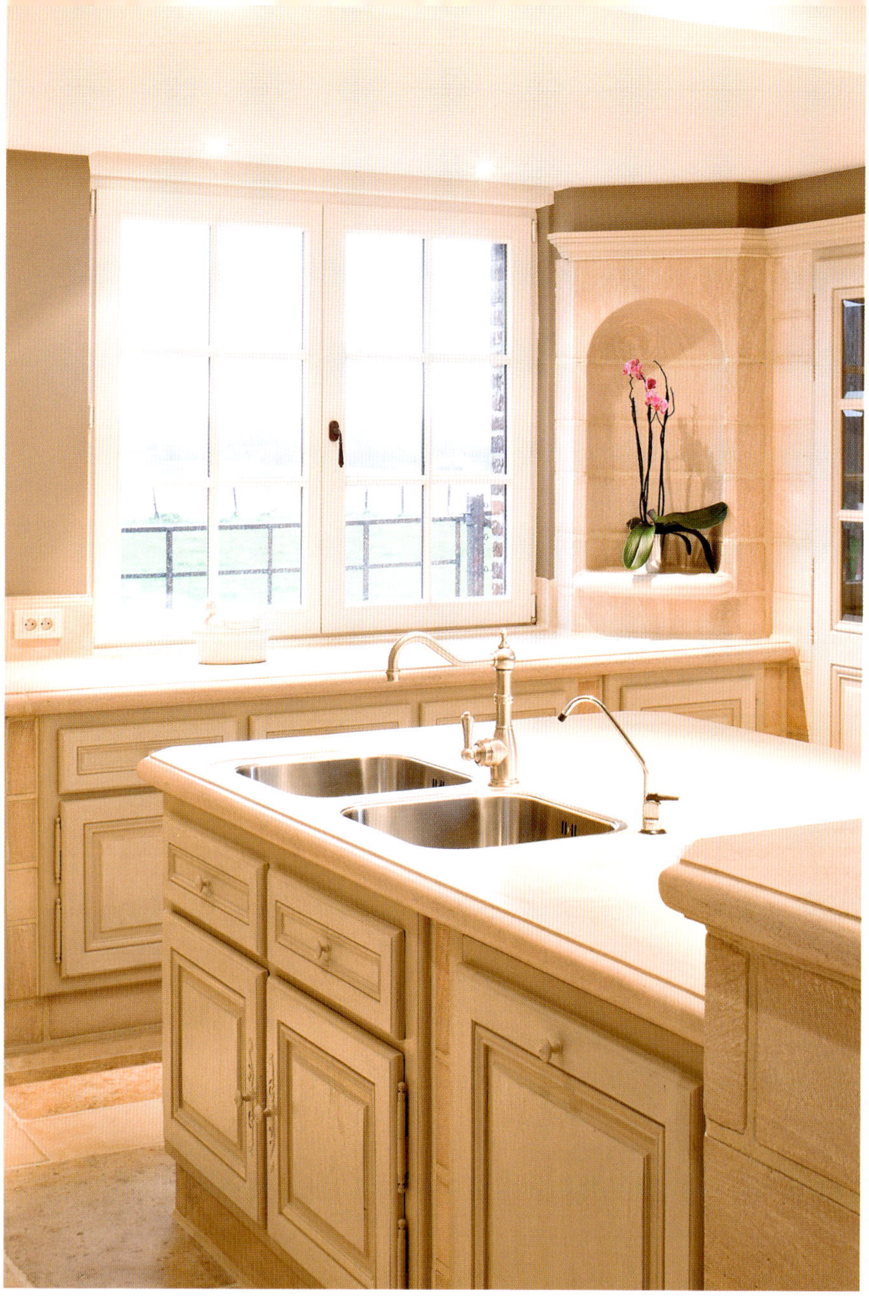

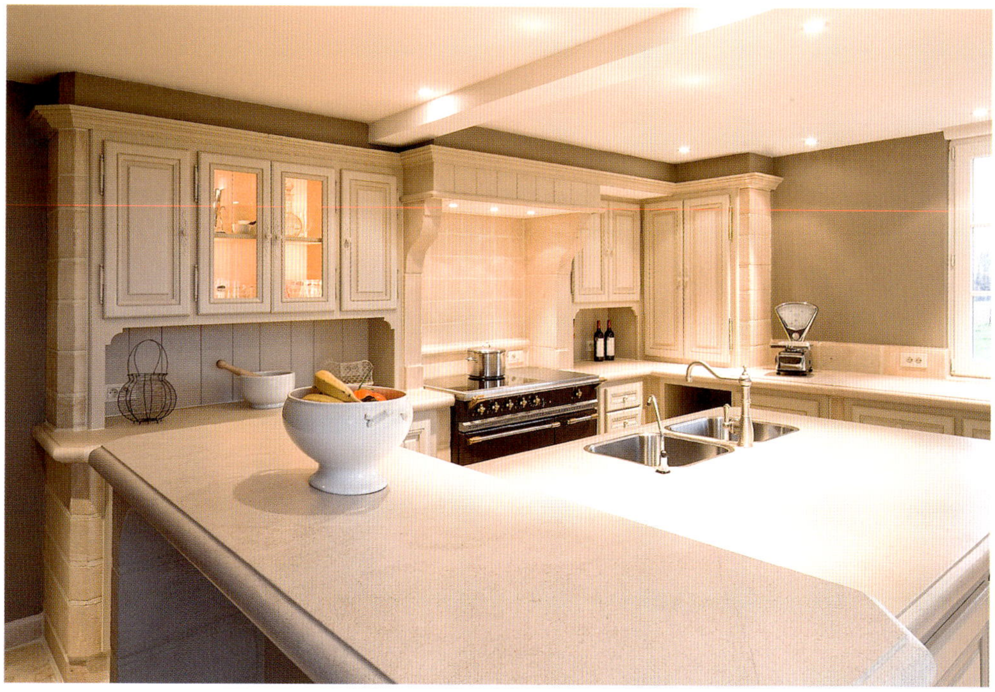

**128-131**
Bourgondisch Kruis' team designed and created this kitchen with old Burgundy stone and solid oak cabinet doors.
The flooring consists of reclaimed second-cut Burgundy slabs which can be placed in any Roman pattern.

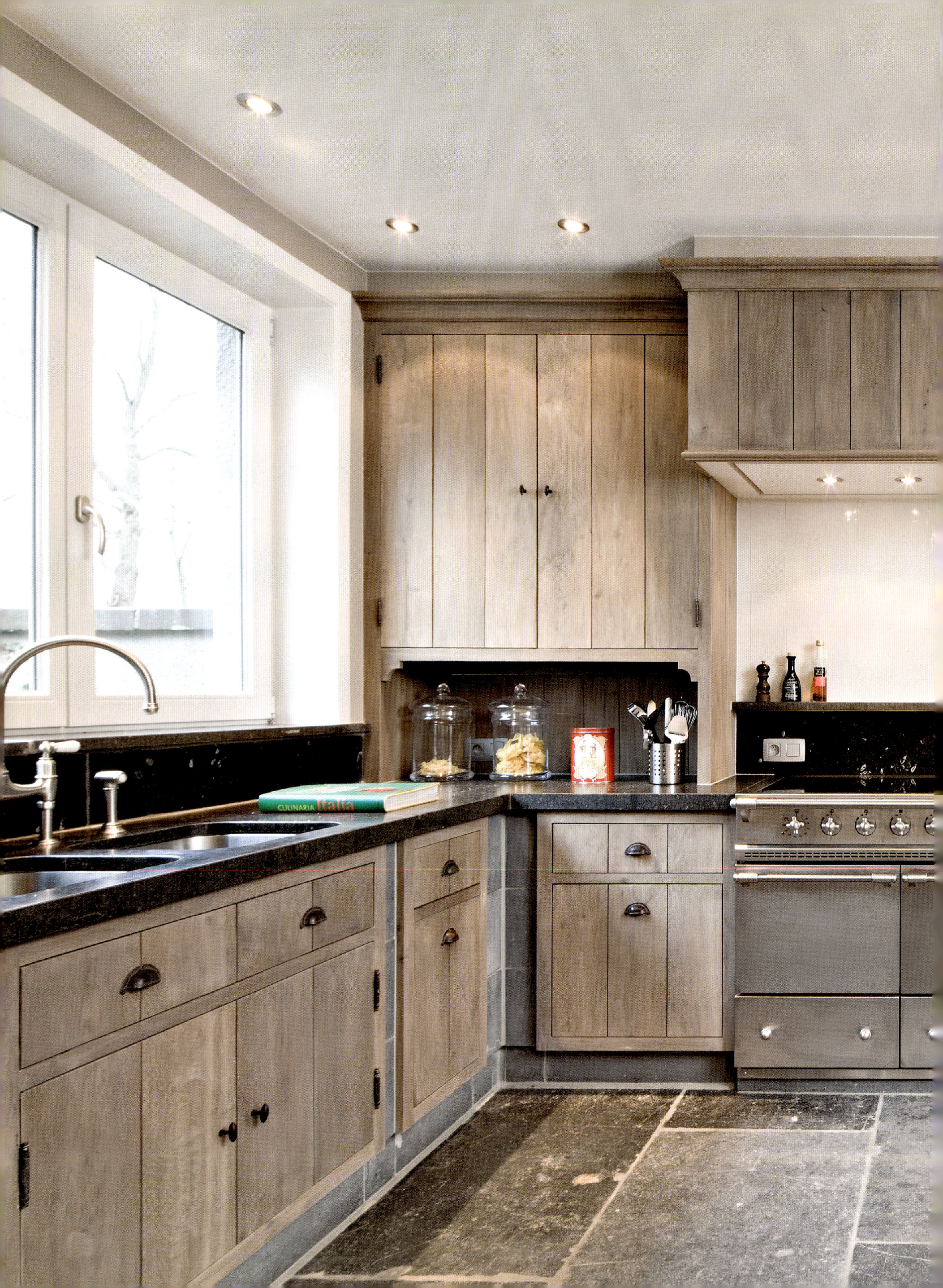
CULINARIA Italia

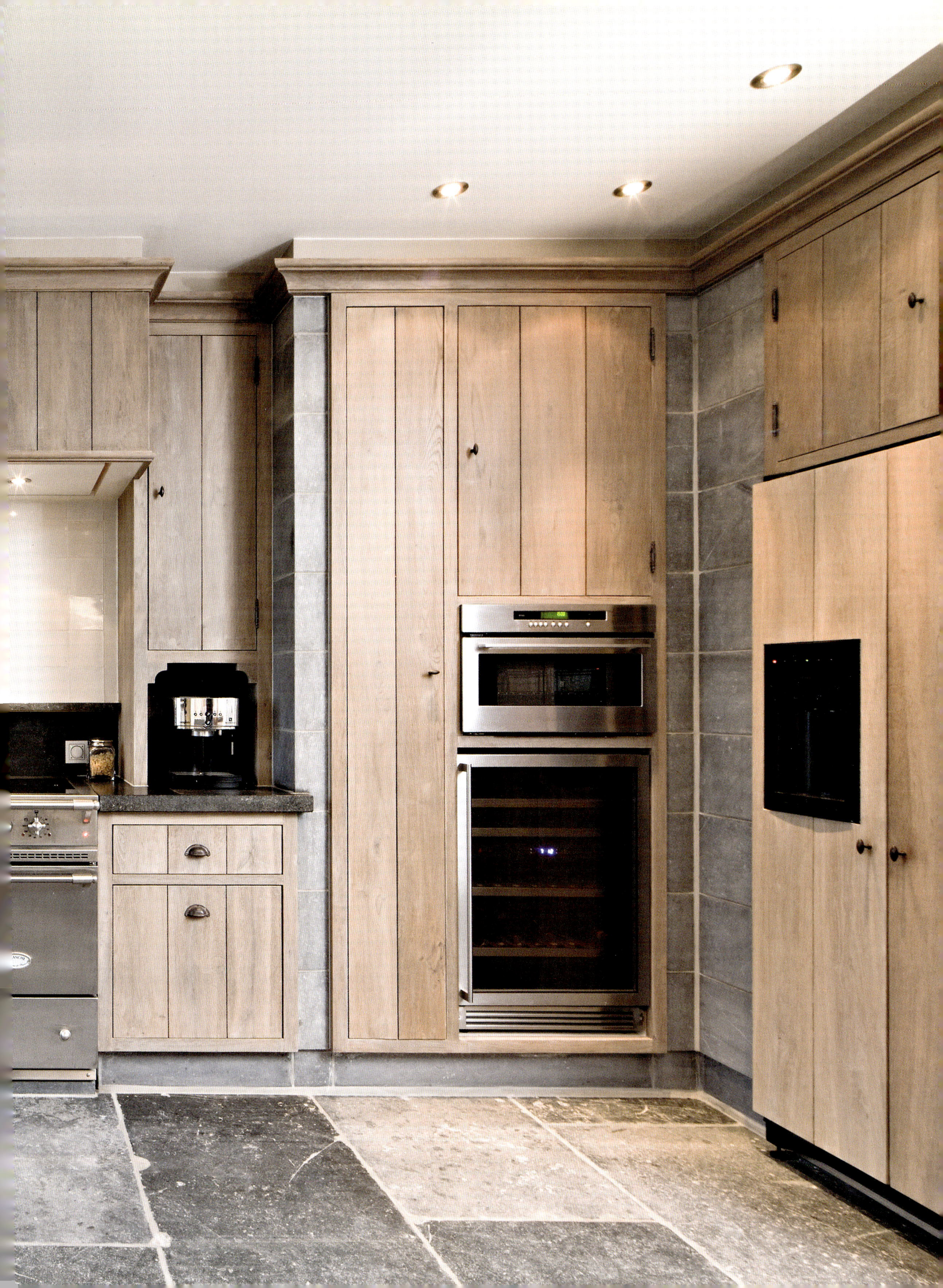

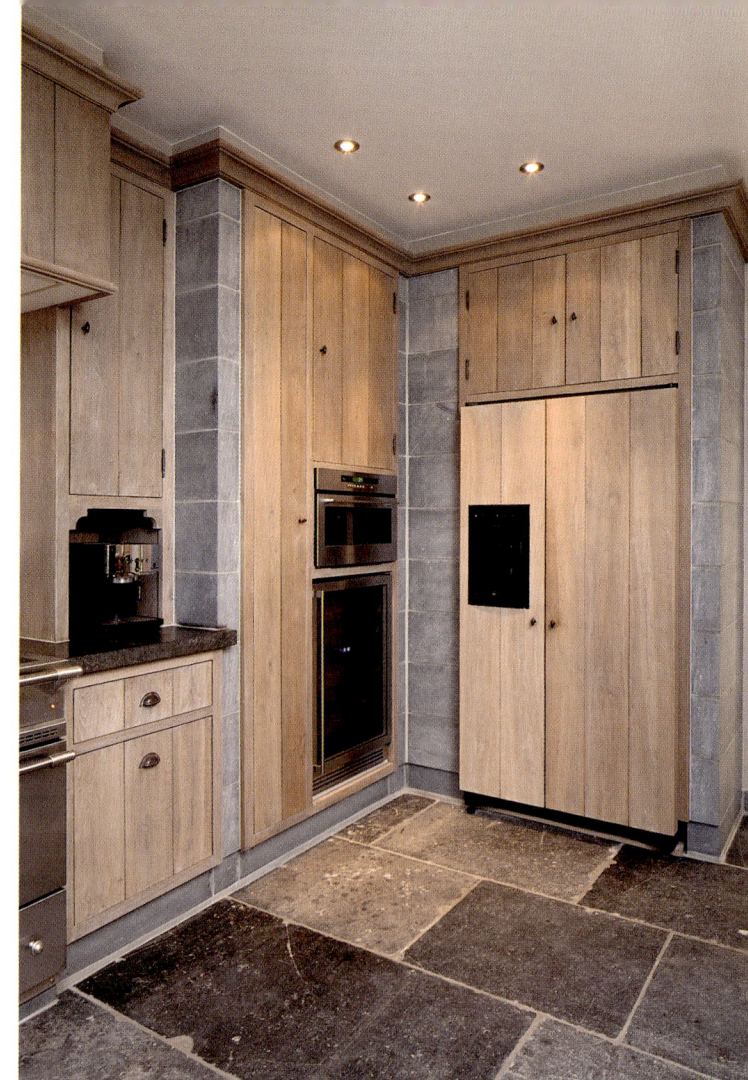

**132-134**
A Bourgondisch Kruis design using weathered oak planking, lightly patinaed and combined with blue hardstone.
The reclaimed blue hardstone floor was laid in 60 cm wide strips.
The stainless steel fronts of the kitchen appliances (including a built-in wine storage unit and oven) and the Lacanche range cooker harmonise with the light patina of the oak planks and the bluestone tiles.

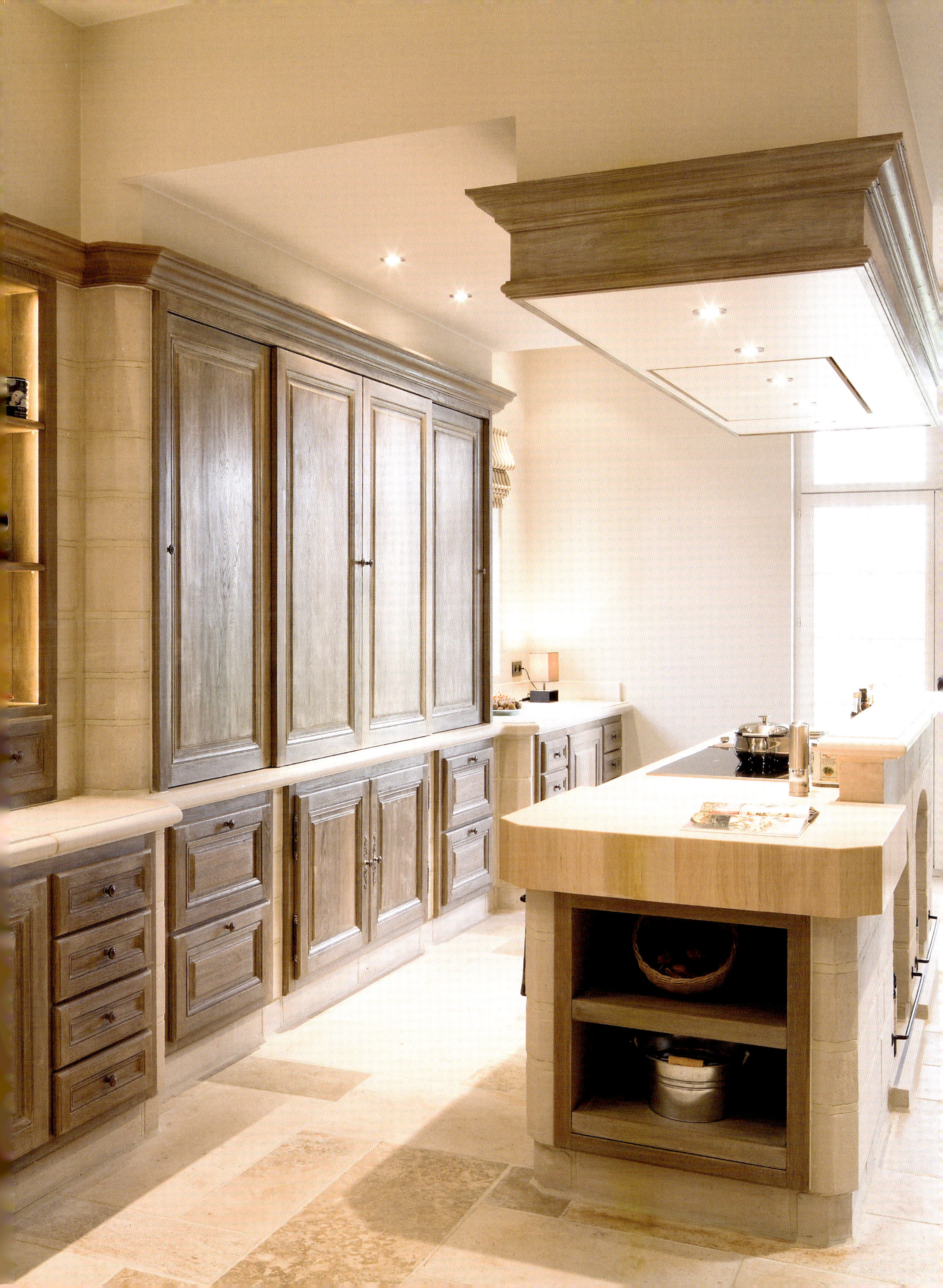

**135-137**
In close consultation with the client, Bourgondisch Kruis opted here for a central cooking island with very opulent display cabinets with large sliding doors.

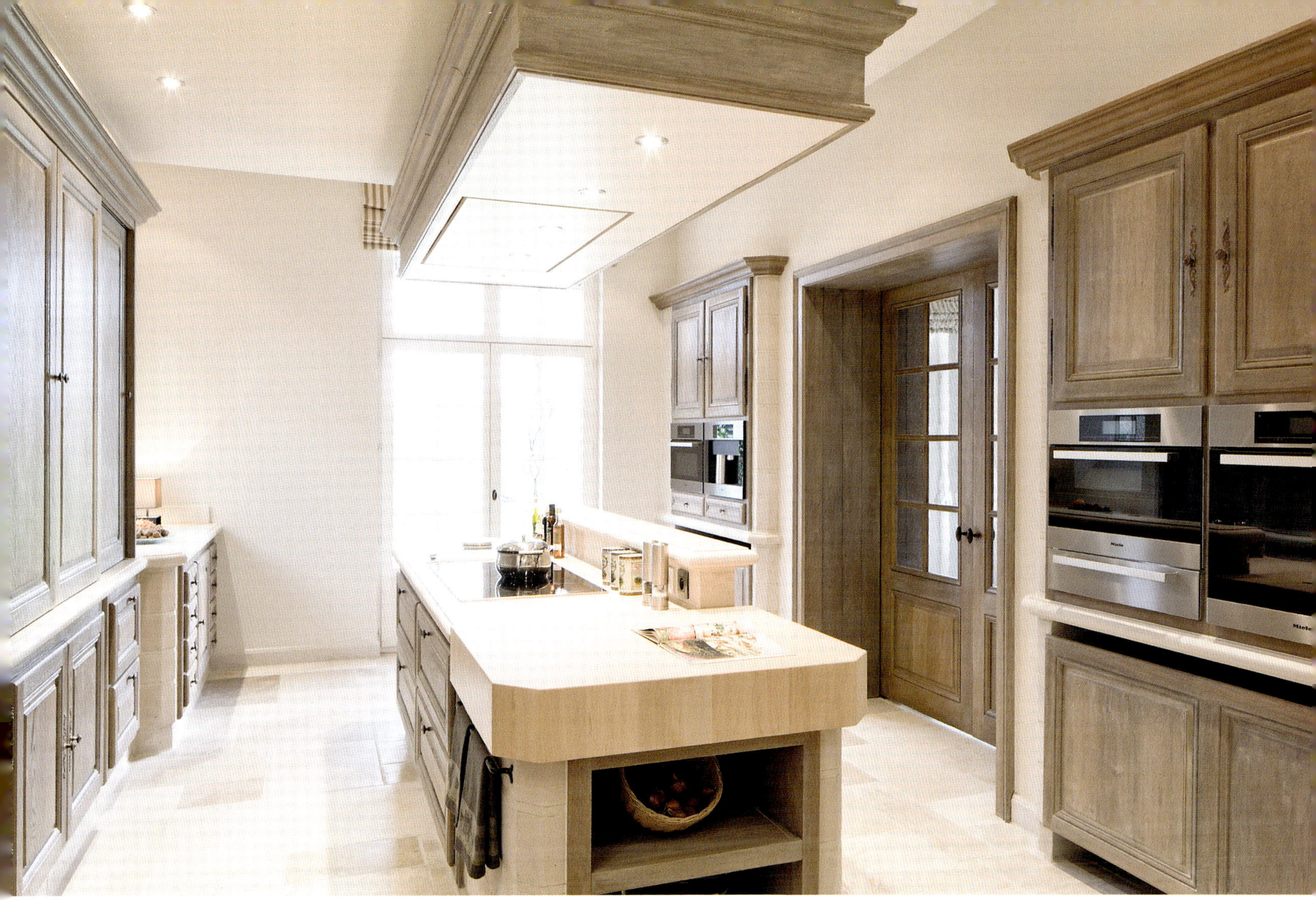

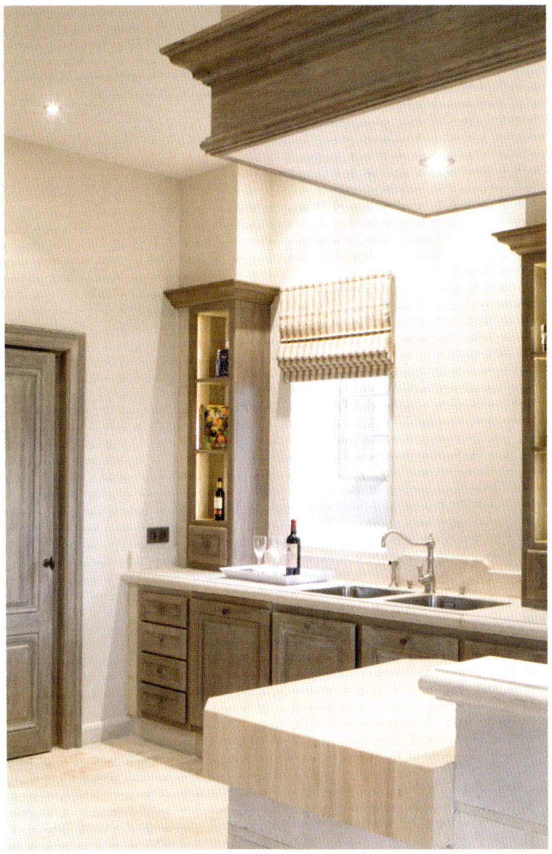

The designers opted here for maintenance-friendly Burgundy slabs in a random jigsaw pattern.
The oak cabinet doors were finished with a light patina that creates an overall fresh and airy impression.

For this kitchen design in a poolhouse, Bourgondisch Kruis opted for worktops made of blue hardstone, cabinets made with 17th-century planking and old square tiles, also made of blue hardstone.

**Bourgondisch Kruis nv**
Darmstraat 20
B - 8531 Harelbeke - Bavikhove
T +32 (0)56 73 16 41
F +32 (0)56 72 96 82
www.bkb.be
www.bourgondisch-kruis.be
info@bourgondisch-kruis.be

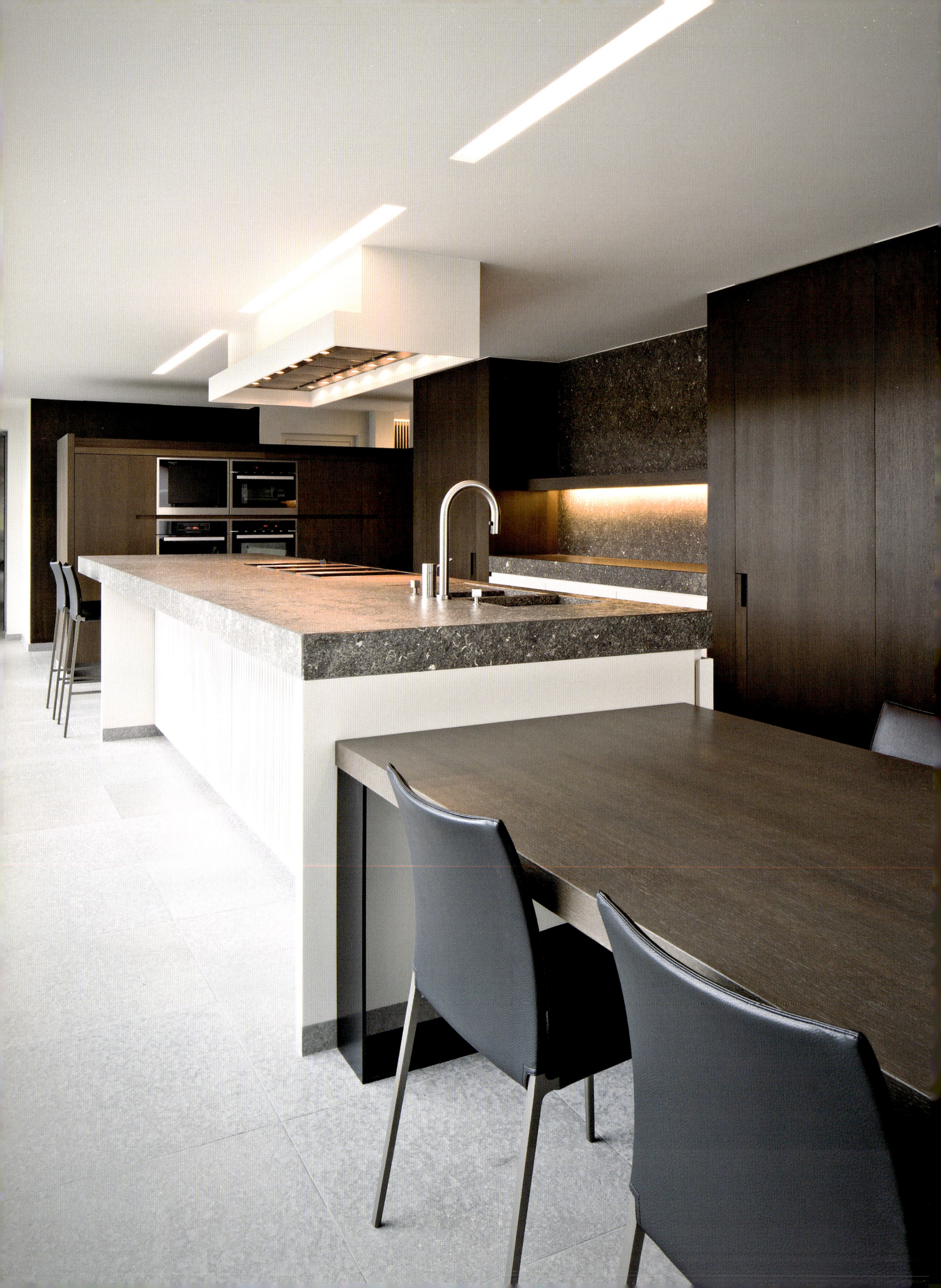

# [ A COMMITMENT TO OPENNESS AND SPACIOUSNESS

For the conversion of a 1960s villa, interior architect Frederic Kielemoes decided to create a sense of openness among the adjacent volumes and with the garden according to a configuration in which the living kitchen forms the central element.

The immense cooking island (510 cm x 130 cm) is covered with a worktop in Gris Catalan, with aged finishing.
The base units are whitewashed and coated with white textured paint.
The other parts are made of brown-stained dark oak.
Kitchen appliances by Küppersbusch. The table and the lighting were made to measure. Lia chairs and Lio barstools, both by Zanotta.

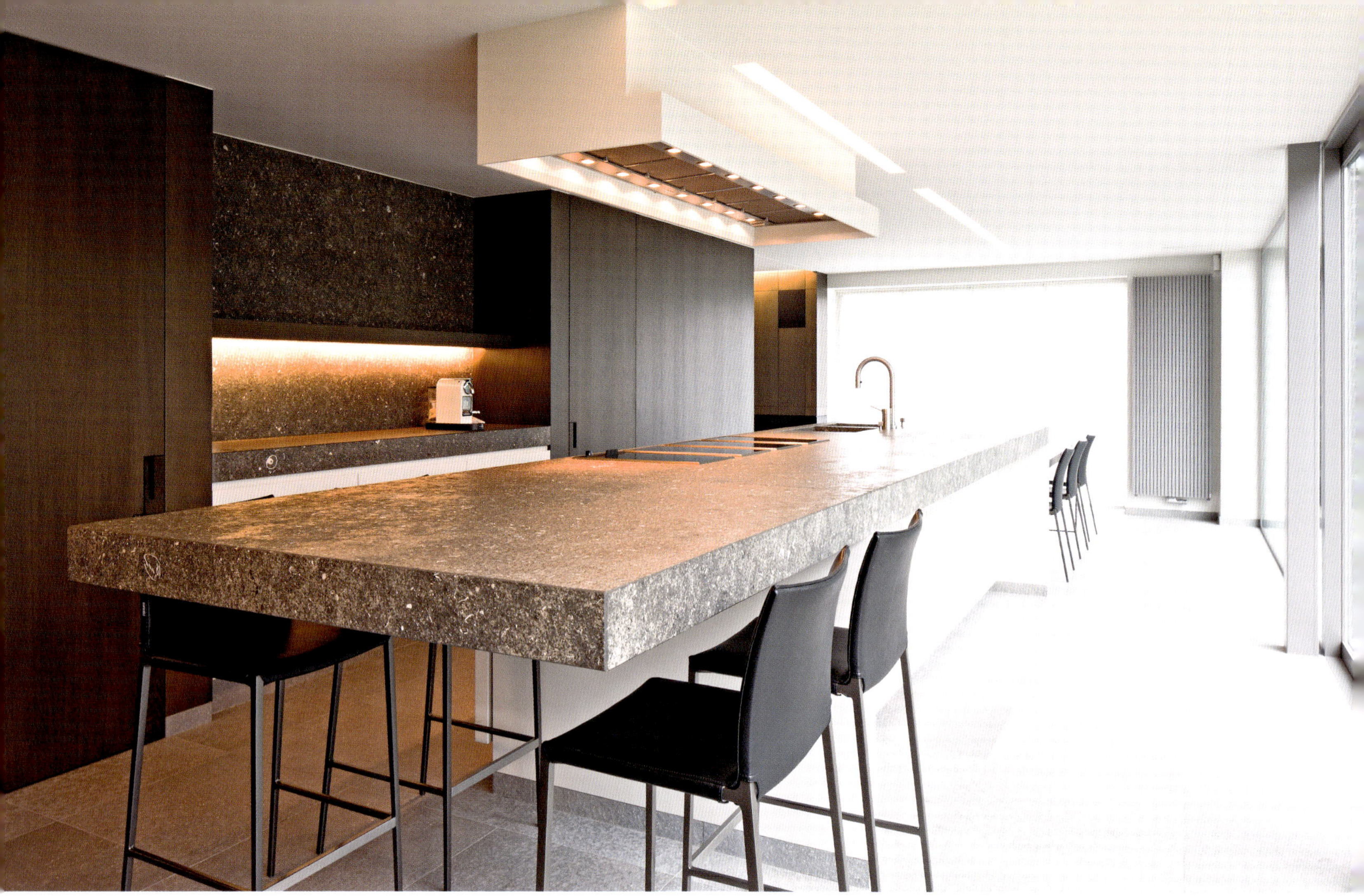

[
**Frederic Kielemoes**
Interior architect
MOB +32 (0)486 40 75 64
www.frederickielemoes.be
info@frederickielemoes.be

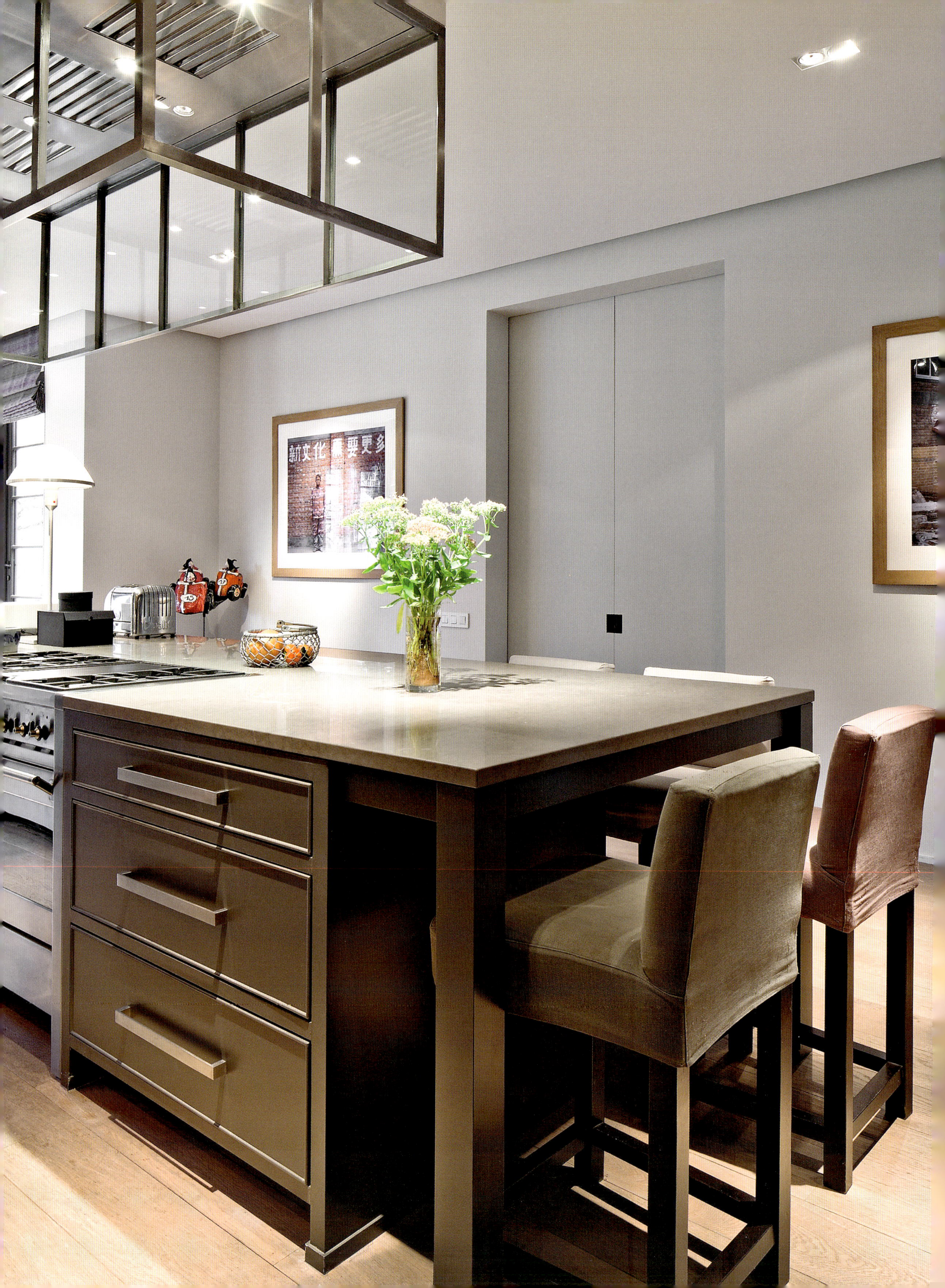

# [ UNRIVALLED CULINARY ERGONOMICS

True to his philosophy, for this new edition Thierry Goffin once again invites us into his elegant world of culinary art, this time to present perfect "culinary ergonomics" with consummate conviviality around the Home Chef.

The Home Chef takes pride of place. It attracts people; they come just to look at it, to gaze in wonder. It becomes a focus of conversation and seems to partake of the atmosphere, but it also creates the atmosphere and irresistibly whets our appetite for good food.

This atmosphere creates the decor for a style which can be contemporary and classic rolled into one.
Fahrenheit often works with renowned decorators and architects like François Marcq, Christophe Decarpentrie, Axel Vervoordt, Marc Corbiau and many others. It creates a perfectly integrated kitchen concept that harmonises with the entire project as conceived by these designers.

This project was designed by Thierry Goffin and created by the cabinetmakers workshop Rigobert, with some additional ideas provided by interior architect François Marcq. As a result, the kitchen forms an integral part of the entire architectural concept in this newly constructed villa in the south of Brussels designed by architect Nicolas de Liedekerke.

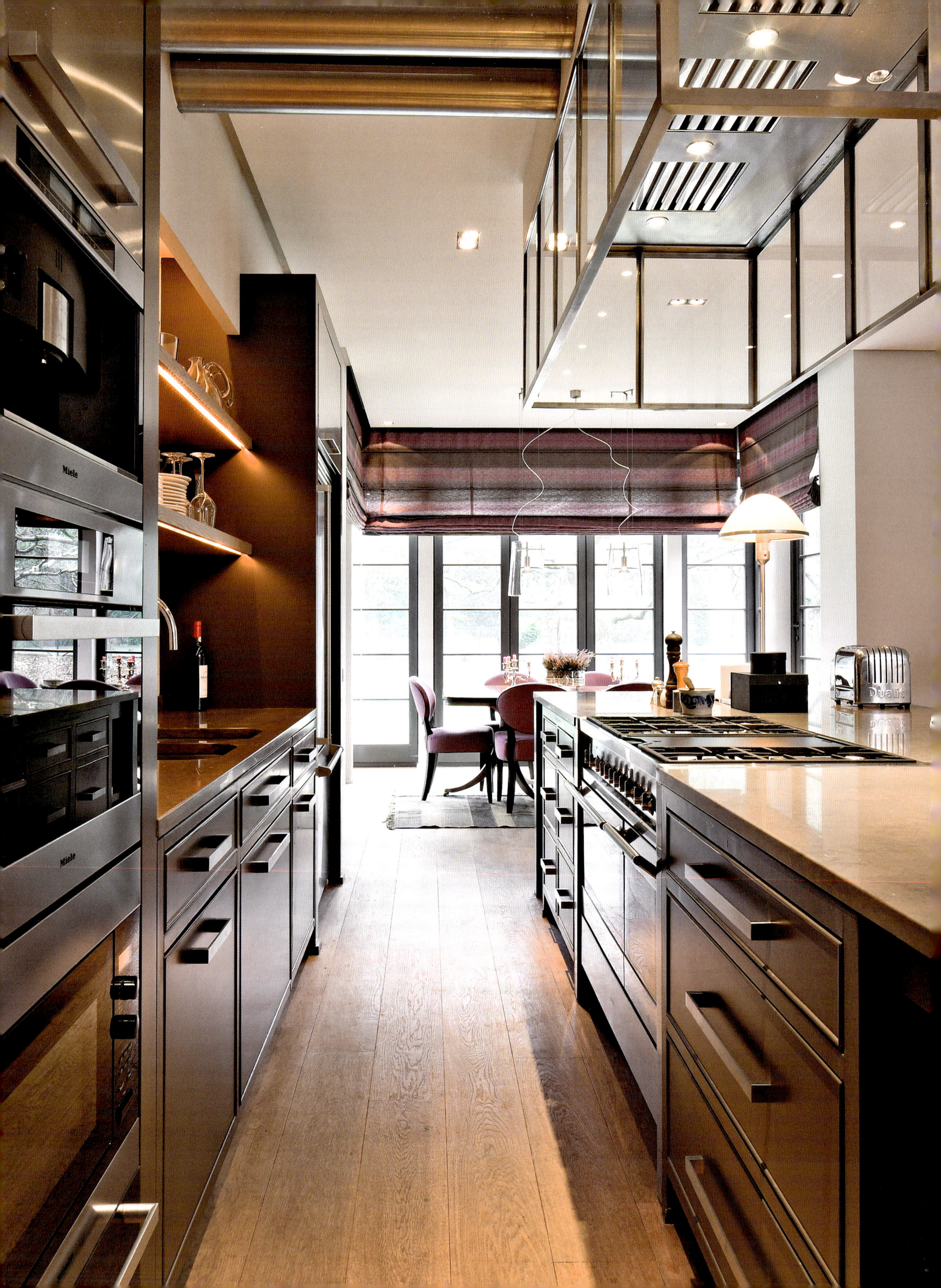

**Fahrenheit nv**
Avenue Louise 83
B – 1050 Brussels
T +32 (0)2 644 28 00
F +32 (0)2 644 27 87
www.fahrenheithomechef.com
fahrenheit@fahrenheit.be

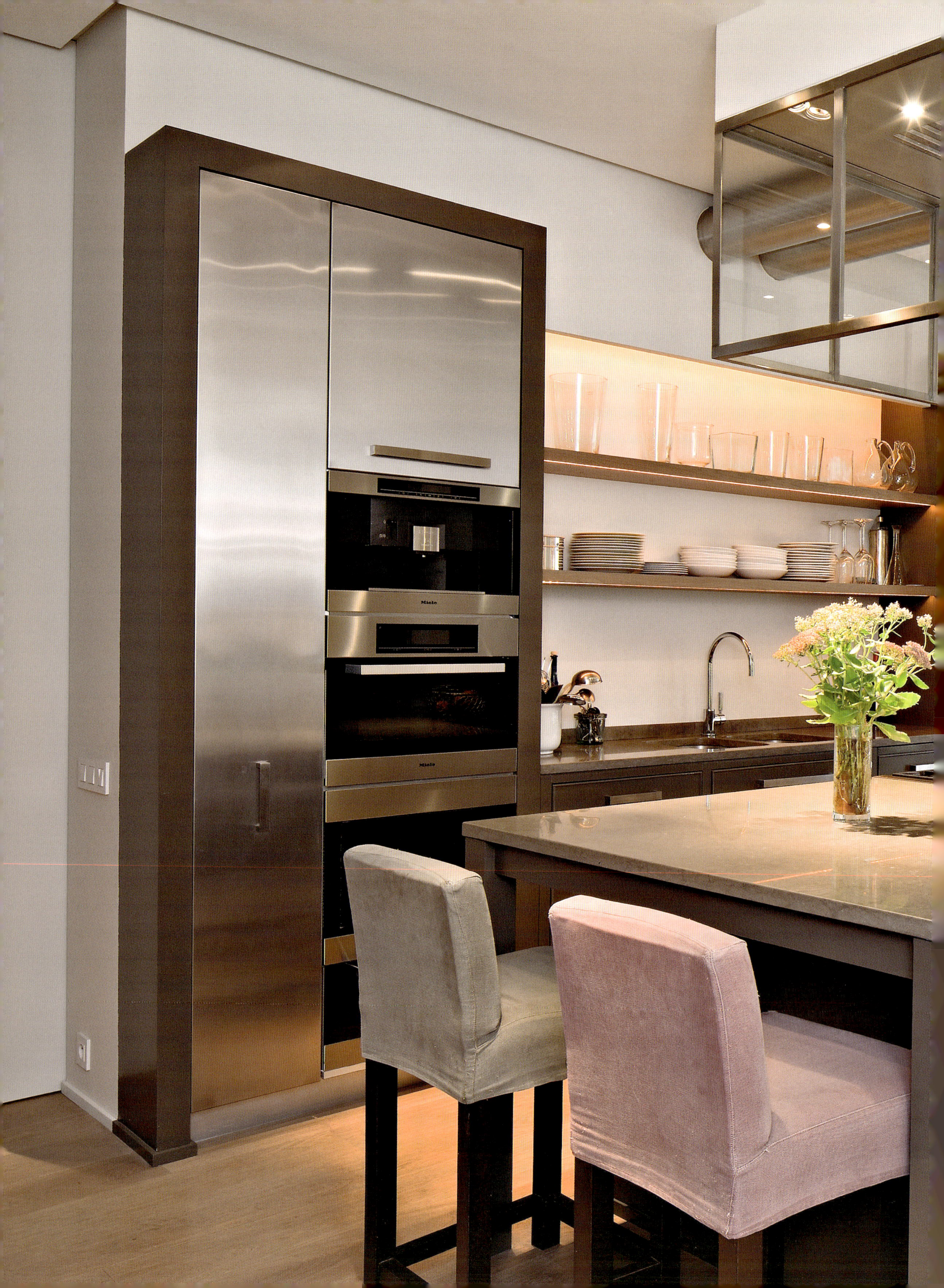

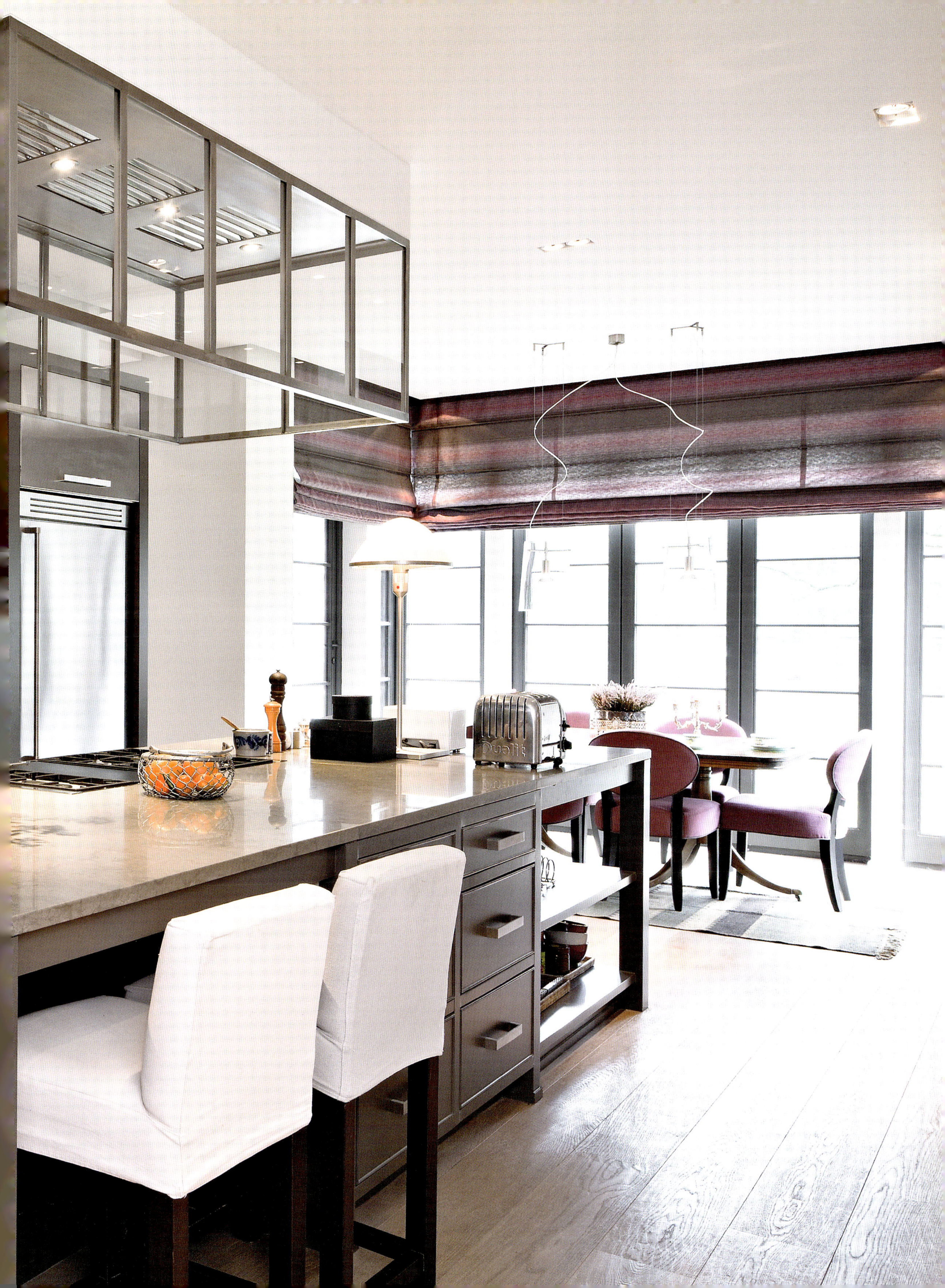
Dualit

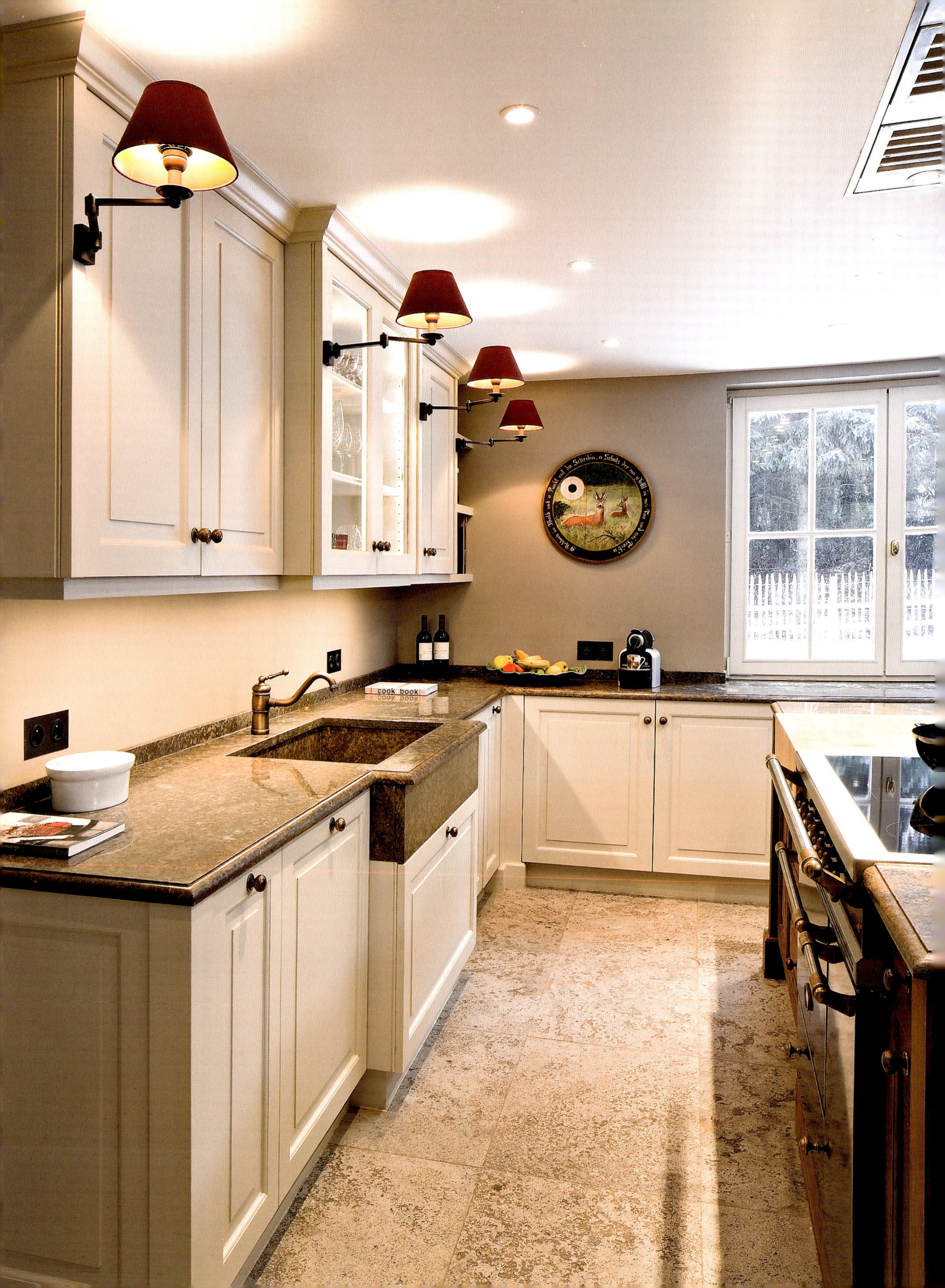
cook book

[ # CLASSICAL STYLE AT ITS BEST

This second kitchen by Fahrenheit (see also p. 144-149), which was part of a renovation project carried out on a villa in the town of Lasne, was designed in the purest classical tradition.

The furniture, made of MDF and painted yellow poplar, perfectly matches the colours of the walls *ton sur ton*. This decorative artifice accentuates the central cooking island, which is made with some truly exceptional pieces of French walnut.

The floors and worktops are made of a natural stone from the quarries of Charles Kreglinger. Different finishings are used: sand-blasted and lather finish for the floor, smoothed and oiled for the worktops. An example of consistency in diversity.

The classic lampshades, which were made to measure by the traditional crafts workshop Artho, add the final finishing touch. Another reminder that every Fahrenheit kitchen is a real living space that makes you want to live to cook, rather than cook to live.

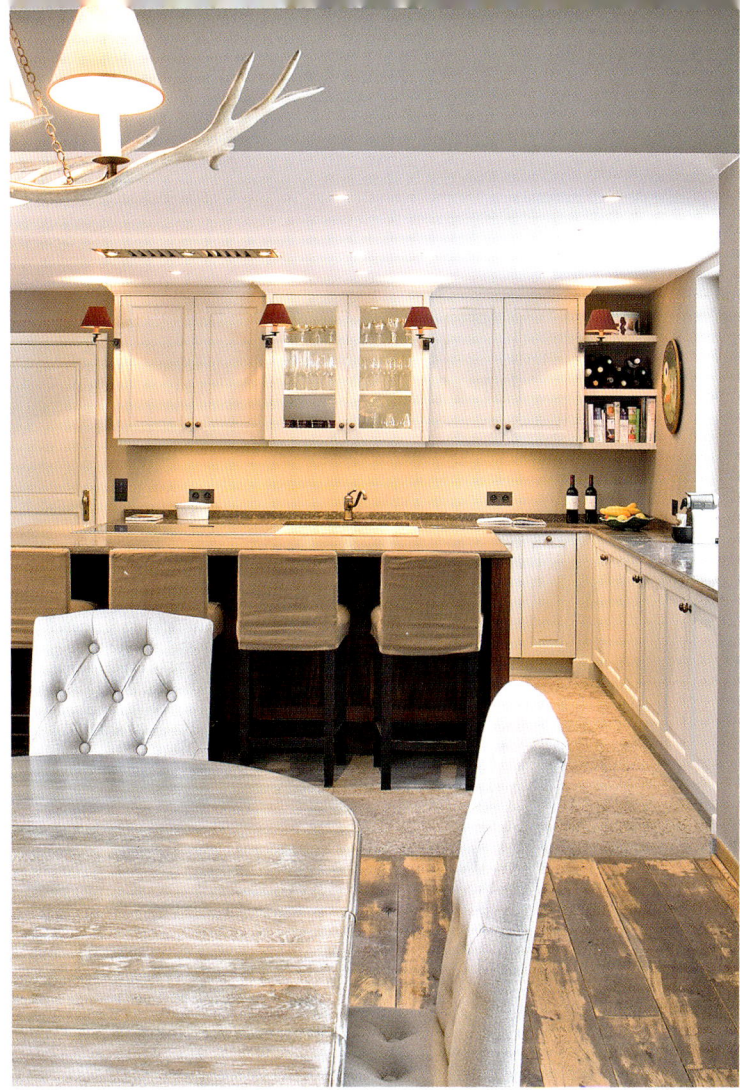

[
**Fahrenheit nv**
Avenue Louise 83
B – 1050 Brussels
T +32 (0)2 644 28 00
F +32 (0)2 644 27 87
www.fahrenheithomechef.com
fahrenheit@fahrenheit.be

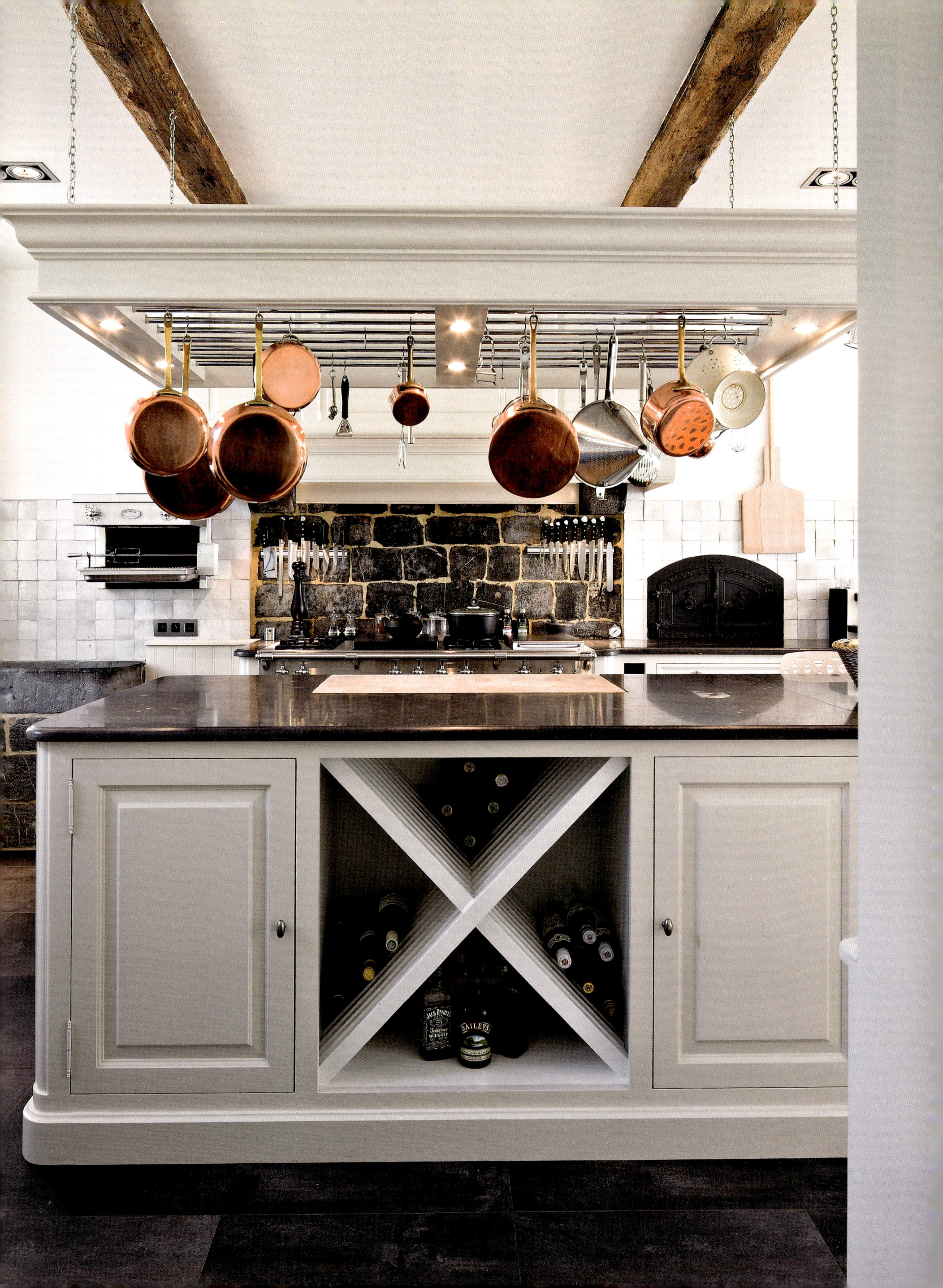
JACK DANIEL'S
BAILEYS

[ # A PERSONALISED APPROACH TO EACH PROJECT

Wood Fashion specialises in the creation of made-to-measure solid wood furniture and beautiful living spaces.

Each project is designed with the client according to his wishes. Whatever the project, Wood Fashion's team submits a personalised design backed up by tried and tested professional know-how and an aesthetic - and unfailingly innovative - vision.

From the initial contact to the delivery of the finished product, Wood Fashion guarantees that the work is followed up by the same person. Wood Fashion is not only a firm of designers but also a furniture manufacturer. In fact, all the furniture is made in its own workshops.

After-sales service is provided by Wood Fashion itself, and this is a very important aspect of each project.

This Wood Fashion kitchen was seamlessly integrated into a 17th-century farmhouse. It looks as if it has always been there. The hanging rack above the cooking island provides plenty of space for pots and pans. In the foreground there is a handy and original bottle rack.

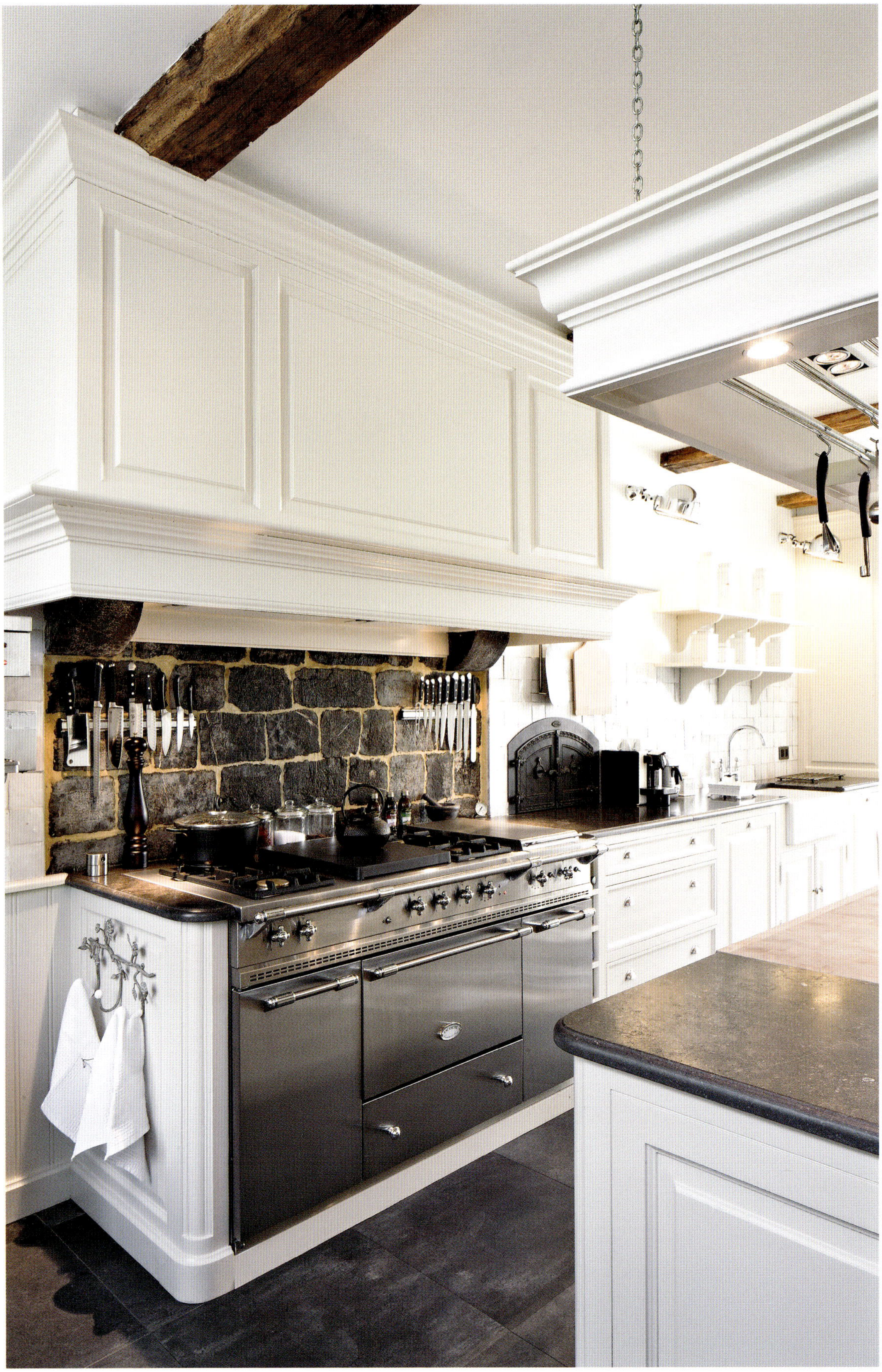

This creation is a tribute to the use of reclaimed building materials.
The original bread oven was reclaimed and renovated, and it is once again in operation.
The edging and the cornice of the old fireplace have also been restored and repainted. Behind the semi-professional stainless steel range cooker, there is an authentic wall made of Belgian blue quarry stone.

A worktop made of Belgian blue hardstone. The chopping block is made of beech wood.
The walls to the left and right of the oven are coated with Moroccan zelliges.

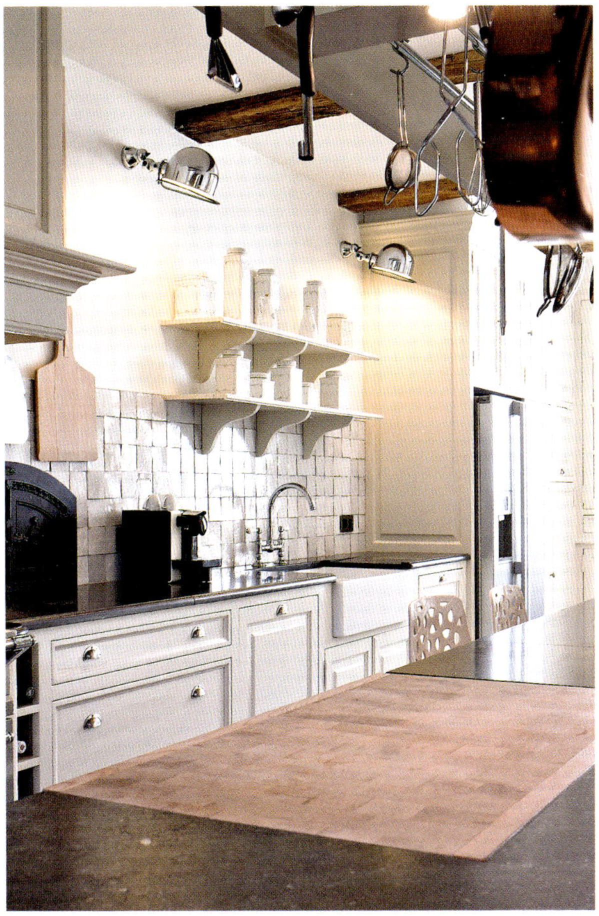
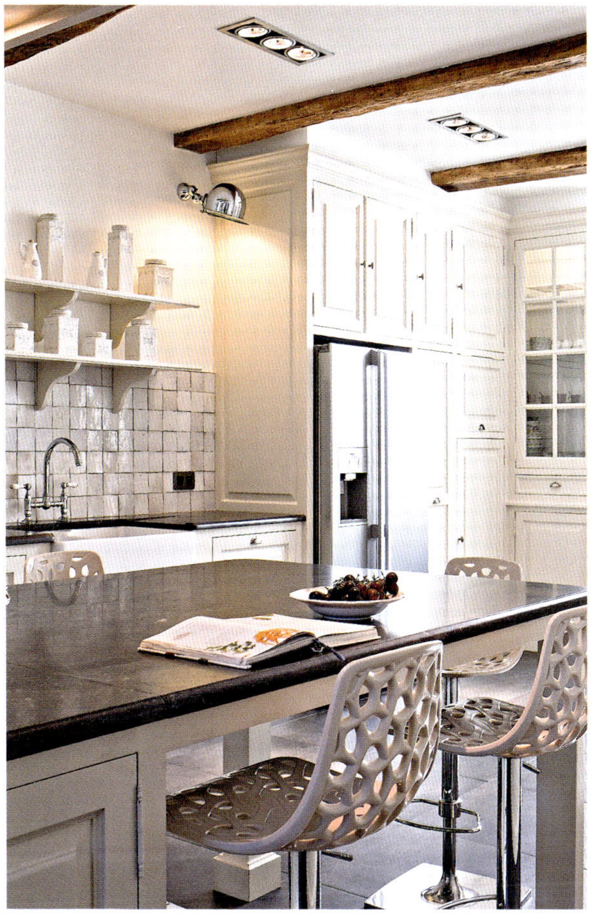
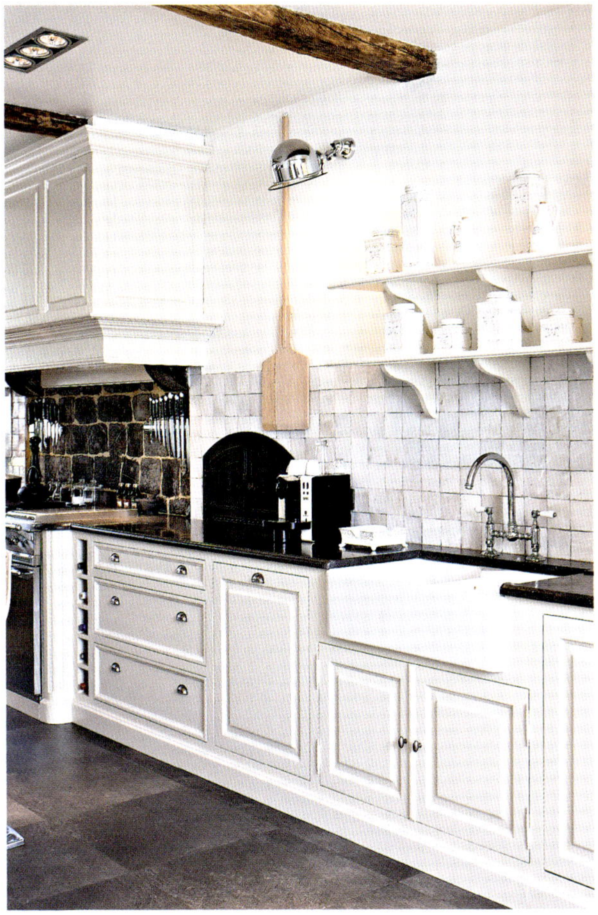
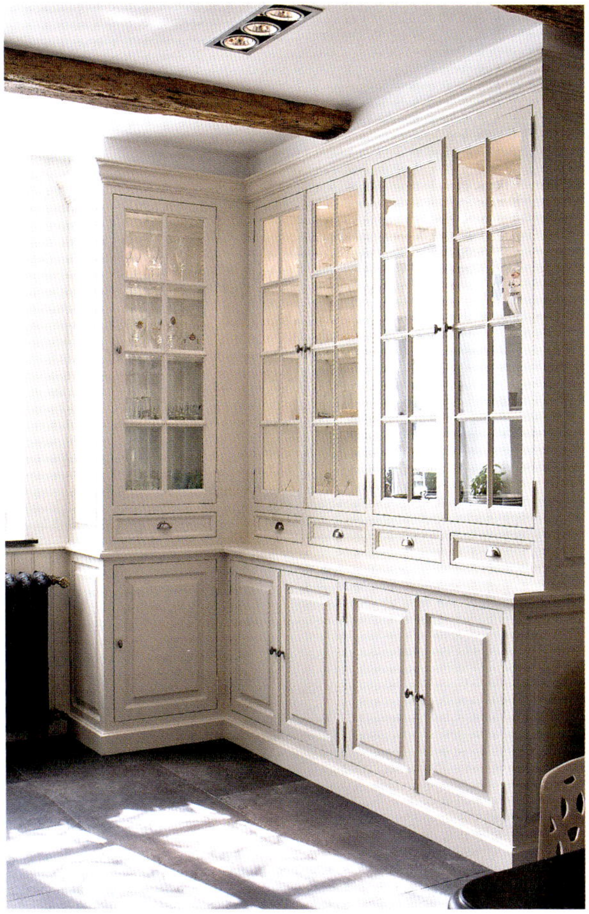

Reclaimed teak and stainless steel worktops.

A stainless steel worktop.

The blue hardstone sinks are recessed.
A draining system is integrated in the solid worktop.
A wooden ladder provides access to the upper shelves of the tall cupboards.

**Wood Fashion**
**Lechat Wood Fashion sprl**

742, chaussée de Bruxelles
B - 1410 Waterloo
T +32 (0)2 387 31 02

1488, ch. de Waterloo
B - 1180 Brussels (Fort Jaco)
T +32 (0)2 374 39 11
F +32 (0)2 374 49 11

Represented by Be.A:
41, rue Mirabeau
F – 14800 Deauville

www.woodfashion.com
info@woodfashion.com

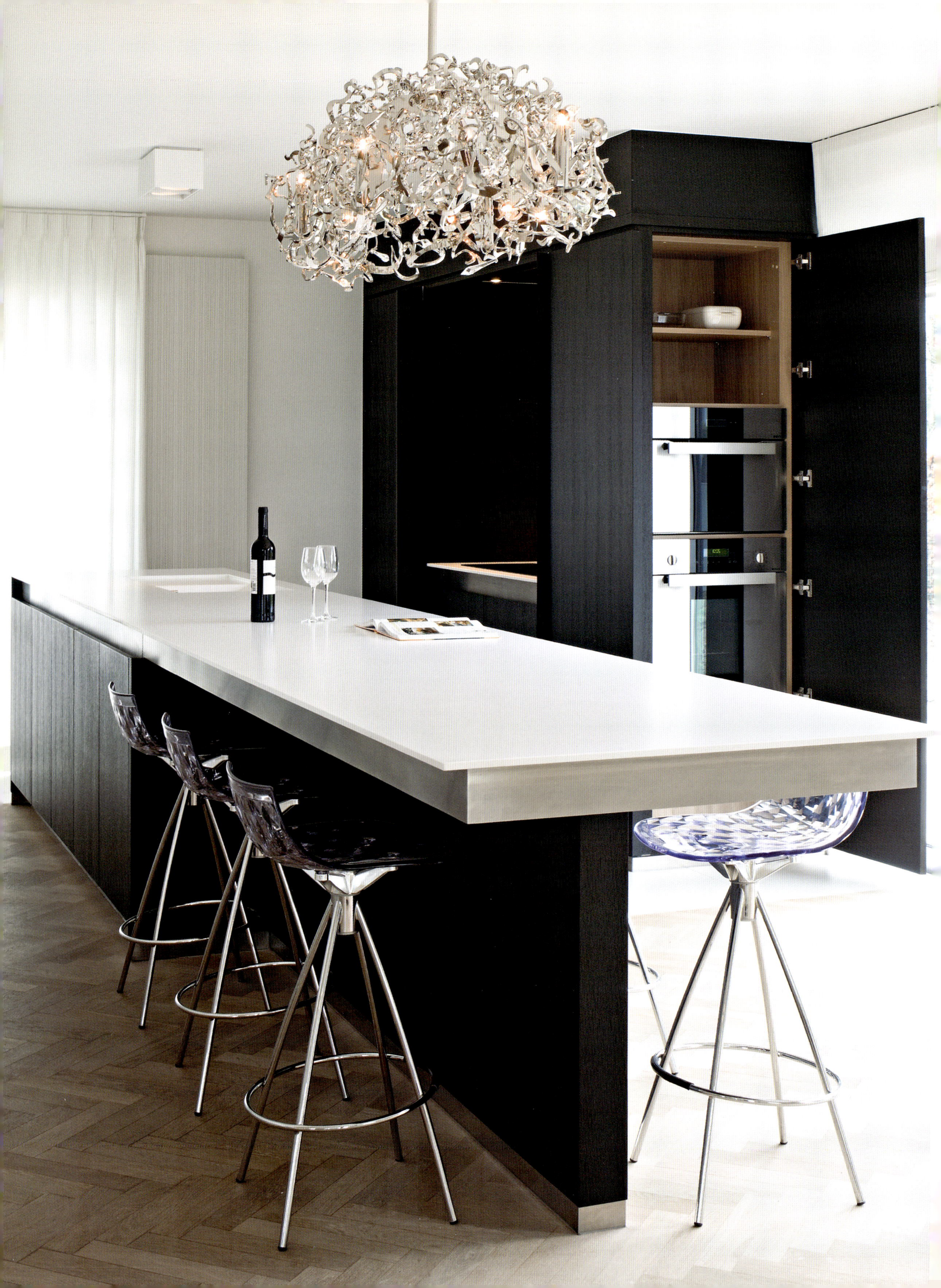

# [ CLIENT-ORIENTED AND INNOVATIVE

For the team of Dekeyzer Kitchen Architecture, everything revolves around a strong relationship of trust with each client.

Trust, of course, is a two-way street, but it means that clients must ultimately get the kitchen of their dreams.

For three generations, Dekeyzer has built up a solid reputation and a passion for high quality customised craftsmanship and beautiful and sustainable materials.

Montréal kitchen, with a worktop and skirting boards made of stainless steel and a dash of ink-black paint.

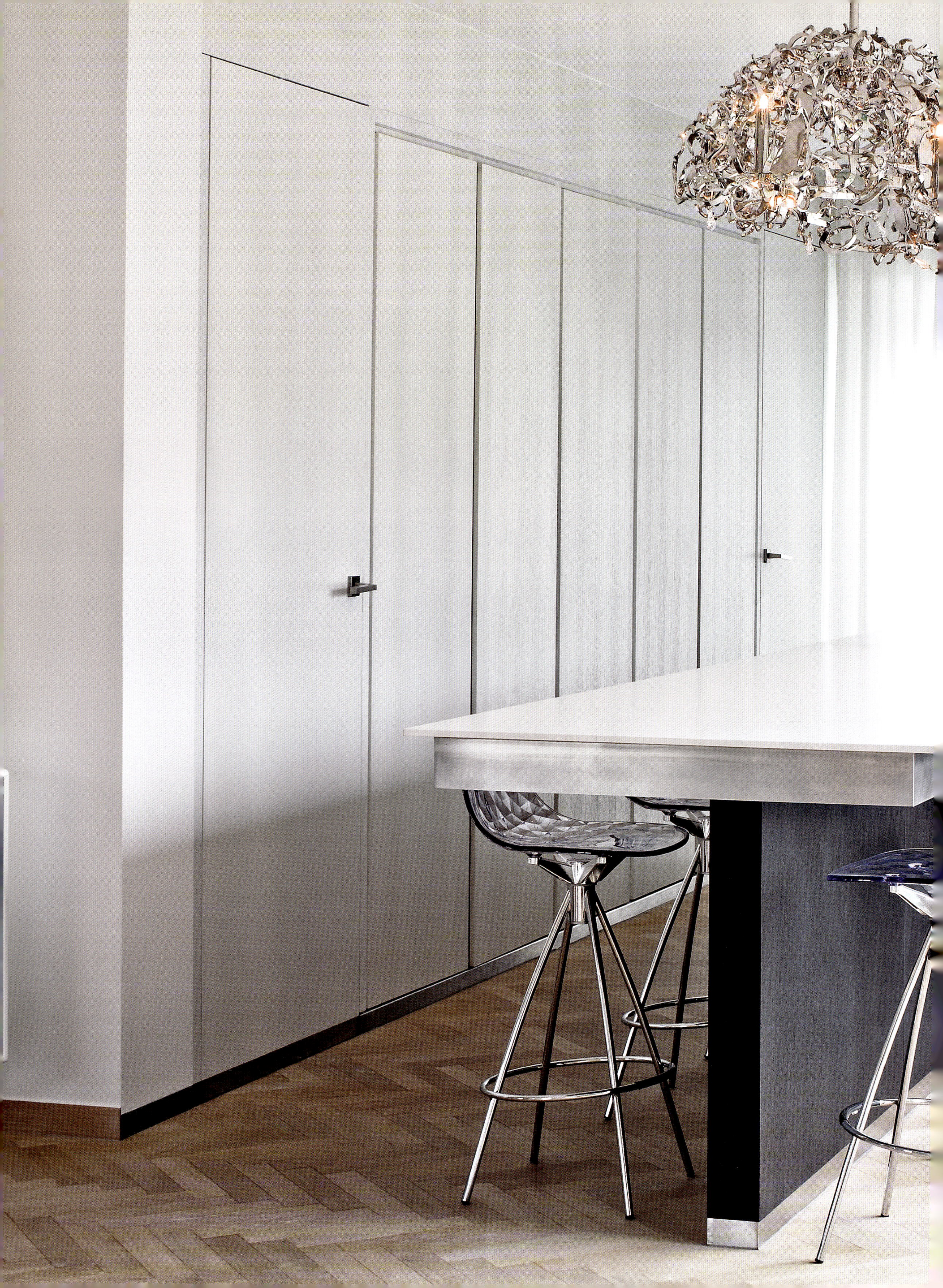

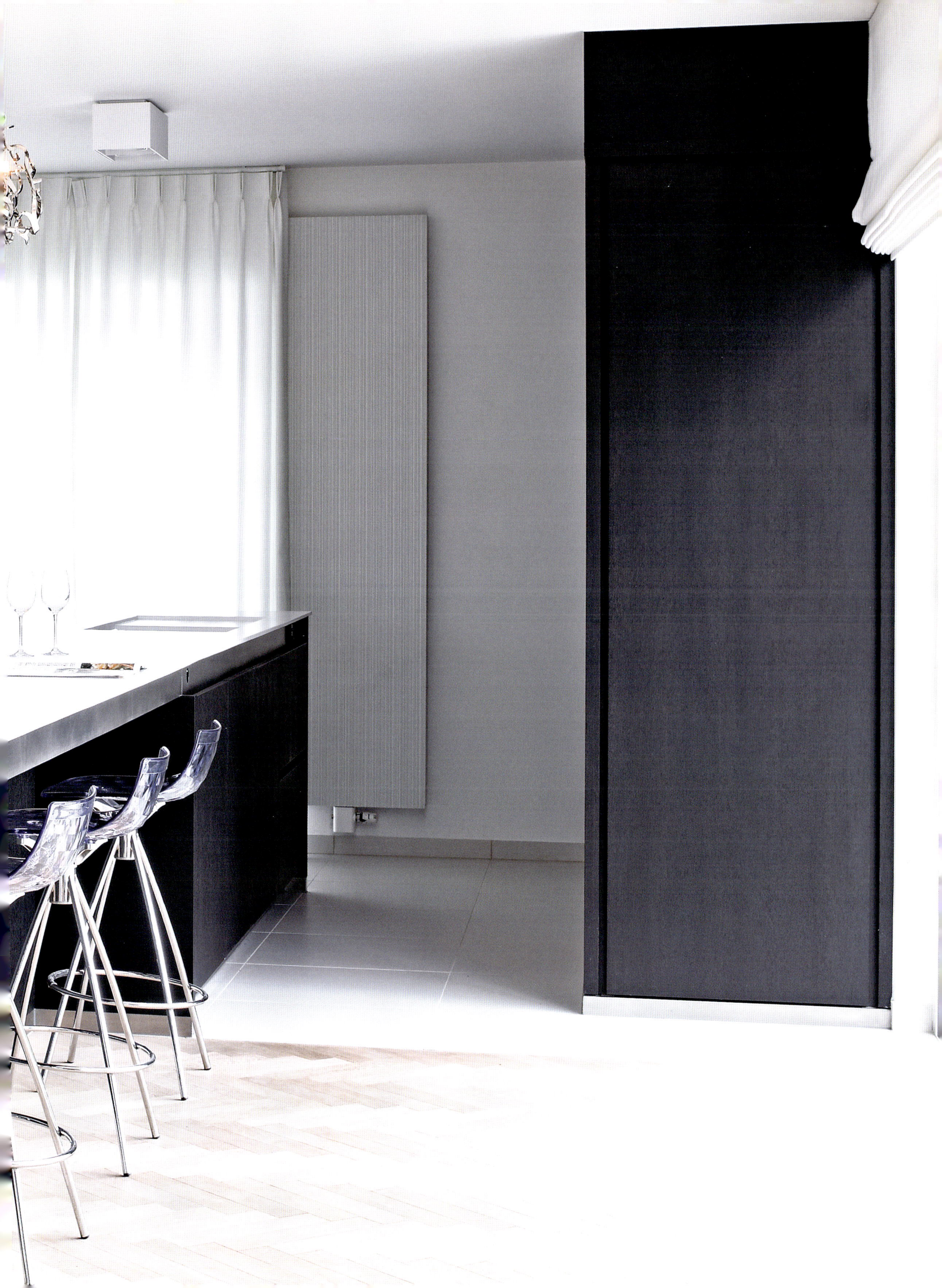

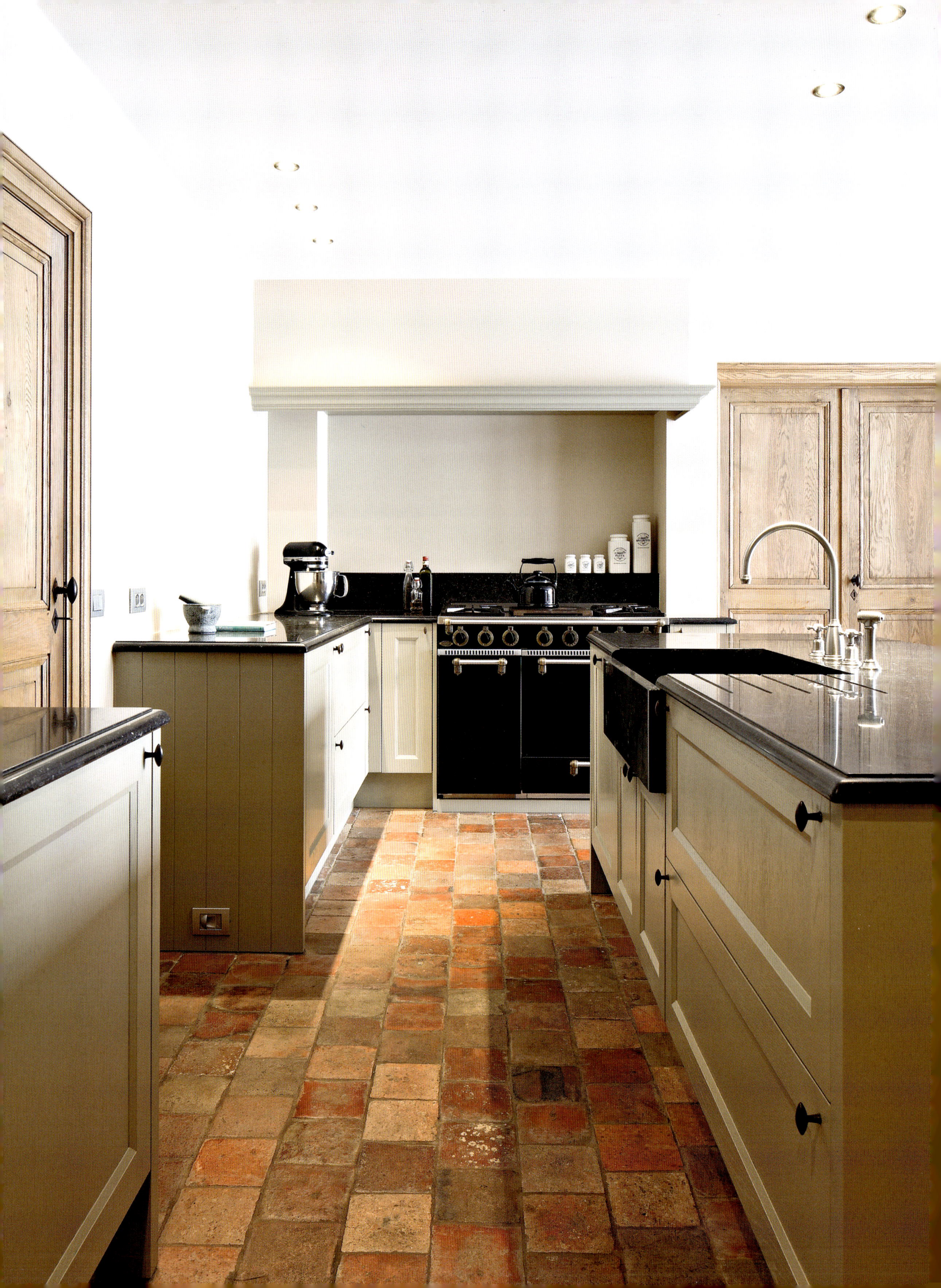

**168-171**
Buckingham kitchen with satin-painted cabinet fronts. The workshops are coated with Hainaut-type blue hardstone.

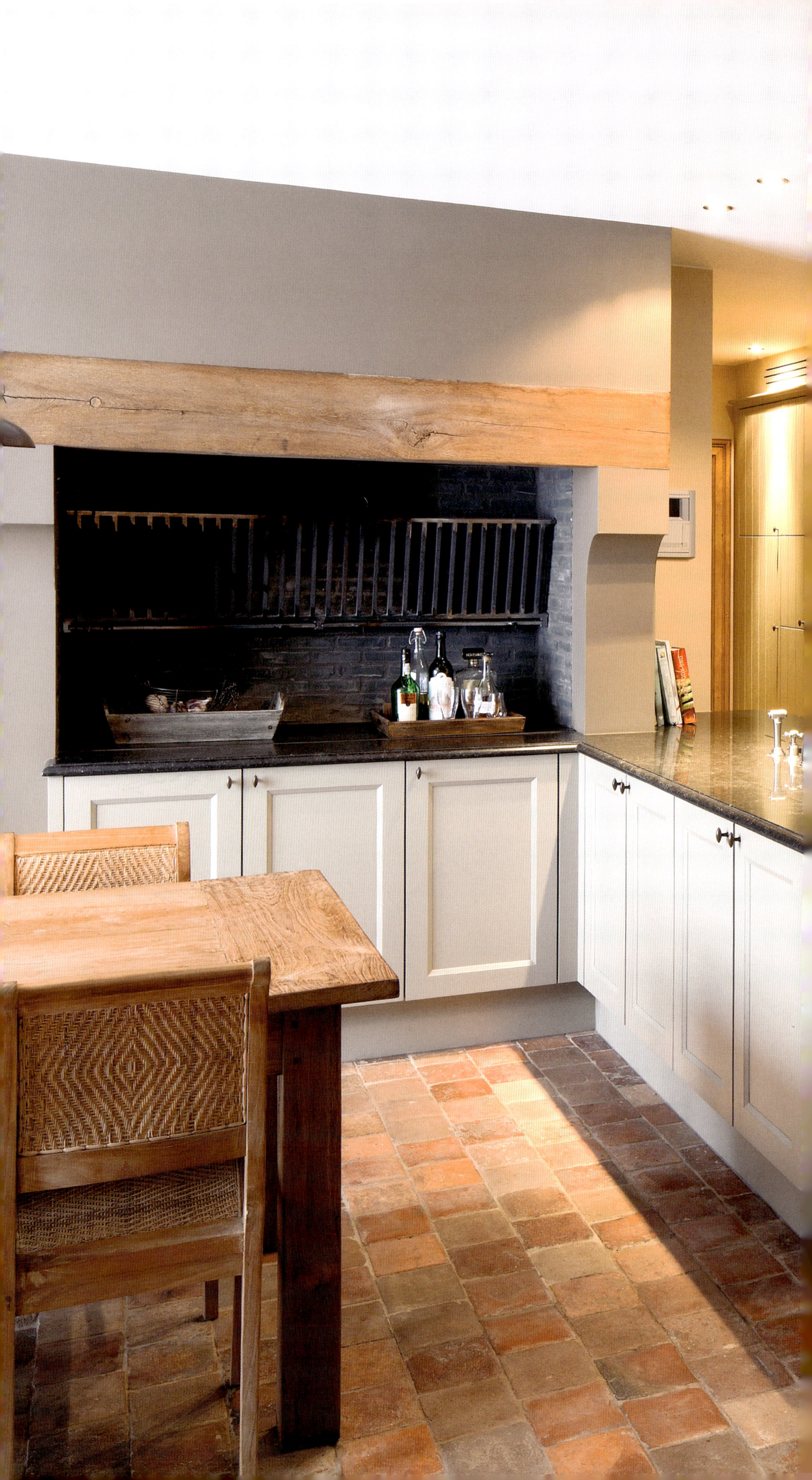

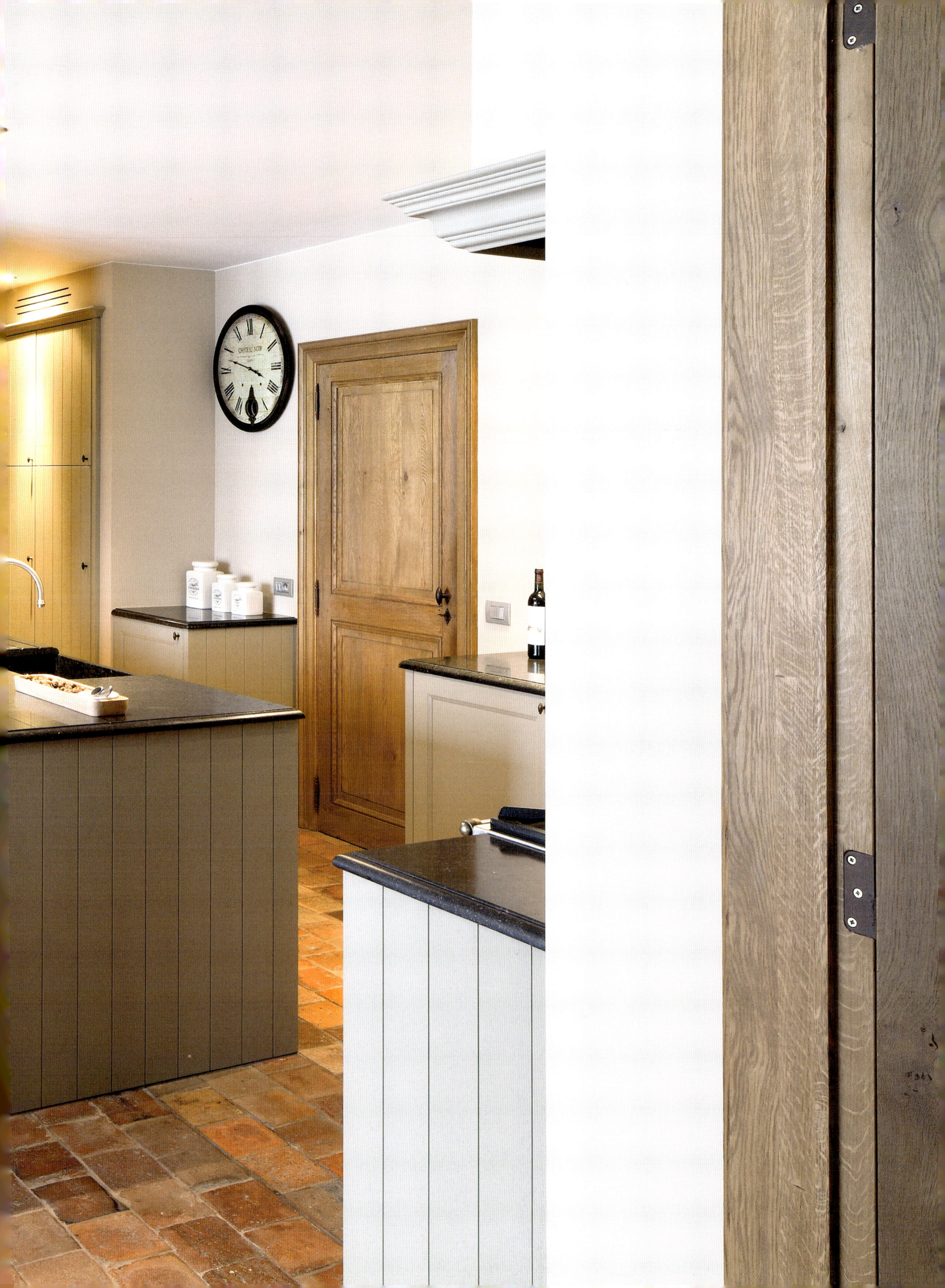

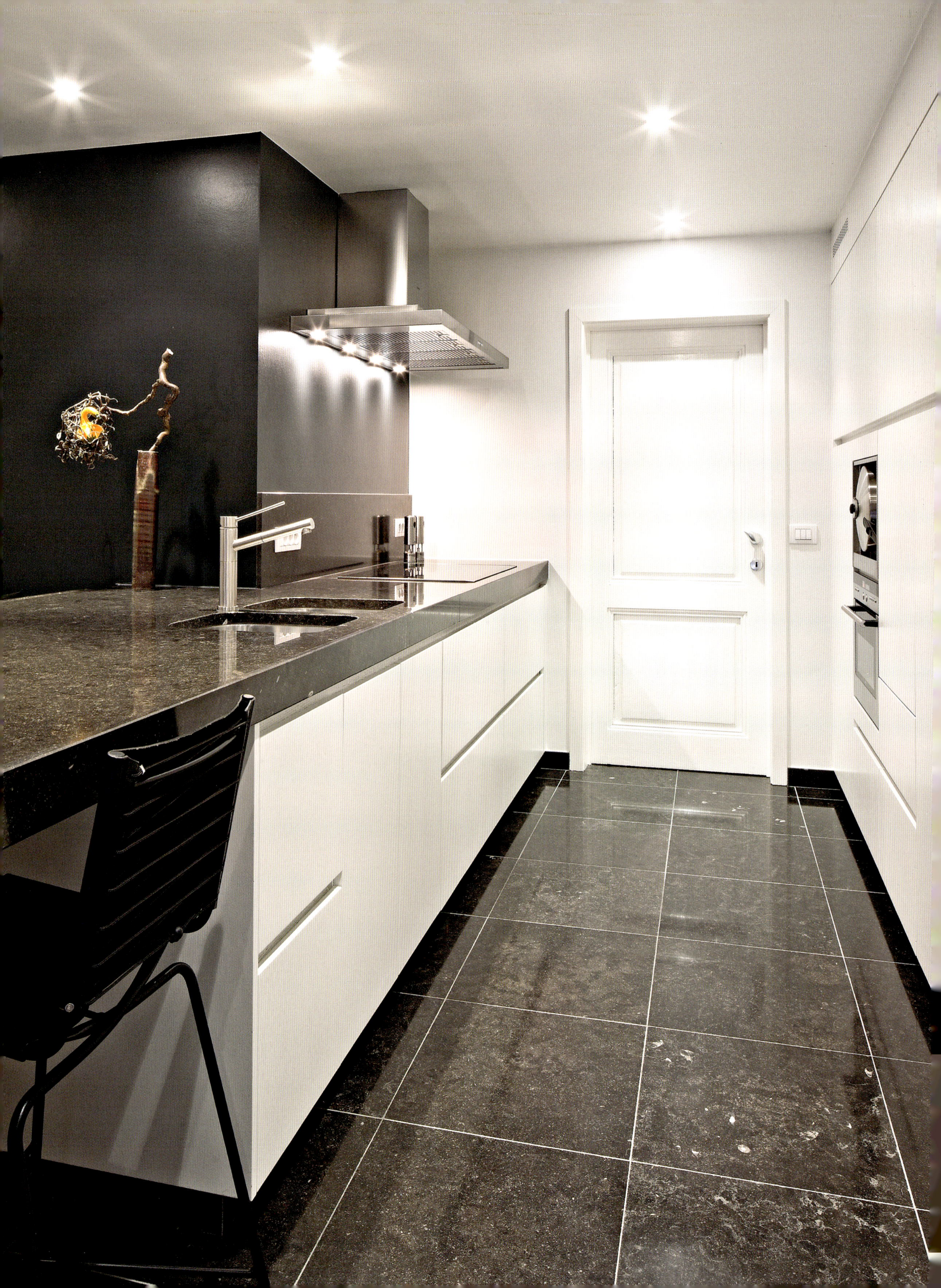

Garda model by Dekeyzer Kitchen Architecture, with a worktop made of smoothed blue hardstone from Hainaut.

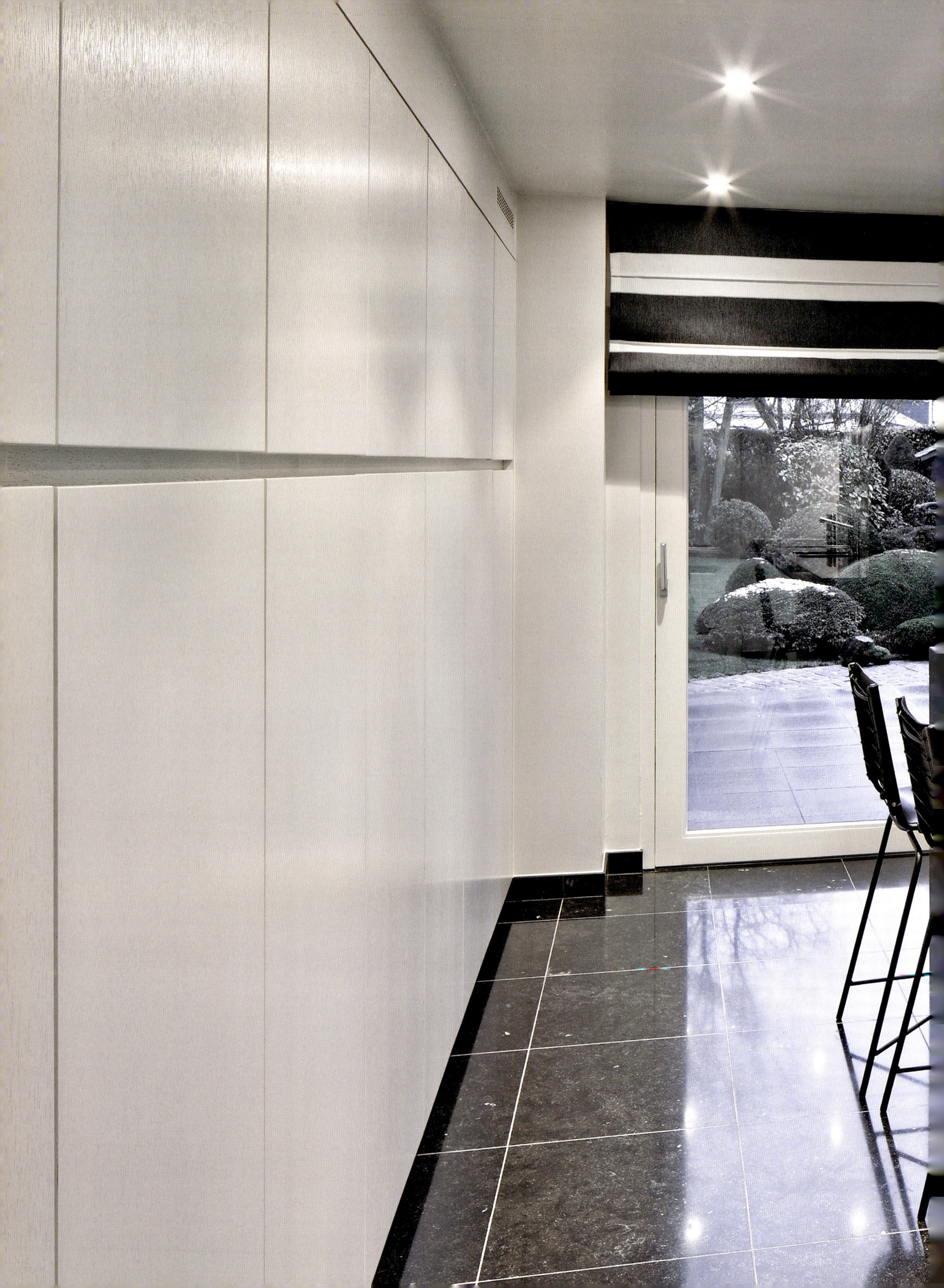

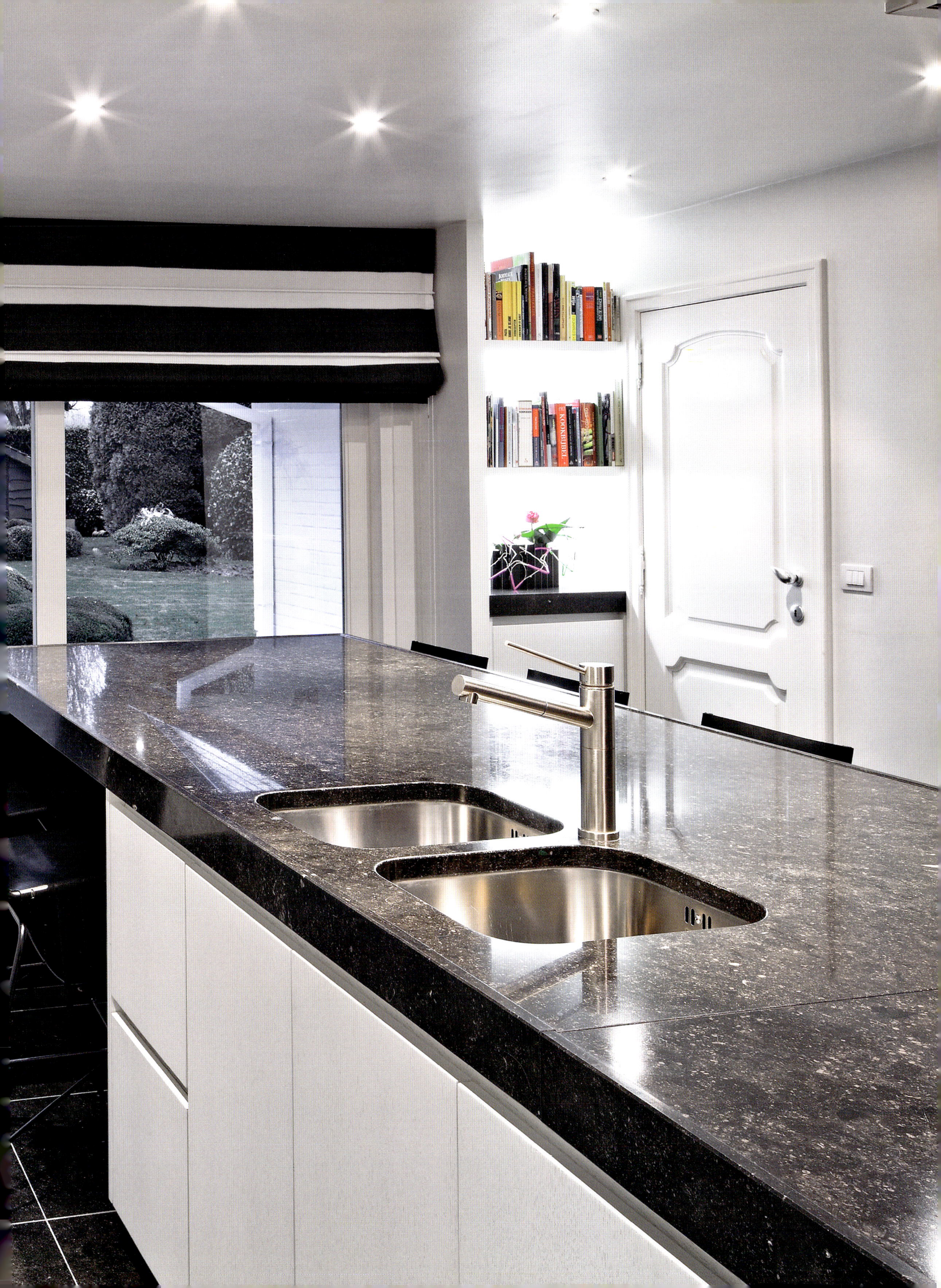

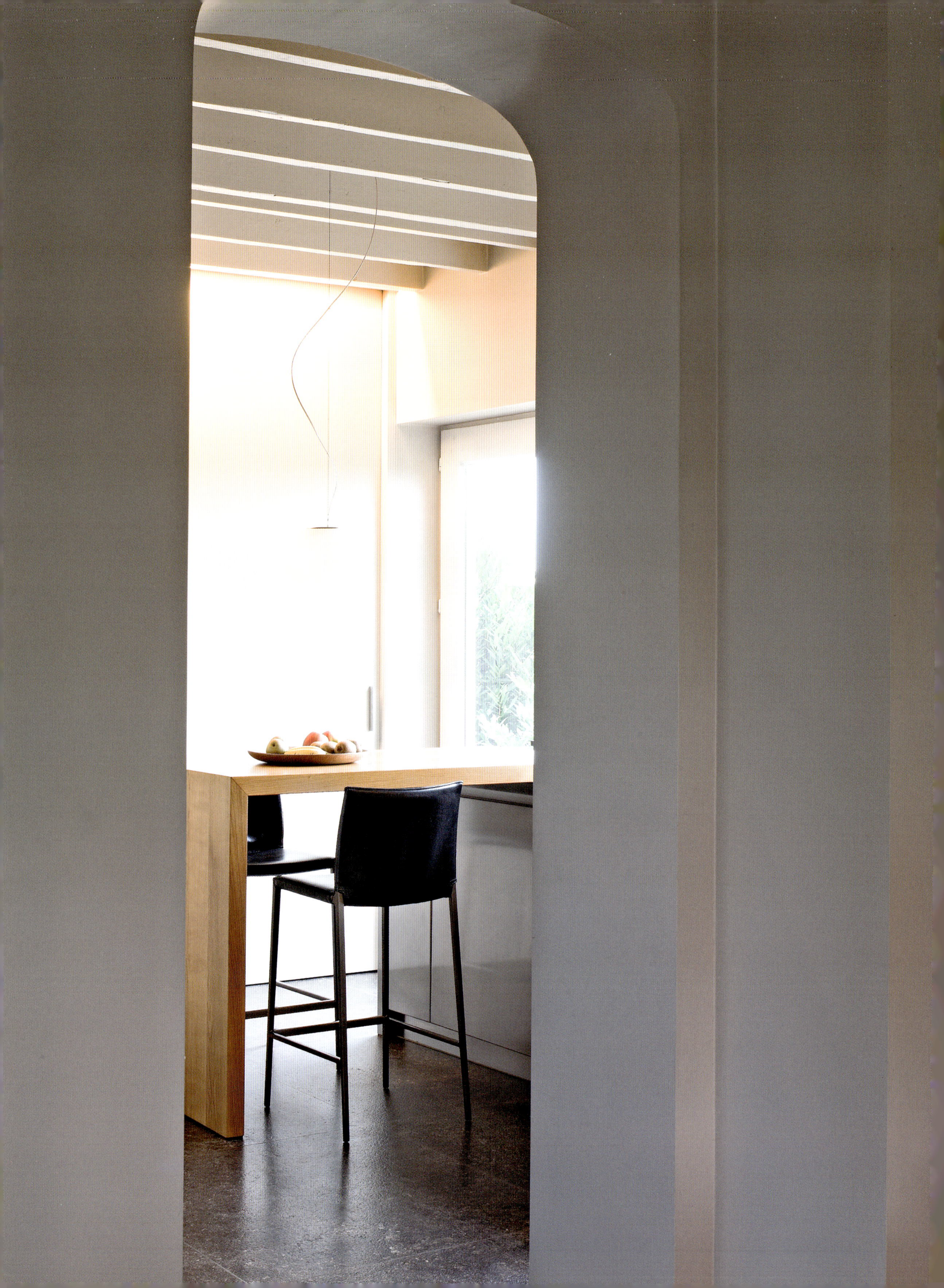

A delicate harmony of warm timber and the austerity of stainless steel in this contemporary kitchen design.

[ **Dekeyzer Kitchen Architecture**
www.dekeyzer.be
info@dekeyzer.be

Showroom Menen (Mon-Sat 10 am - 12 noon & 2 pm - 6 pm)
Industrielaan 55
B – 8930 Menen
T +32 (0)56  52 13 40

Showroom Sint-Martens-Latem
(Mon-Sat 10 am - 12 noon & 2 pm - 6 pm)
Kortrijksesteenweg 1
B – 9830 Sint-Martens-Latem
T +32 (0)9  241 54 54

Showroom Roeselare (Mon-Sat 10 am - 12 noon & 2 pm - 6 pm)
Diksmuidsesteenweg 370c
B – 8800 Roeselare
T +32 (0)51  260 680

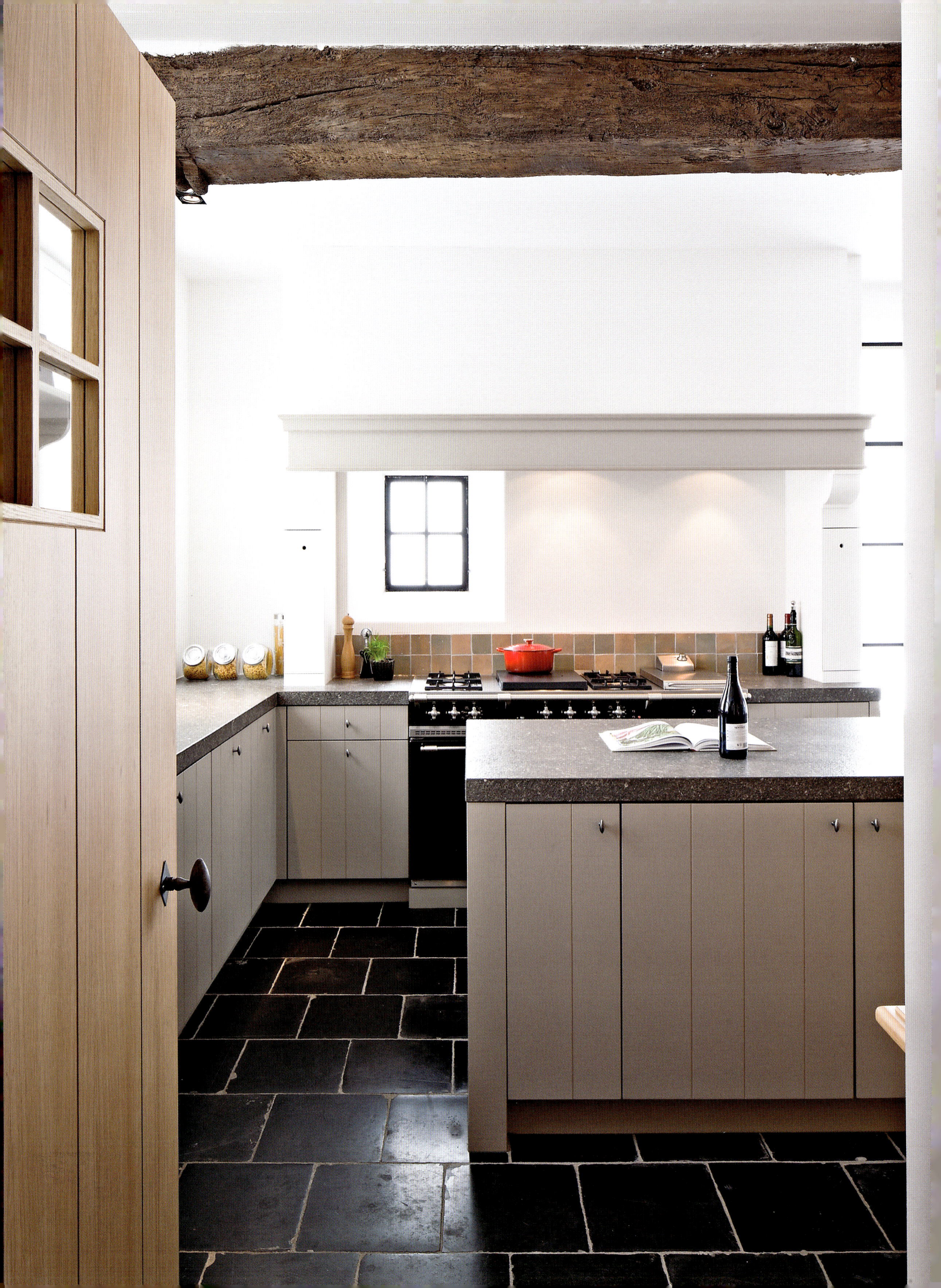

[ # A BLEND OF COSINESS AND *JOIE DE VIVRE*

The living kitchens created by Frank Tack are always a study in character and refinement. They exude a certain timelessness, creating a pleasant environment to cook, work or enjoy a chat with a few friends over dinner…

All the furniture designed by Frank Tack is unique, and each piece is created using the most noble materials.

Whether it be a classic design, country-style or something more austere, there is an indissoluble link between the design and the creation and between the client's wishes and the end result. Frank Tack's kitchens are something very special: a blend of cosiness and unadulterated *joie de vivre*.

Frank Tack designed and created this convivial living kitchen with its black range cooker by Lacanche in a fully restored farmhouse.
The designer opted for a combination of natural oak and painted oak, with an exclusive natural stone to form the worktops: Gris Catalan Anticato with straight edging.
The existing small window and the extra spice racks in the pillars were incorporated into the structure of the extractor hood.

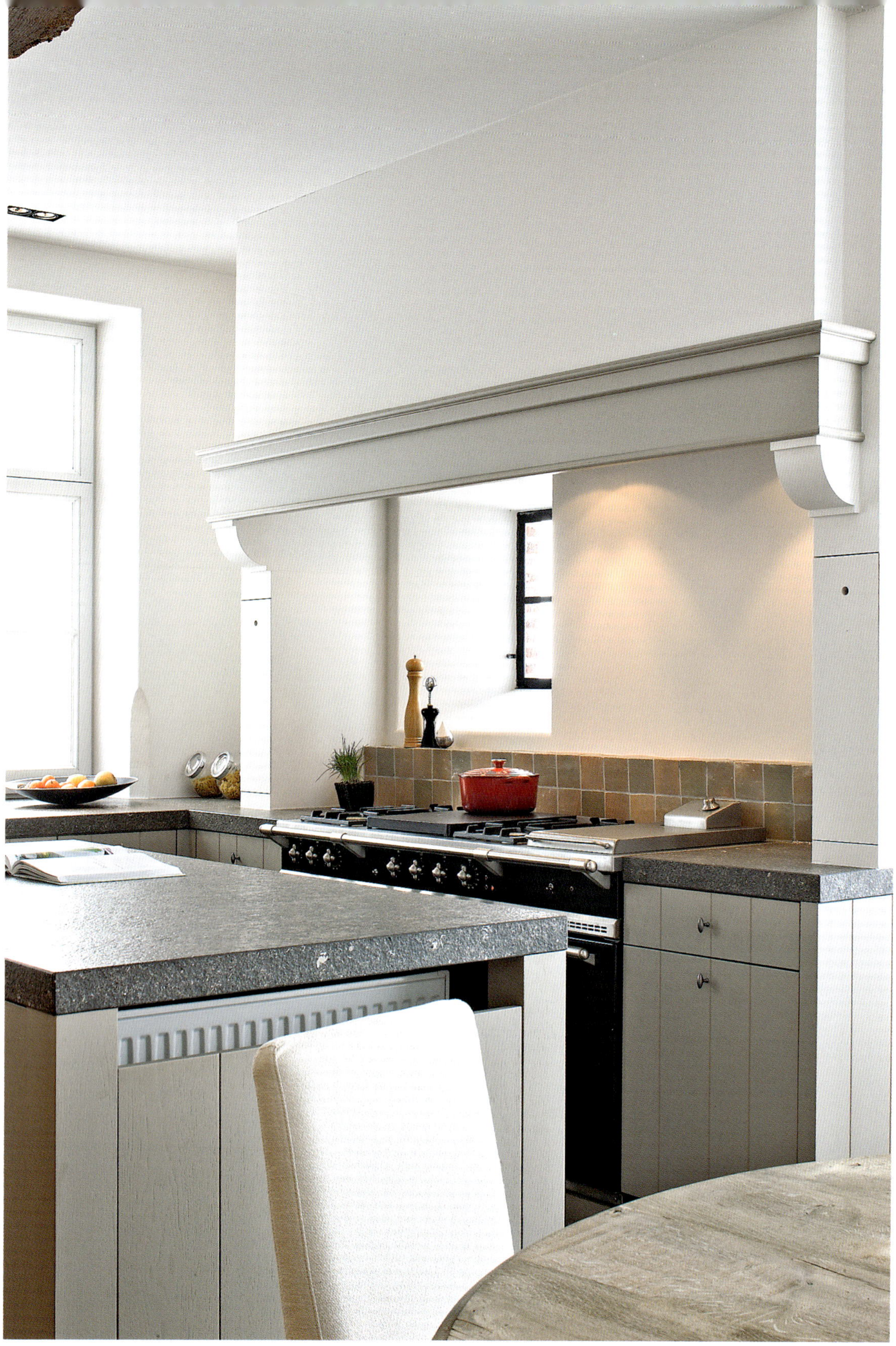

An inside door with peephole, with on the right a guillotine cabinet that conceals the standalone appliances (coffee maker, toaster, etc.).

Tap by Perrin & Rowe.

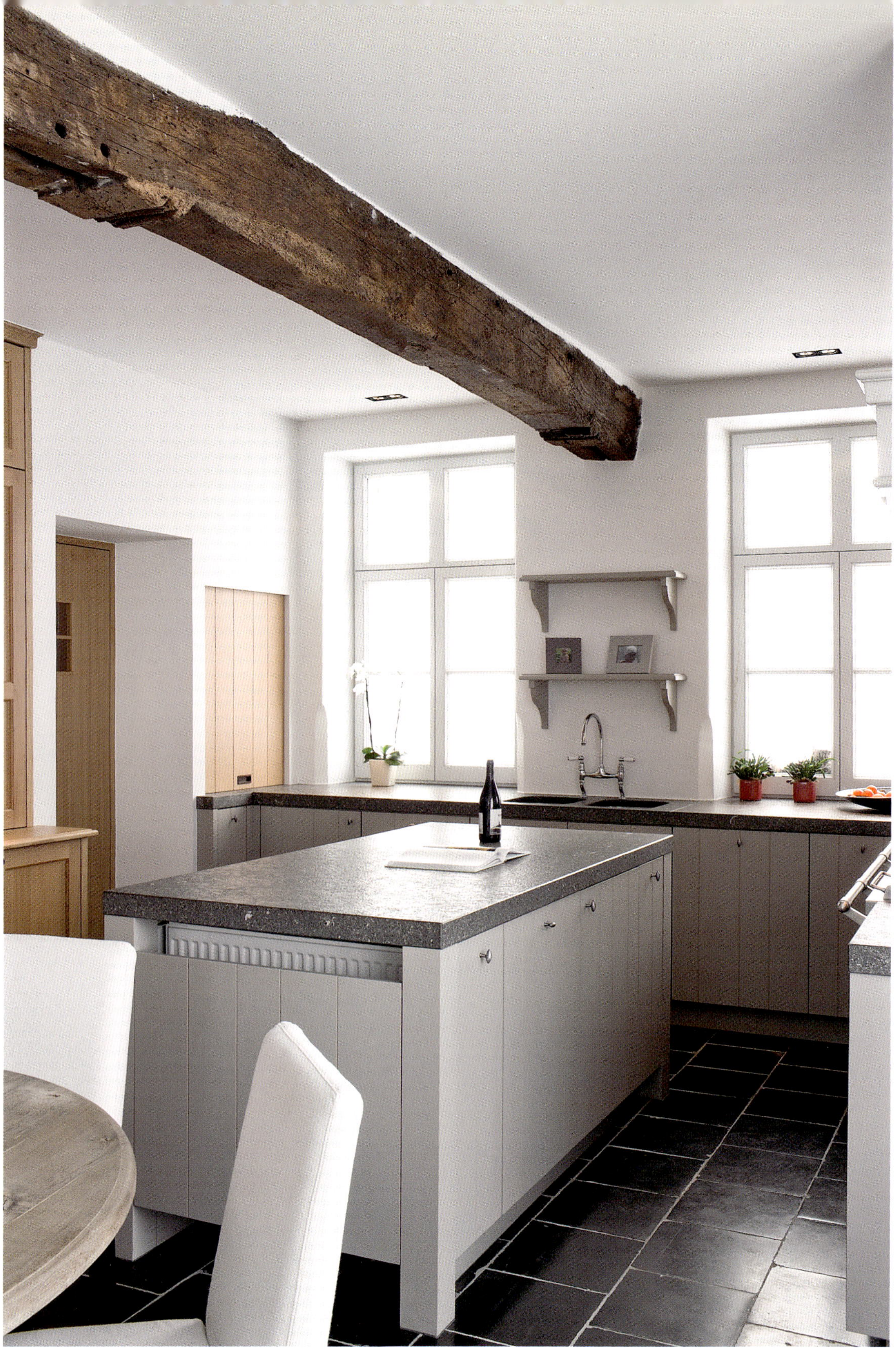

The display cabinet is a combination of glass and framed doors.
Frank Tack has here combined somewhat old materials (the ceiling beam, floors, table, etc.) with new elements, such as the lighting and the kitchen furniture.

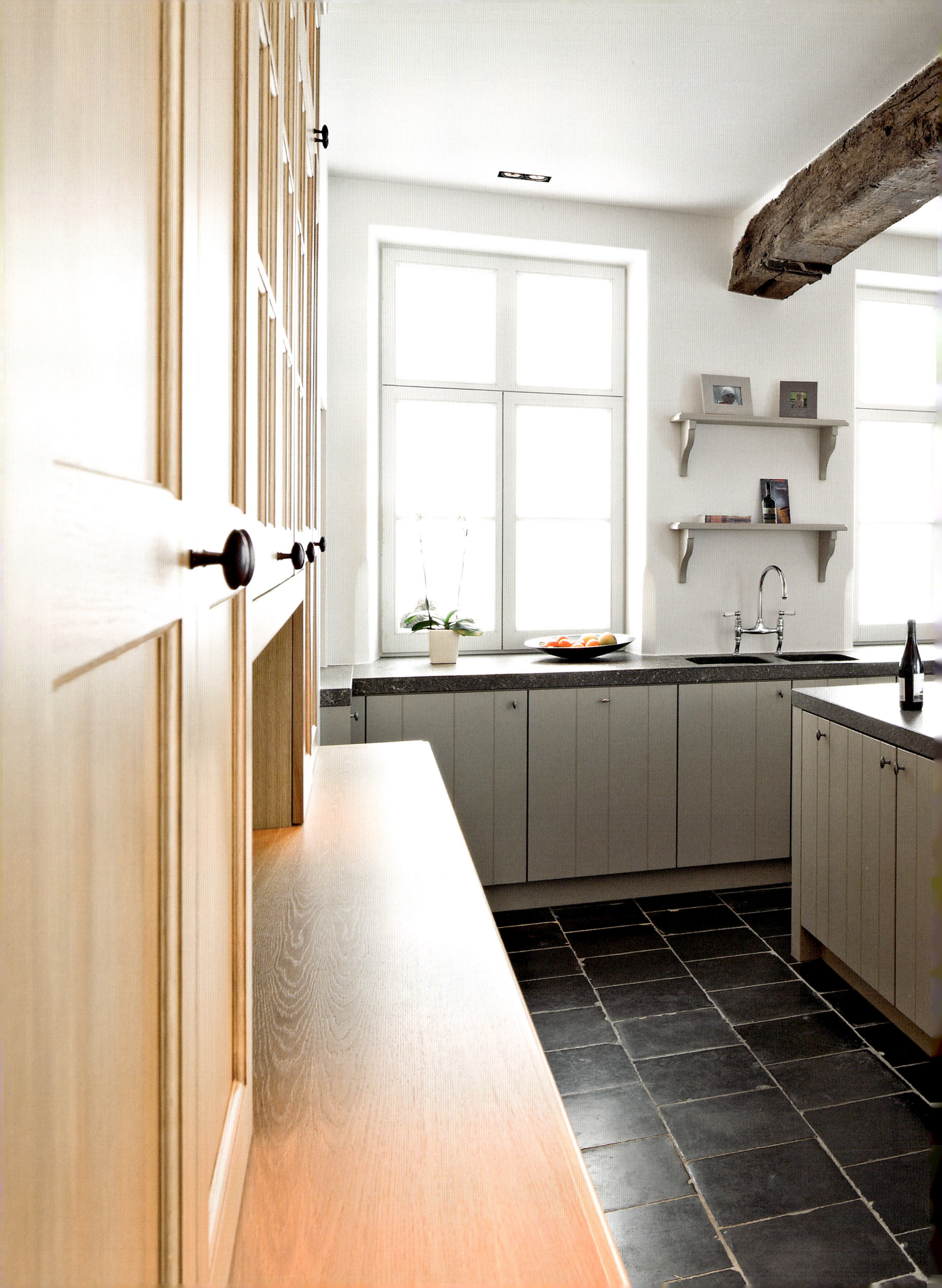

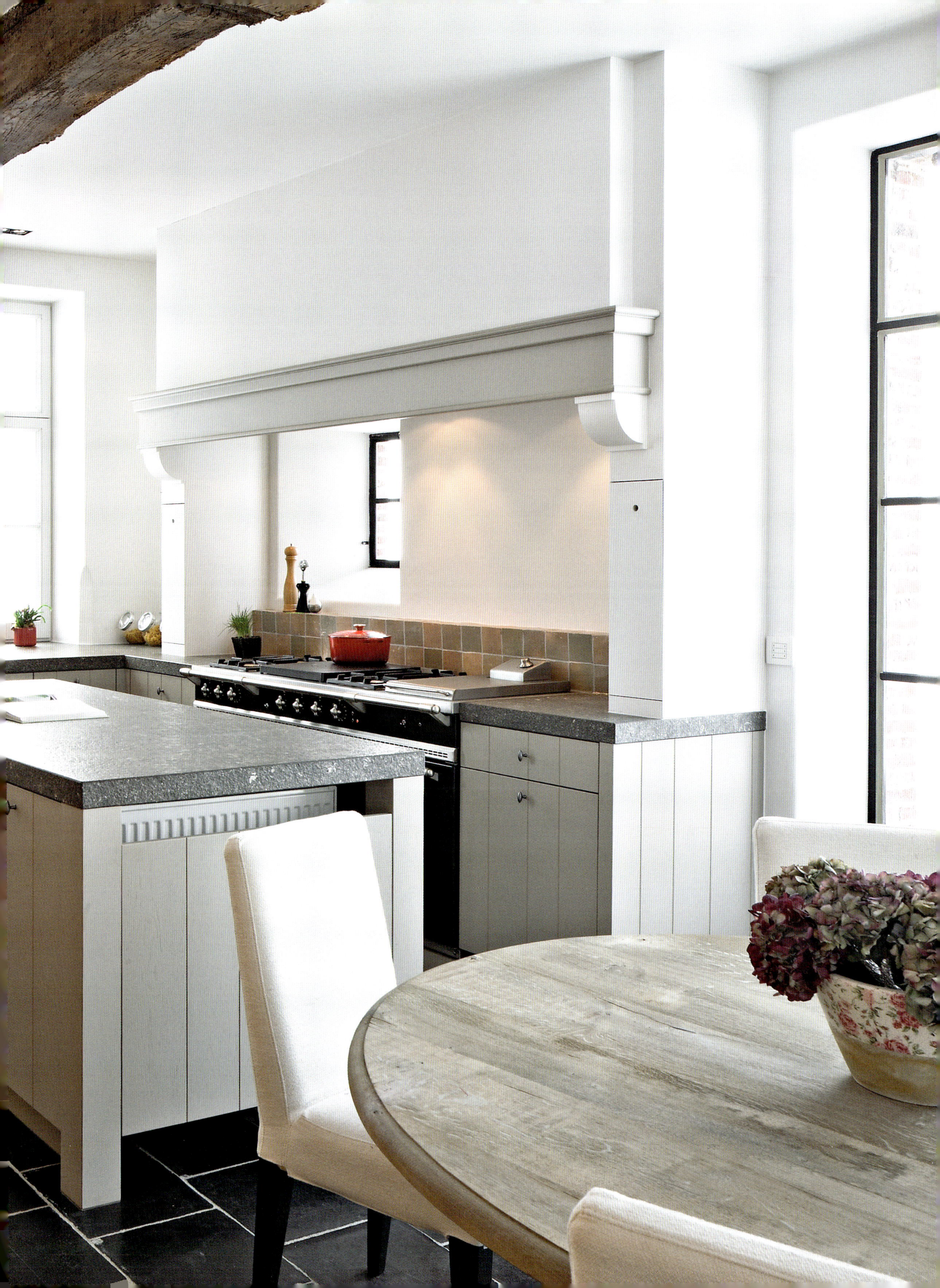

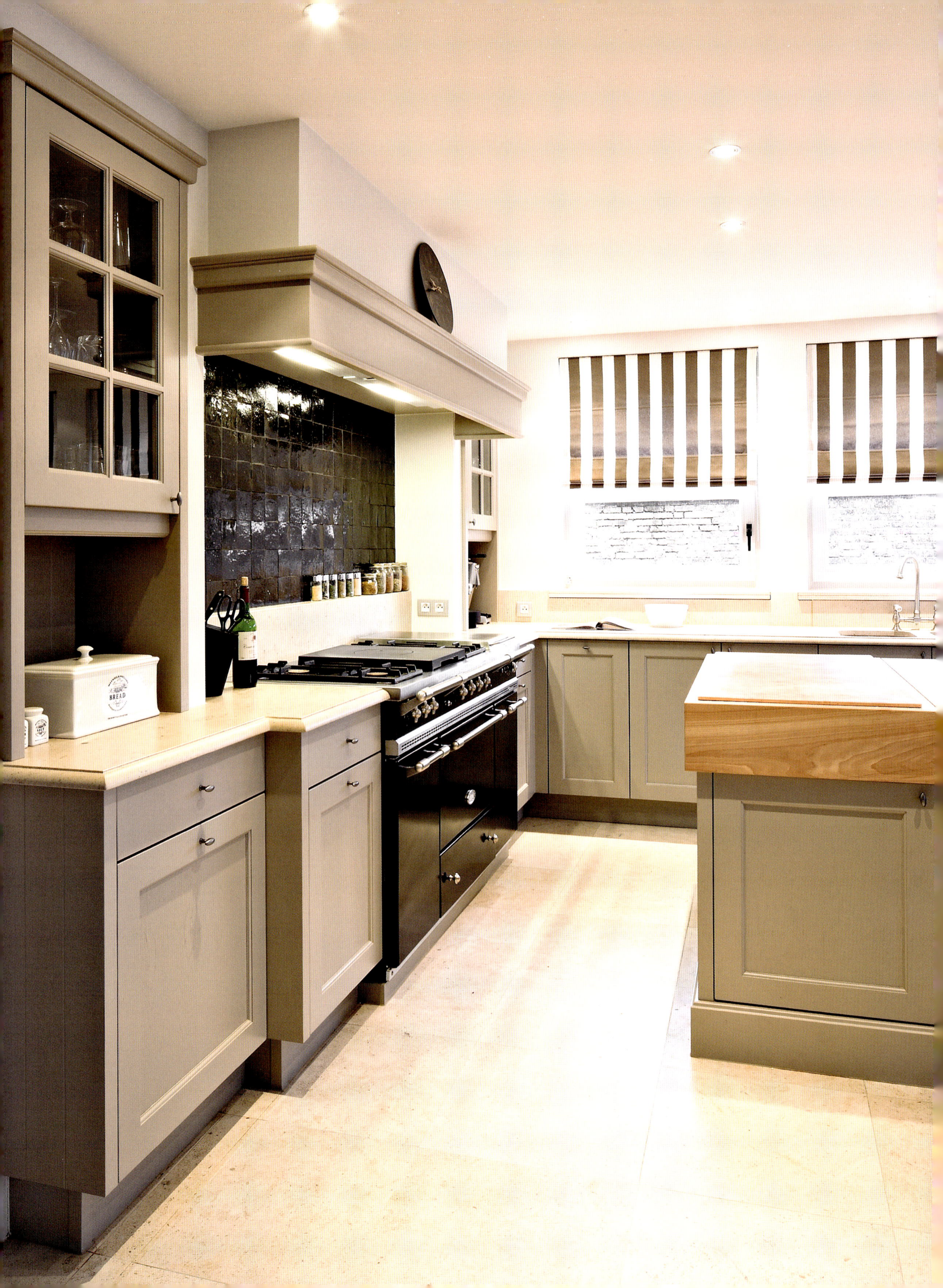
BREAD

This kitchen in painted oak is the epitome of functionality: all the appliances are neatly concealed behind a full wall unit.

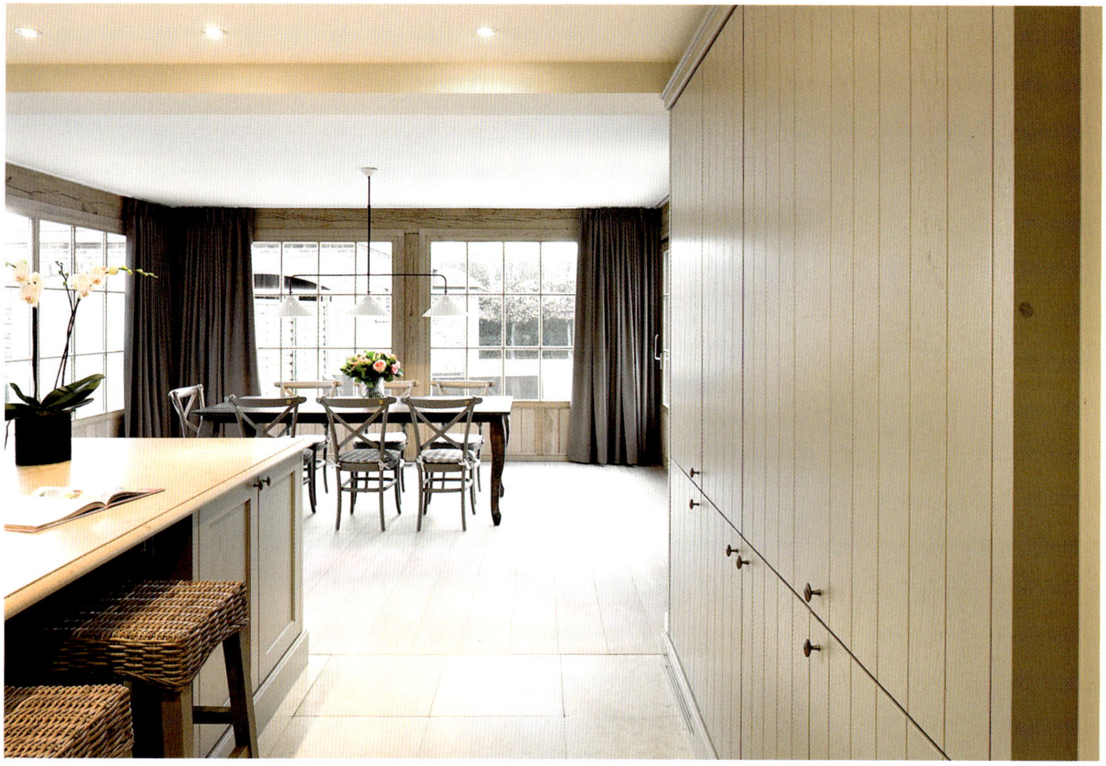

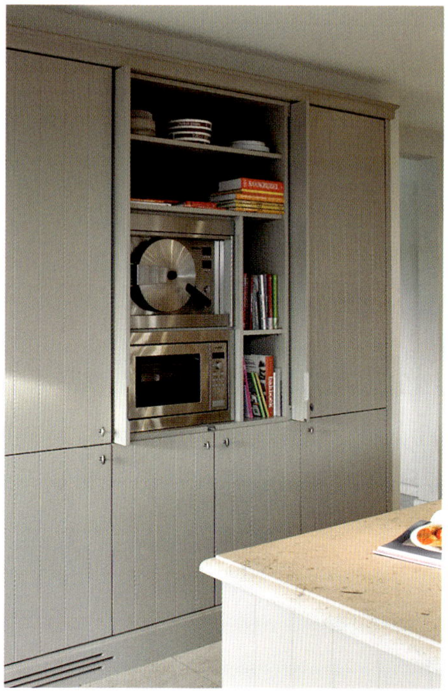

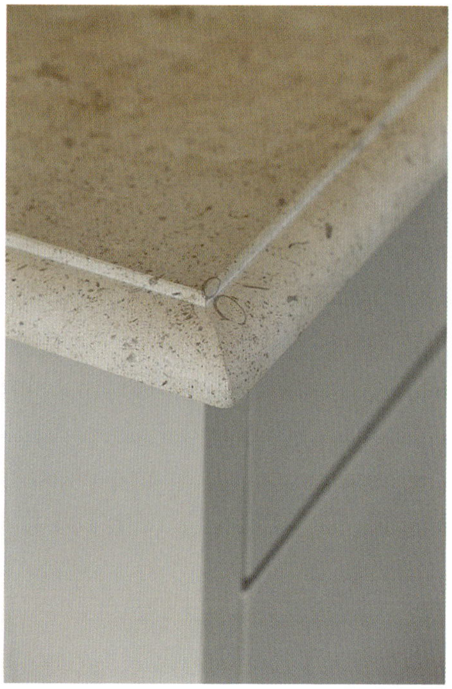

The eye-catching chopping block creates an impression of functionality in harmony with the worktop created in Massangis Clair (a French limestone) which is finished with a bevelled edge.
The black Lacanche range cooker is perfectly placed by the wall clad with black Moroccan zelliges.
For this design, Frank Tack has opted for framed doors with a few glass touches here and there.
Tap by Perrin & Rowe.

**Frank Tack**

**Kitchens and furniture  / design and production**

Grotstraat 74

B - 8780  Oostrozebeke

T +32 (0)51  40 47 18

F +32 (0)51  40 61 40

76, avenue de Villiers

F - 75017 Paris

www.franktack.eu

By appointment.

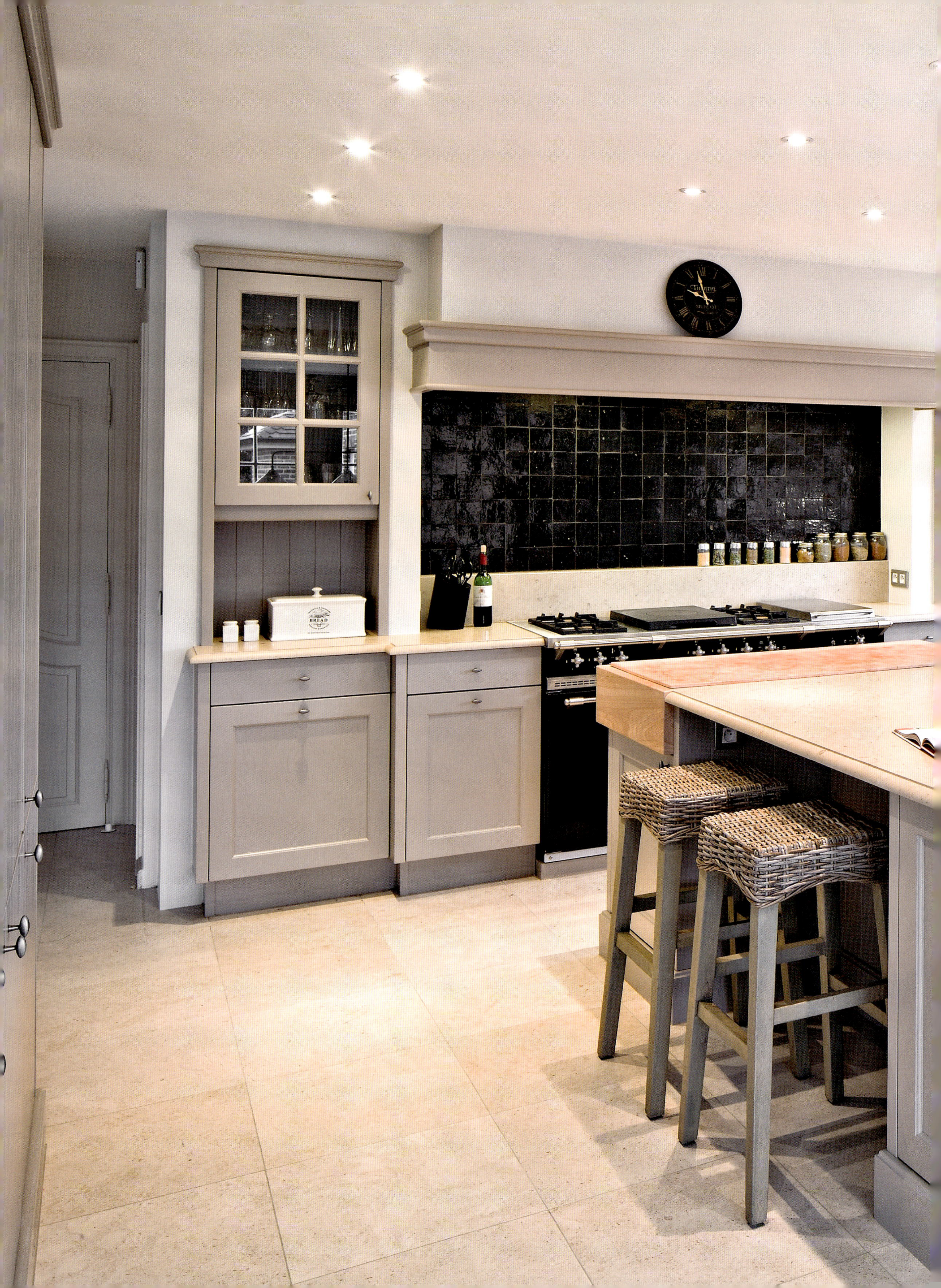
BREAD

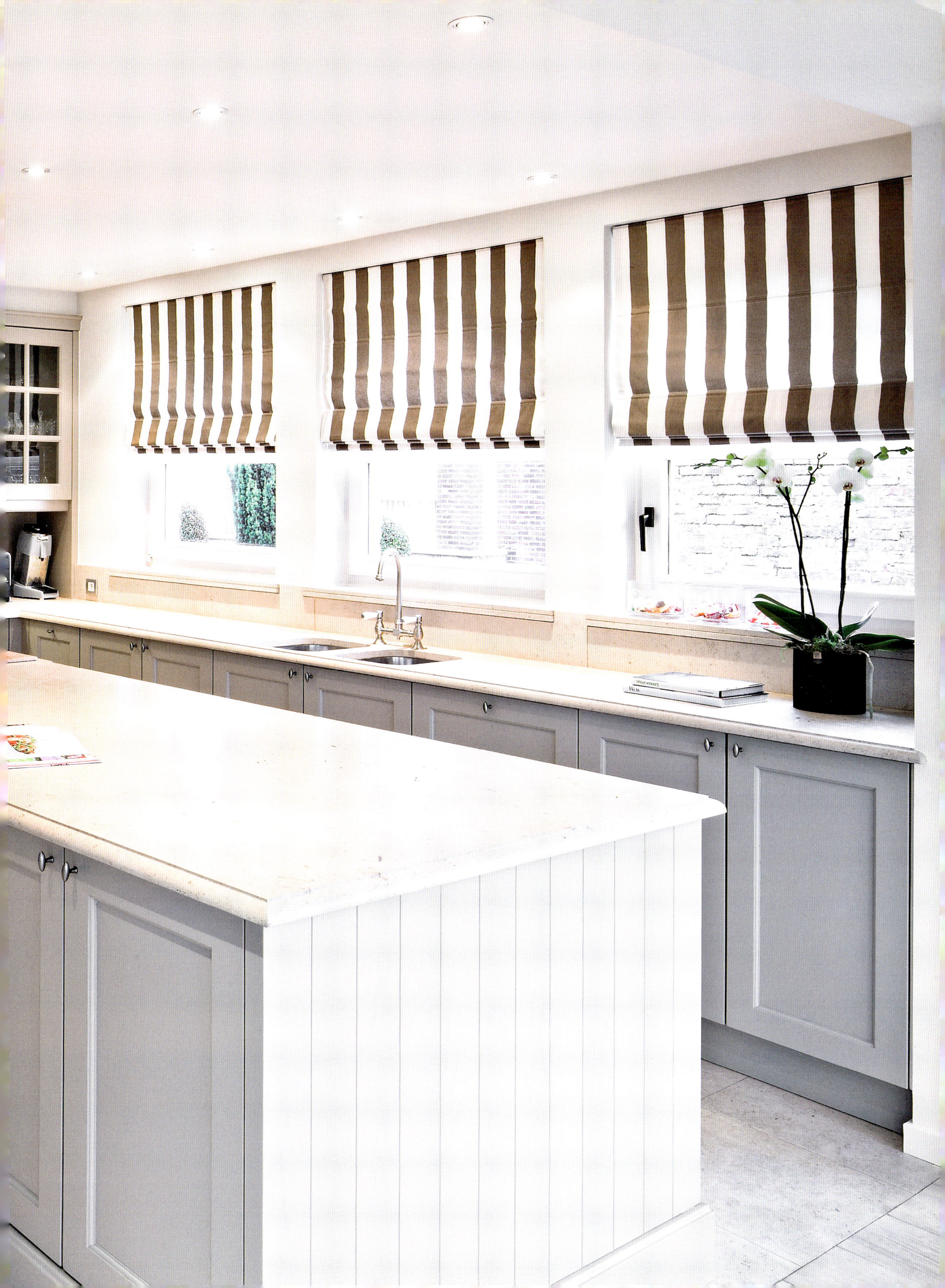

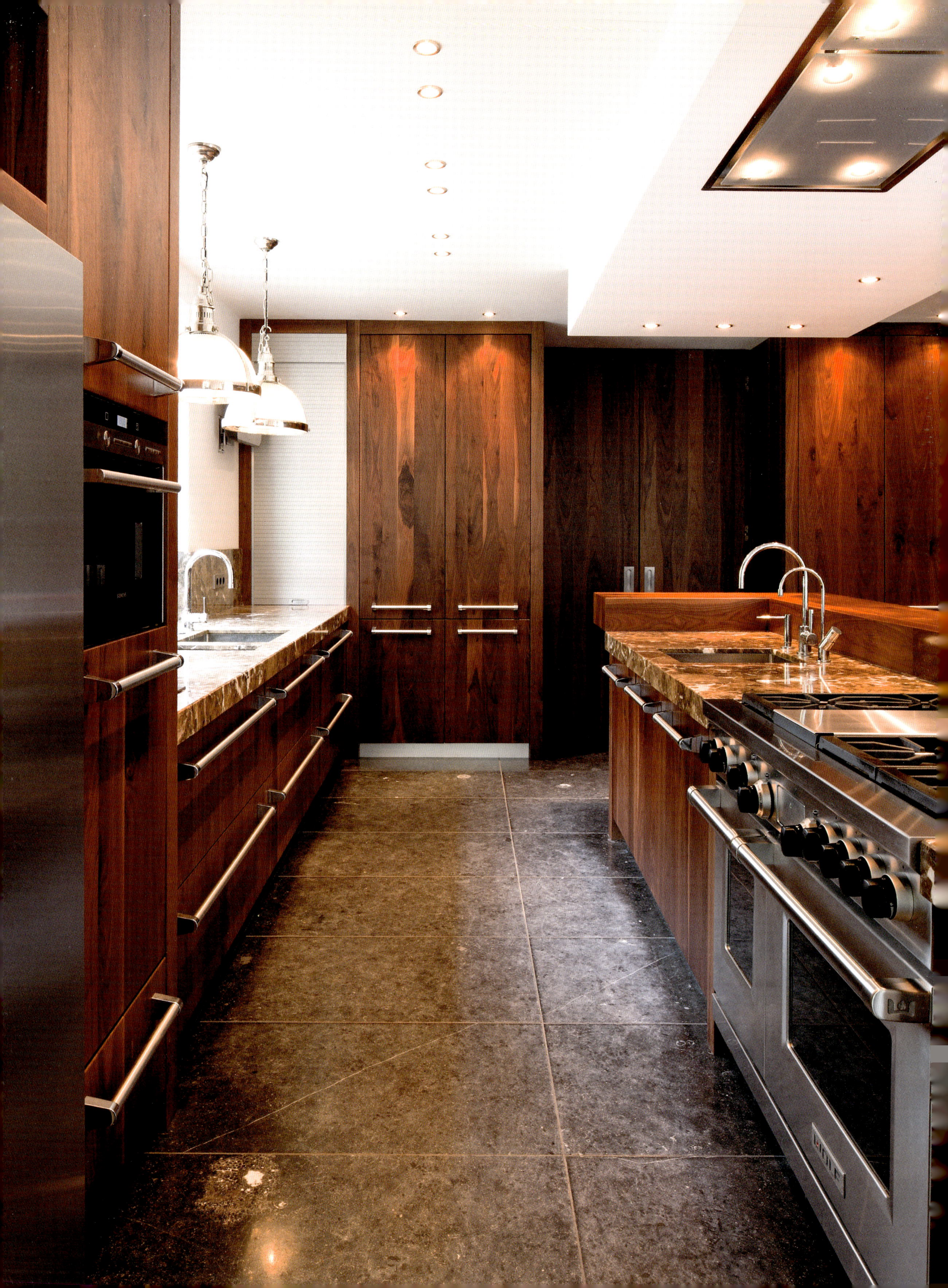

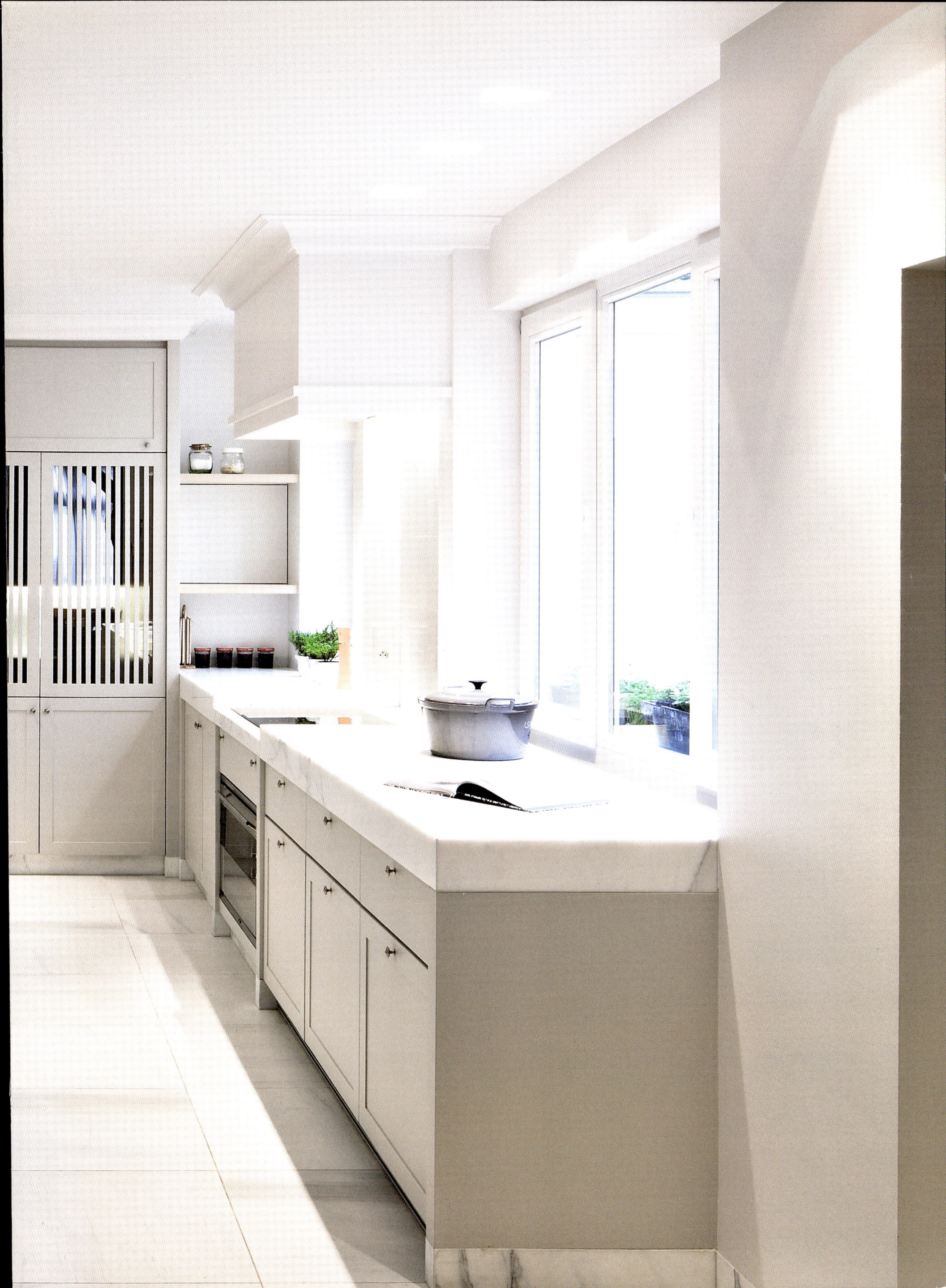

PUBLISHER
BETA-PLUS Publishing
www.betaplus.com
info@betaplus.com

PHOTOGRAPHY
Jo Pauwels
12-17  Karel Moortgat
22-27  © obumex
88-89  © indu+
92-93  © indu+
139    © Bourgondisch Kruis

GRAPHIC DESIGN
POLYDEM bvba
Nathalie Binart

TRANSLATION
Belga Translations

January 2011
ISBN 13: 978-90-8944-089-1

© All rights reserved. No part of this publication may be reproduced or transmitted in any form or by any means, electronic or mechanical, including photocopy, recording or any other information storage and retrieval system, without prior permission in writing from the publisher.